THE LEGITIMACY CLASH

Challenges to Democracy in Multinational States

In the coming decade, we may see the advent of multinational federalism on an international scale. As great powers and international organizations become increasingly uncomfortable with the creation of new states, multinational federalism is now an important avenue to explore, and in recent decades, the experiences of Canada and Quebec have had a key influence on the approaches taken to manage national and community diversity around the world.

Drawing on comparative scholarship and several key case studies (including Scotland and the United Kingdom, Catalonia and Spain, and the Quebec-Canada dynamic, along with relations between Indigenous peoples and various levels of government), *The Legitimacy Clash* takes a fresh look at the relationship between majorities and minorities while exploring theoretical advances in both federal studies and contemporary nationalisms. Alain-G. Gagnon critically examines the prospects and potential for a multinational federal state, specifically for nations seeking affirmation in a hostile context. *The Legitimacy Clash* reflects on the importance of legitimacy over legality in assessing the conflicts of claims.

ALAIN-G. GAGNON is Canada Research Chair in Quebec and Canadian Studies and professor in the Department of Political Science at the Université du Québec à Montréal.

The Legitimacy Clash

*Challenges to Democracy
in Multinational States*

ALAIN-G. GAGNON

UNIVERSITY OF TORONTO PRESS
Toronto Buffalo London

ISBN 978-1-4875-4754-7 (cloth)   ISBN 978-1-4875-4757-8 (EPUB)
ISBN 978-1-4875-4755-4 (paper)   ISBN 978-1-4875-4756-1 (PDF)

Library and Archives Canada Cataloguing in Publication

Title: The legitimacy clash: challenges to democracy in multinational
    states / Alain-G. Gagnon.
Names: Gagnon, Alain, author.
Description: Includes bibliographical references and index.
Identifiers: Canadiana (print) 20220412278 | Canadiana (ebook) 20220412332 |
    ISBN 9781487547547 (cloth) | ISBN 9781487547554 (paper) |
    ISBN 9781487547578 (EPUB) | ISBN 9781487547561 (PDF)
Subjects: LCSH: Multinational states. | LCSH: Federal government. |
    LCSH: Democracy. | LCSH: Majorities. | LCSH: Minorities.
Classification: LCC JC311 .G34 2023 | DDC 320.54 – dc23

We wish to acknowledge the land on which the University of Toronto Press
operates. This land is the traditional territory of the Wendat, the Anishnaabeg,
the Haudenosaunee, the Métis, and the Mississaugas of the Credit First
Nation.

University of Toronto Press acknowledges the financial support of the
Government of Canada, the Canada Council for the Arts, and the Ontario Arts
Council, an agency of the Government of Ontario, for its publishing activities.

Canada Council **Conseil des Arts**
for the Arts **du Canada**

ONTARIO ARTS COUNCIL
CONSEIL DES ARTS DE L'ONTARIO

an Ontario government agency
un organisme du gouvernement de l'Ontario

Funded by the   Financé par le
Government   gouvernement
of Canada   du Canada

Contents

Figures

Acknowledgments

The idea to write this book took shape during my sabbatical in Paris in 2017. I was dividing my time between my duties as holder of the Chaire de recherche du Québec contemporain at the New Sorbonne University and my responsibilities as a visiting professor at Sciences Po Paris. In addition to continuing my research and mentally recharging, I was able to organize a series of thought-provoking lectures on cultural and legal pluralism at the New Sorbonne University and, with my colleague Alain Dieckhoff, director of the Center for International Studies, a stimulating series of conferences at Sciences Po Paris, called "The Future of Nations: Continuity and Breaks." The conferences at Sciences Po are directly related to this book. The speakers were asked to discuss contemporary research on nationalism and ways of living together in democratic multinational contexts. Those talks triggered further discussions with colleagues, including Uriel Abulof, Carles Boix, Gérard Bouchard, Craig Calhoun, Alain Dieckhoff, Jan Erk, Jonathan Fox, Jule Goikoetxea, Daniel Salée, and Pierre de Senarclens, that strongly inspired me and above all convinced me that I had to write this book.

However, the book could not have been written without the help of many people, whom I would like to thank here. To begin with, there are the graduate students on whom I tested my initial ideas. Whether at UQAM's Department of Political Science, the biennial summer institute on democracy and diversity, or conferences and workshops, their feedback has always been generous and welcome. Among those whose comments have had the greatest impact on this book, I would like to mention my colleague Geneviève Nootens (Groupe de recherche sur les sociétés plurinationales) and post-doctoral student Félix Mathieu (Universitat Pompeu Fabra, Barcelona), whose suggestions helped make the text more cohesive, and also doctoral student Jérémy Elmerich (UQAM/Université polytechnique Hauts-de-France, Valenciennes), who explained significant aspects of European policy to me. I would also like to thank post-doctoral student Dave Guénette (McGill University), who documented important legal issues that might otherwise have remained obscure.

At the Canada Research Chair in Quebec and Canadian Studies, there is of course Olivier De Champlain, who has been senior coordinator of research from 2005 to 2021. He is always ready to share his knowledge and suggest new avenues to give our work the greatest possible analytical depth. I would also like to take this opportunity to recognize the contributions of PhD students whom I have had the privilege of supervising in recent years until the successful defence of their theses: Paul May (2013), Alexandre Germain (2015), Étienne Schmitt (2016), Valérie Vézina (2016), Jean-Charles St-Louis (2018), Jean Rémi Carbonneau (2019), Marc-André Houle (2020), Félix Mathieu (2020), and David Sanschagrin (2021). My discussions with them provided an opportunity to hone my reasoning and analysis. Many other PhD and post-doctoral students, including Oscar Berg, Audrey-Anne Blanchet, Antoine Brousseau Desaulniers, Jeremy Elmerich, Dan Freeman-Maloy, Guillaume Lamy, Benoît Morissette, Dan Pfeffer, Marc Sanjaume-Calvet, David Sanschagrin, Gustavo Santafe, Arjun Tremblay, and Catherine Viens, also helped me to refine and flesh out my arguments.

The funding bodies, the Fonds de recherche du Québec – Société et culture (FRQSC) and the Social Sciences and Humanities Research Council (SSHRC), must also be thanked for their stubborn defence of research budgets, which are perennially under attack. Academic research – both by professors and by students at all levels and in every discipline – needs to be supported and promoted to provide the new cohorts entering university with the best possible training, and also to disseminate knowledge as widely as possible.

For the English version of the book, I would like to thank Mary Baker for translating the acknowledgments and epilogue, and Benjamin Waterhouse for translating the introduction, chapters 1–7, and the conclusion. Quotes are presented in their English version wherever possible but have mostly been translated from French. I would also like to thank the Secrétariat du Québec aux relations canadiennes (SQRC) for a generous translation grant. Special thanks also to Dan Quinlan, acquisitions editor with University of Toronto Press, for his kind prodding throughout the book preparation, as well as UTP's manuscript reviewers for their particularly relevant comments and suggestions.

Lastly, on a more personal note, I would like to thank my spouse Louiselle Lévesque and our son Vincent for being there and for their joie de vivre and encouragement. This book is dedicated to them above all.

THE LEGITIMACY CLASH

Introduction

I have chosen 2021 as the year to complete the triptych that began with *The Case for Multinational Federalism: Beyond the All-Encompassing Nation*,[1] published in 2010, and continued with *Minority Nations in the Age of Uncertainty: New Paths to National Emancipation and Empowerment*, published in 2014. The decade from 2020 to 2030 could well create the conditions needed to see multinational federalism emerge on the international stage. Given the growing unease shown by major powers and international organizations at the idea of creating new states, one path that deserves serious consideration leads towards this multinational form of federalism.

Many political communities within plurinational states have relations that are characterized by social tension, and this fact deserves special attention. Examples include Ethiopia, which became a leader in Africa after adopting the approach of plurinational federalism, and Iraq, which established the mechanisms associated with federalism. Similarly, in the heart of Europe, Spain is attempting to break away from its sui generis model of the State of Autonomies. Also in Europe, the United Kingdom's exit from the European Union reflects the discomfort felt by many governments facing a loss of state sovereignty.

Recent decades have demonstrated that the experiences of Canada and Quebec have had a key influence internationally on the approaches taken to manage national and community diversity. Today it is impossible to read the work of leading practitioners in political philosophy, law, or political science without seeing references to Canadian and Quebec authors. Special mention goes to the work of Charles Taylor, Geneviève Nootens, Will Kymlicka, and James Tully in political theory, John Borrows, Eugénie Brouillet, Peter Russell, and José Woehrling in constitutional law, Gérard Bouchard and Brian Young in history, and Linda Cardinal, Jane Jenson, and Guy Laforest in political science.

An examination of the way in which national diversity is managed in Quebec and Canada is currently at the heart of the political and social debates in Germany, Belgium, Spain, the United Kingdom, the Maghreb, most countries in the Near and Middle East, Southeast Asia, China, Indonesia, Japan, and beyond. This can be seen in the many studies that followed publication of the Reference re Secession of Quebec (1998) and the report of the Consultation Commission on Accommodation Practices Related to Cultural Differences (Bouchard and Taylor 2008). Clearly these have been two high points in the country's political life, and each has had widespread repercussions in the public debate. In a more concrete way, the studies undertaken following the Reference and the Bouchard-Taylor report have created tools for decision-makers in states dealing with the challenge of accommodating their national diversity. This can be seen, for example, in the stubborn refusal of the central government in Spain to recognize the right of the Catalan government to consult the population on its political future or, less aggressively, in the opposition of the governments led by Theresa May and Boris Johnson to a referendum organized by the Scottish government during the endless negotiations on Brexit.

By way of introduction to this book, I would like to make a few brief comments about the contribution made by the members of the Research Group on Plurinational Societies (known by its French acronym GRSP) to the building of a plural and pluralist society through the emergence of a form of democracy that is open to deliberation and inter-community discussion. The members of the team I have directed since it was founded in the fall of 1994[2] have always made their expertise available to other countries and to public decision-makers and international organizations. They have made a key contribution in several crucial areas and addressed large-scale societal issues. I should add that the team brings together researchers from various fields (Canadian politics, comparative politics, political philosophy, law), working on topics relating to national diversity within liberal and democratic societies. Its most recent work has focused on majority nationalism (2003–8) and the dynamics of trust and mistrust within plurinational societies (2008–13). Since 2014, the members of the team have paid particular attention to matters connected with constitutionalism and constitutional policies in plurinational states – in other words the political dynamics of calls for constitutional reform. This program of work focuses on attempts to amend constitutions in order to transform the rules of the political game and sometimes the actual operation of the state. The objective of the current program, of which this analysis forms a part, is to explore three research paths: (1) the quality of the proposals for constitutional reform put forward by political actors within multinational democracies; (2) the elements that condition deliberations and mobilization on constitutional issues; and (3) the effect of these processes and actions on efforts to reform and extend the democratic exercise. The work will be supported by input from the field of comparative studies and several case studies targeting, primarily, the cases of Scotland and the United Kingdom, Catalonia and Spain, and the Quebec-Canada dynamic, along with relations between Indigenous peoples and various levels of government in the (con)federation.

More broadly, the GRSP program is laid out along three axes. Axis 1 proposes a review of the normative foundation for constitutional policy and the repercussions of certain ideas (internal and external self-determination, the quest for justice and stability, the search for a balance between individual and community rights, etc.) on the evolution of constitutionalism. The projects conducted by my colleagues in this field aim (1) to highlight the place occupied by rights in the emergence of liberal constitutionalism, (2) to identify contemporary issues for deliberation in a plurinational context, and (3) to extend the theorization of constitutional policy. The researchers most closely involved in Axis 2 study the political institutions that structure constitutional reforms and the role played by various political actors. They pay particular attention to the processes for developing constitutional dynamics, while taking advantage of comparative analysis (institutional contexts, actors and interests present, opposing political ideas) over the long term. The researchers involved in Axis 3 analyse the influence of the legal rules (in constitutional and international law) and study the political use of law for constitutional reform. This research field looks more specifically at the contribution made by constitutions to the well-being of the population, as well as the judicialization of political life.

My own triptych project advanced as part of the work of the other GRSP members, which explains my gratitude and academic debt to them for having generously shared and willingly agreed to compare their ideas and world views over a period of twenty-five years. I can only hope that this dialogue will continue and grow with input from researchers with such a rich and diverse range of interests.

Within the GRSP, my own work has tended to focus on the creation of the conditions conducive to the establishment of multinational federalism in countries where national diversity constitutes the main political asset underlying the pact on which the sovereign state founds it legitimacy.

In *The Case for Multinational Federalism: Beyond the All-Encompassing Nation* (Gagnon 2010) I tried to highlight the normative aspects that are often neglected in the work of federal studies specialists, whose view is frequently limited to empirical, technical, or descriptive considerations that are unlikely to reveal the concerns of minority populations within sovereign states. In fact, it is essential to understand the traditions underlying these states and the principles on which their actions are founded. This dimension is often ignored by the people who hold power within federal states, and this is why it is important to reassess our ways of looking at and doing things. Otherwise, the legitimacy of the political elites in positions of authority will only be lessened. It is important to act now, to extend and broaden democratic practices. These are the objectives that guided me during the writing of this book.

Contribution to the Field of Knowledge

The main contribution made by *The Case for Multinational Federalism* was to set up the main normative elements promoted by contemporary liberal philosophies in order to reveal communities and their accreditation within larger wholes (Tully 1999). Respect for the normative elements of justice, equality, liberty, fraternity, and solidarity is ultimately intended to guarantee the stability and, above all, the preservation of the state, while establishing its legitimacy. Another goal was to contrast three key principles at the centre of political action: the community principle, the equality principle, and the democratic principle. Each principle can receive more or less emphasis, depending on whether the federation opts for the plurinational path[3] or the territorial path as the main reference for resource allocation and the sharing of power.

In Canada, the majority nation has generally appeared unwilling to support the community principle but has nevertheless admitted that Quebec could rely fully on the democratic principle during episodes of high political tension. This was the case for the May 1980 referendum on sovereignty-association, the referendum on the 1992 constitutional agreement (Charlottetown), and the October 1995 referendum on the proposal for sovereignty-partnership.[4] In Belgium, since the early 1970s, the political actors have been willing to accept the community principle (Van den Wijngaert 2011), while deepening the state's power to share and extend sovereignty in international relations (Paquin et al. 2006) and seeking – in the case of the prosperous Flemish community – to sidestep the egalitarian principle in the field of social security (Béland and Lecours 2008, 2012).

The trajectories followed by Belgium and Canada are surprising because, although the two countries have taken separate paths, both have experienced significant political tension over the last half-century for different reasons. The comparative study that Dimitrios Karmis and I conducted in the mid-1990s, when Belgium and Canada were, once again, searching for a winning formula to achieve state stability, showed that different formulas for constitutional adjustment could lead to similar results. In Belgium, the political actors promoted cultural and linguistic compartmentalization to reduce contact between the political communities, while in Canada the central government consistently supported universalizing measures through the establishment of social programs, health care programs, and other initiatives. However, the results have been similar: greater fragmentation in identity. In both cases, the decisions taken have fuelled identity disconnection, either because of an excess of universalism or because of too many specificities or particularisms (Karmis and Gagnon 2001).

The second book in the triptych, *Minority Nations in the Age of Uncertainty* (Gagnon 2014), adopts a more philosophical stance. At the time I hoped to encourage political and social actors to rethink the functioning of the state and the allocation of key state functions in light of the expectations and needs expressed by minority nations in multinational states. The aim was to require states, as they have been constituted over the years, to rethink the basis of their power relations in order to meet the national affirmation needs of the political communities at the origin of the constitutional compact. In this second book, I highlighted two main ideas: first, that liberal nationalism – perhaps more than any other expression of liberalism – carries within it the essential characteristics for the implementation of more complete democratic practices and, second, that the federal ideal can be realized only in liberal democracies that have reached the most advanced stage.

This was a partial response to the numerous criticisms of the dangers that nationalism posed for contemporary societies. However, to take the position defended by Yael Tamir in her imposing book *Liberal Nationalism* (Tamir 1993), it is important to reconcile the concepts of nationalism and liberalism, especially since they both derive from the same vein (Canovan 1998). This kind of interpretive approach makes it possible to go beyond the classical theories of liberalism inherited from the Enlightenment and to put more emphasis on a new current of humanist thought (Todorov 2008). The most complete formulation of these classical theories of liberalism is undoubtedly John Rawls's scholarly analyses published since the early 1970s.[5] Tamir adds an essential element to these theories by linking liberalism and nationalism.

Unlike Rawls, and although I appreciate his contribution to the conception of individual liberalism for the achievement of greater equality among citizens and a more adequate representation of political communities, I believed that authority relationships needed to be re-thought, first, in terms of national pluralism. In my world view, this is the first defining element of the state, without which societies fail to realize their full potential and render their actions all the more illegitimate.

Not everything can be reduced to the individual, but rather must be thought of in terms of a fair balance between individual desire and projects of a community nature. As Joseph Yvon Thériault (2019) suggests in *Sept leçons du cosmopolitisme : agir politique et imaginaire démocratique*, individuals must belong to a society and grow within it, creating an urgent need to respect the principle of equality between the political partners at the origin of the federative compact.

Legal expert Christophe Parent has produced one of the most insightful analyses of the multinational federal state. He accurately points out that

> only the existence of territories with their own identity makes it possible to consecrate national identities. This territorial autonomy makes it possible to uphold the collective rights of a nation to its language and culture, ensuring that the linguistic and cultural security offered by the territory preserves a balance for a nation that has become a national minority and a federated majority. In this way, the multinational state affirms the principle of a pact between equal nations, not mere tolerance of a national minority. In short, the multinational state enshrines a collective framework based on the equality of its constituent members and not on a principle of recognition of national differences. (Parent 2011, 79; translation)

It is important for national communities to feel that they are living a shared collective experience and to wish to extend this project of co-construction of identity over the long term. This project will be even easier to implement if the members of the political community share a history and a memory.[6] Federalism has significant potential for the scenario of a pooling of resources on a defined territorial basis. This is what made Will Kymlicka say, "The fundamental reality of political life, dating back to the seventeenth century, is the co-existence of distinct national groups on Canadian soil: Aboriginal, French, and English. Many of the pivotal episodes in Canadian political history have centred on attempts to renegotiate the relationships among these national groups. And these relationships remain the most serious threat to the stability of the country" (Kymlicka 1998, 130).

These comments by Kymlicka have lost none of their relevance two decades after they were first published in English. The sense of urgency –

analysed by Guy Laforest at the same time (Laforest 1995) – has gradually faded away since then in federal and provincial offices in Canada, even though Quebec, almost forty years after the fact, has still not endorsed the repatriation of the Canadian Constitution that was imposed on it.

The underlying goal at the heart of the second volume of this triptych – *Minority Nations in the Age of Uncertainty* – was to suggest that political actors should think about inter-community relations in terms of equal representation rather than power relations. In other words, the aim was to imagine ways in which people in minority political communities could have the same opportunities for self-realization as their compatriots in the dominant national group.

Each nation has its own characteristics and brings together groups and individuals with multiple identities. How can we ensure that each of these sociological realities has a voice in the establishment of public policies, in the adoption of societal choices, and in the relationship between the various traditions present in the territory? This is a major challenge, since it requires dividing power and making it accessible to a greater number of groups, and, as a result, allowing the development of various national projects.

In *Minority Nations in the Age of Uncertainty*, I also wanted to define the main principles that would make it possible to shape a theory of federalism that is respectful of traditions, while at the same time proposing a clearly defined normative approach – which is too often neglected among practitioners of federalism. At all stages in my research, I have emphasized the concepts of shared sovereignty, federal culture, and compact.

Inspired by authors such as Gérard Bouchard, Eugénie Brouillet, Guy Laforest, José Maria Sauca, Ferran Requejo, Yael Tamir, Charles Taylor, and James Tully, I have tried to focus on the essential ethical considerations needed to *make a society* (Thériault 2007). The first consideration is a "sense of proportion" and a search for a fair balance between the stakeholders in the federal compact. Stated otherwise, this means ensuring that inter-community relations are dictated by a willingness to give each party in the federative compact the essential powers needed for full self-realization.

My second goal was to create a climate conducive to the development of social relationships based on respect. This condition is more likely to be met when the partners in the compact create opportunities for friendly contact. These moments ensure that political actors, and the populations they represent, accept the challenge of engaging with rather than ignoring each other – also known as solitude – which impoverishes inter-community interactions and reduces the possibilities for discussion that are so fundamental to life in society. The third goal concerns the need to be hospitable and to create the conditions needed for coexistence within federal entities – a genuine attempt at the accommodation of nations, societal cultures, political forces, and legal traditions.

Turning now to the present book, it is devoted to a discussion about ways to promote the establishment – both in the Western world and in the East – of models open to the recognition and empowerment of nations within plurinational states, as the optimal political path. The goal is not to set out a program of research but rather to take stock of the state of contemporary federal thinking, drawing on the Canadian and European experiences as well as the evolution of international institutions in connection with the affirmation of the principle of shared sovereignty or co-sovereignty. These notions have become popular in Europe and in several federal countries. The discussion makes it possible to establish a basis for designing approaches to accommodation and affirmation for nations within democratic federations of a plurinational nature.

Overview of the Book

This book is divided into seven chapters. In chapter 1, I lay the groundwork for a better understanding of how contemporary states have developed their ways of dealing with the rights of minority nations. More broadly, I want to assess how societal and political dynamics can work together when legality and legitimacy are placed in opposition to each other in complex political spaces. The chapter closes with some conceptual clarifications that will be used throughout the analysis.

In chapter 2, I discuss the successive implementation of several major national policies by the central government in Canada, with the goal of making itself the sole constituent power in the country, to the detriment of multinational federalism. The primary intention is to reduce the member states of the Canadian federation to the role of mere executors with no tangible powers, disinherited from their own sovereignty.

Chapter 3 contains an analysis of (1) the multination as the concrete expression of fully constituted political subjects, even though they are not constitutionalized in Canada, and (2) the adoption of relational sovereignty to address one of the most fundamental challenges to the sustainability of complex democratic societies: the association of peoples within a single state.

In chapter 4, I propose a critical reading of the political order in Canada in light of constitutional changes and changing power relations. I first discuss the existence of competing historical narratives and show how political actors go about imposing some narratives and disqualifying others, depending on whether or not they correspond to their own reading of reality. This discussion will help explain why the central government in Ottawa, relying on constitutional patriotism, is almost invariably satisfied with the adoption of minimalist recognition policies. To close the chapter, I will comment on the position taken by the Justin Trudeau government that Canada has reached the stage of a post-national state. This transition from a colonial state (Delâge and Warren 2017) to a bi-national state, from there to a multicultural state within a bilingual framework, and finally to a post-national state would make Canada the first country to present itself on the international scene in such an ahistorical way.

In chapter 5, I continue the discussion from the previous chapter about the challenge of respecting diversity in all its forms to achieve the full realization of an advanced liberal democracy. I briefly discuss the phenomenon of societal, ethnocultural, religious, linguistic, and national diversity as a strong expression of contemporary society. Here the value of diversity for fragmented societies will be assessed.

Chapter 6 looks at the evolving practices of international organizations in recognizing the right to self-determination of nations that wish to emancipate themselves from their current sovereign state. It discusses the types of regime in place, the sharing of sovereignty (unitary or federal state), and various attributes (regional context, political culture, national history, etc.). From my perspective, sovereignty can be divided and powers can be shared between levels of government. In this chapter I also examine how recent years have seen both advances and setbacks for nations seeking recognition as members of international organizations, while the sovereign states that manage them are increasingly reluctant to expand the circle of nations formally recognized in the form of states.

In chapter 7, the last chapter of the book, I explore in greater depth the strengths and potential of the multinational federal state for nations seeking affirmation where international authorities are increasingly reluctant to see new states emerge. It is important to focus on enabling scenarios for nations seeking recognition. This can be done in various ways. If not all nations can have their own state – given the large number of national groups – it is crucial to imagine scenarios that give them substantial powers within the plurinational state. This affirmation of plurinational diversity and, above all, of its legitimacy is the key idea underlying the whole of this book. It is an idea that I hope will make the plurinational equation more robust, with the central objective of mitigating and ideally countering the structural political imbalances that exist within complex democratic federations.

Chapter One

Laying the Groundwork: Legality, Legitimacy, Fair Democracy

Despite the etymological link with the concept of legality, legitimacy (from the Latin *lex, legis,* "law") means something completely different when the underlying principles are taken into account. Legitimacy, unlike legality, is not concerned with the application of laws, or compliance, but instead with an assessment of the underlying moral values for a political decision or choice. In this area the courts play an essential role, since judges must rule on the validity of a given law and, by extension, the standards it enacts. And judges, to retain the respect and esteem of the general public, have an interest in acting impartially, without giving preference to either party in the disputes brought before them. Although they act within a specific legal (and constitutional) framework, the courts play a key role, particularly in maintaining the linguistic, political, or societal balances negotiated or renegotiated within a democratic state.

Given the political tensions that have characterized inter- and intra-state relations in Europe over the last decade, worries about the democratic health of several member countries appear justified. The most immediate cause for concern among observers of the political scene is the situation in Spain. During the last fifteen years, the country has faced movements for national affirmation of varying intensity, after finding an ingenious way to leave the Franco years behind in the late 1970s by establishing a regime that highlights the political autonomy of the regions and recognizes some as "historic nations." In response to these tensions, the central Spanish state has adopted an intransigent position under which "there is no legitimacy beyond legality" (Bossacoma i Busquets 2020, 275). This uncompromising attitude has the sole aim of disqualifying social and political opponents within the state of autonomies, and even of presenting their public actions as a reprehensible form of disloyalty that needs to be severely punished by the courts.

In this way, legitimacy and legality are placed in opposition to each other, with no negotiation possible, deliberately creating a dead end with consequences that can lead only to a weakening of the social bond.

In the opinion of a Spanish jurist of Catalan "nationality," Pau Bossacoma, this creates a form of "constitutional fundamentalism" (Bossacoma i Busquets 2020, 275) that blocks all ways out of the political crisis tearing Spain apart for a decade and a half. From Madrid's point of view, the only possible option is unconditional obedience to the status quo, making the constitution a sort of a sacred text. In other words, the only conceivable "way out" from the current impasse is to comply with the Spanish Constitution as the sole expression of both popular sovereignty and an apparently monolithic constituent power.

Although all analysts understand that legality is a form, and also a source, of legitimacy, in a democratic context it would be too limiting to adopt such a formalistic, narrow, and self-serving position on the principle of legitimacy. The issues of justice and equity must also be taken into consideration if all individuals are to have a role to play in political representation. In short, the political pole must be given as much importance as the legalistic pole.

Nation-Building

The stubborn refusal to recognize the existence of their own nationalism is what makes Spain, France, Italy, and, to a degree, Canada so different from other Western liberal democracies. To counter majority-based nationalism, the political communities they include may develop counter-hegemonic strategies (Forsyth 1994, 23) or, in a more forthright way, seek to establish their own sovereign state. The situation is different in Bolivia (Sichra 2014), Ethiopia for some time (Fessha 2016), the United Kingdom (Brown Swan and Cetrà 2020), and several consociational democracies (Lijphart 1999, 2008), where tension is relieved by ongoing political negotiations that yield encouraging results and even make a contribution to political stability.

In this chapter I will describe the main sources of legitimacy in liberal democracies, before assessing the degree to which they may conflict. On this point, philosopher Daniel Weinstock (2004) has noted a phenomenon specific to these democracies, which he describes as an expression of "republican fear" – an anxiety that community pluralism could eventually threaten the majority nation and, by extension, the very stability of a liberal democracy. For Weinstock, the emphasis should be placed not so much on the presence of a common identity or the existence of shared values, but instead on the conditions that help establish a society based on mutual respect and trust. There is a clear link here with the work conducted by the researchers at the Research Group on Plurinational Societies (GRSP).

A monist vision of the nation state has gradually been given precedence by the political authorities in Canada over a vision that could – and, from my point of view, should – have shown more sensitivity to national pluralism. The political authority that the member states of the federation were recognized to hold, until the Second World War, has been gradually dissipated to the benefit of the political centre (Macdonald Commission 1985). The monist vision received a slight jolt in August 1998 when the Supreme Court of Canada, in Reference re Secession of Quebec (1998), recognized the democratic principle as a key underlying principle of the constitutional order that guarantees both the proper operation of political institutions and respect for the political communities that cohabit in Canada. To recapitulate, the Supreme Court affirmed in article 66 of the ruling that "the relationship between democracy and federalism means, for example, that in Canada there may be different and equally legitimate majorities in different provinces and territories and at the federal level. No one majority is more or less 'legitimate' than the others as an expression of democratic opinion" (*Reference re Secession of Quebec* 1998, para. 66). In this 1998 decision the judges also took care to specify the fundamental principles, defined as being of equal importance, that should inform, organize, and strengthen the relationship. These are the four fundamental markers for its interpretation: (1) federalism, (2) democracy, (3) constitutionalism and rule of law, and (4) protection of minorities.[1] We are a long way here from the biased and intransigent position adopted by the Constitutional Court of Spain to deal with repeated demands for constitutional negotiation from political players in the Basque region and Catalonia, in particular since the early 2000s (Payero-López 2020).

On 11 September 2008, the Constitutional Court of Spain, acting in accordance with the centralizing forces at work in Madrid and echoed in several Castilian regions, declared that the decision by *lehendakari* (president) Juan Jose Ibarretxe to hold a referendum on the political future of the Basque Country inside or outside the Spanish state was unconstitutional. In a unanimous decision, based on clause 149 (1) (32) of the Spanish Constitution under which "the State holds exclusive competence over … authorization for popular consultations through the holding of referendums," the judges at Spain's highest court ruled against the holding of a referendum (Lazaro 2008). All the arguments deployed were based on legal considerations, with no attention paid to the cultural, political, and societal issues. However, a decision on whether or not to hold a referendum on the future of a historic nation, in this case the Basque nation, lies in the political domain and, as a result, should be freely discussed in the political arena. Political representatives have a duty to take on this responsibility on behalf of their constituents. In a context of this kind, two legitimacies (one emanating from the central state and one from the regional state representing the autonomous community) must have an opportunity to seek and, in the most optimistic scenario, achieve a democratic and negotiated settlement.

The intentions of Juan Jose Ibarretxe were clear. In his view, the central Spanish government and the other autonomous communities had to be forced to begin constitutional negotiations to review the functioning of the state of autonomies from top to bottom. Clearly Ibarretxe's plan was inspired by the sovereignty-association formula (Sauca 2010; Lecours 2012) promoted in Quebec throughout the decade 1970–80 by former premier René Lévesque and the militants of the Parti québécois, in a debate in which citizens were offered two legitimate proposals for society. Using all the means at its disposal, the federal government in Ottawa managed to beat the sovereigntist forces on the political field and won the first round. The second confrontation came in 1995, when the sovereigntist forces led by Premier Jacques Parizeau lost their second referendum-based attempt. Quebecers had freely decided their political future after having an opportunity to gauge the merits of the two options presented at the referendum. The debate did not centre on legal arguments but on the intrinsic value of two legitimate political projects.

The most recent developments in Spain – this time in connection with the future of Catalonia – do not reflect the democratic approach taken in Canada during the referendums of 1980 and 1995 and in the United Kingdom during the 2014 referendum in Scotland. The intransigent position taken by the Spanish government involves opposing all forms of political contestation from the autonomous communities, with no possibility of appeal. The only option offered is for political leaders to adhere unconditionally to the rules set (once and for all) at the end of the Franco era.

This view of the necessary relationship between the political centre and the autonomous communities involves declaring "subversive" (Curko 2016) (1) any attempt to renegotiate the constitutional arrangements without having first obtained approval from the central government, or (2) any proposal that diverges from the existing constitutional text. In short, the autonomous communities face a double lock, and any constitutional change that is not initiated by, and to the advantage of, Madrid is impossible. Any attempt by the autonomous communities to make a change could lead to accusations of disloyalty from the central regime. The constitution is viewed as a sort of immutable mechanism that cannot be set aside and deprives the constituent nations of their freedom for the benefit of the encompassing nation (Tully 1999).[2] It is this refusal to recognize the freedom of the constituent states, combined with the introduction of a direct, uniform, and identical relationship with each citizen, regardless of his or her national attachment or allegiance, that is the problem.

Essential Conditions for Political Stability

The legitimacy of a political regime depends, not on brute force, but on a number of key principles. I will limit myself here to four essential conditions for political stability: freedom to act, informed loyalty, ethical diversity, and judicial impartiality. Each of these conditions emphasizes elements that are consistent with the quest for greater social cohesion within political communities, rather than the use of coercion by the *unitary state* (Fazi 2020). The conditions have the same normative value and must be pursued jointly.

First, it is important to emphasize the capacity of political regimes to guarantee each community's *freedom to act*, allowing it to achieve its full potential at the cultural, economic, political, and institutional level. This freedom of action is essential to either building or rebuilding, as the case may be, the bond of trust between political partners within the state and involves regularly respecting and encouraging democratic deliberation as well as the quest for individual and community autonomy. In short, citizens are free to act within their environment and the universe of meanings that gives true meaning to their own existence as political subjects. Jorge Cagiao y Conde (2014, 295) has said of the current period, marked simultaneously by cultural diversity and a quest for unity, "We are perhaps free to choose, but always in a context of defined choices that both limit and guide our freedom." With that proviso, it is important to emphasize that *freedom to act* will be sustainable and bear fruit only if it targets individual and community autonomy and, at the same time, the greatest possible equality between individuals. This definition of the freedom to act involves merging what Isaiah Berlin describes as the positive conception of freedom with a negative conception in order to ensure the protection of individual rights and freedoms (Berlin 2002). A policy of recognition must be established to promote the emancipation of individuals (positive freedom) while moving towards the creation of a political regime with as little constraint, interference, and domination as possible (negative freedom).[3]

Once this first condition has been met, the bond of trust will be consolidated and will allow the second condition to emerge. The political authorities at various levels (local, regional, national, supranational, international) will be able to expect *informed loyalty* from their constituents. The goal is not to obtain blind, unconditional loyalty, but to establish political practices that enhance respect for the political entities concerned. This informed loyalty should lead to greater trust in political leaders among the general population. This trust must always be conditional, in order to create a climate conducive to permanent negotiation in a democratic regime (Tilly 2005). The intensity of the loyalty will vary, depending on the context, the power relationships present, and the previous experiences of each of the political communities called upon to cohabit within the same sovereign state.[4]

The third condition concerns the prevalence of *ethical diversity* within pluralist democratic societies. Diversity results from the establishment of conditions that are conducive to the exercise of group-differentiated rights, to use the expression aptly proposed by Will Kymlicka, to ensure that the members of political communities (both minority and majority) can enjoy full cultural, political, institutional, economic, and social emancipation. Support for this conception of what is right can, in the presence of national pluralism, help promote the establishment of a social project at a human scale, not to suppress rights or oppress populations, but to give back to political communities their dignity and their ability to represent themselves fully (Tierney 2004).

Ethical diversity is at the heart of the debate about the moral right to political self-determination – whether internal or external. The scholarly community can rely, in particular, on the work of political scientist Dimitrios Karmis, who has devoted a great deal of energy to exploring the ethical issues found across all liberal democracies. He invites us to view national identity as an emancipatory ethical project, measured by the criteria of "three levels of pluralism on a rising scale: (1) possible inclusion, (2) symbolic inclusion, and (3) deep inclusion" (Karmis 2004, 91). This leads him to distinguish pluralism as a "sociological fact" and then as the expression of a "political ideology."

Next, Samuel LaSelva (2018, xvi) offers an insightful reading of the evolution of political arrangements in Canada when he suggests that "in 1867 and 1982, it [Canada] reached beyond the British and American models, devised (however imperfectly) constitutional arrangements to accommodate 'the rights of others,' and in that way contributed to the ethics and practice of constitutionalism in a divided world." LaSelva's reading presents Canada not as a continuation of the British or American models, but as the expression of a sui generis model (41–2) that is potentially responsive to the needs of Indigenous nations, minority groups, and communities of destiny.

The fourth condition concerns *judicial impartiality* and is often overlooked in other analyses, even though it is a sine qua non requirement for full implementation of the three previous conditions. In the absence of judicial impartiality, the balance that must be maintained between individuals, groups, and political communities can fail under stress for lack of state neutrality.[5] The lack of impartiality may force some political communities, deprived of their full rights, to challenge the political authority of the sovereign state. In a situation of this kind, political differences will highlight the sovereign state's lack of moral authority, and its inability to offer solutions that are not based on coercion or violence, weakening the democratic principles that should form the very foundation of the political regime.

This is why we can agree, like philosopher James Tully, that the judges of the Supreme Court of Canada did not exercise sufficient restraint when they defined the constitutional obligations of the central government that permitted the repatriation of the Constitution in the early 1980s. Surprisingly, the Supreme Court judges – in a split decision in 1980 – agreed not to require unanimous agreement from the provinces before authorizing repatriation, helping to lift the main obstacle for the central government. This hazardous decision, which was to have considerable consequences, deprived Quebec's National Assembly of its full freedom to act with the other partners in the federation and reduced its power as a national community that had become culturally and politically rooted over the long term (Gagnon and Iacovino 2007).

My colleague Guy Laforest has written several analyses of the role played by the Supreme Court of Canada, drawing inspiration from British philosopher John Locke. Laforest states that the move to repatriate the Constitution was driven by a desire to "strengthen allegiance to Canada, [and] promote Canadian identity" (Laforest 1990, 630). It was a significant action taken to entrench Canadian citizenship. Laforest also notes that "the price to be paid to complete the repatriation operation was considerable. From a 'Lockean' standpoint, we could affirm that the events of the fall of 1981 and the spring of 1982 rendered the Canadian government institutions illegitimate" (630) and, we might add, clearly so for the Quebec nation.[6]

Reference re Secession of Quebec (1998) later attenuated and partly corrected what I consider to be a grave historical injustice for Quebec. As stated previously, the *Reference* recognized the existence, within Canada, of two national majorities, one English-speaking and one French-speaking, each holding its own legitimacy. Similarly, each had the right to devise its own political future while respecting the other.[7]

The way in which the repercussions and consequences of the 1998 *Reference* are interpreted varies widely, and we will return to this question later. However, it would be remiss of me not to mention how political scientist David Sanschagrin views the *Reference*, especially since he refuses to believe in the Supreme Court's impartiality. Rather, Sanschagrin considers that the Supreme Court is a powerful tool in the hands of the sovereign state: "The symbolic violence exercised by the state via the judicial branch proved to be insufficient. The [1998] *Reference* stated, on the one hand, the 'obligation to negotiate' and, as it were, the existence of a Quebec *demos*, while on the other hand making it subject to the principles of federalism, democracy, protection for minorities, and constitutionalism and the rule of law. The essential was preserved" (Sanschagrin 2019, 222).

As noted in the introduction to this chapter, the situation in Canada contrasts strongly with the situation in Spain, where the central government constantly attempts to impose its own wishes on all the political communities otherwise known as autonomous states. The Government in Madrid claims legitimacy for itself alone and declares itself the sole defender of the democratic rights of citizens living in Catalonia. Political scientist Marc Sanjaume-Calvet rightly considers that this position shows a clear lack of consideration for the legitimate demands of elected politicians and representatives of civil society in Catalonia.[8]

> The events in Catalonia show the difficulties faced both by federal governments and by legal or moral theories on secessionism and federalism. The Spanish executive led by Mariano Rajoy, and the main state-wide parties (PP, PSOE, Cs) reject both the right to hold a referendum in Catalonia and/or the existence of a "just cause." On the one hand, their discourse is based on the Constitutional Court's interpretation of the 1978 Constitution, stating the existence of a unique sovereignty and framing a self-determination referendum as unconstitutional. On the other hand, the fact is that state-wide parties appoint the central State institutions (including judges) and hold a qualified majority both in Congress and the Senate, effectively blocking any constitutional reform. (Sanjaume-Calvet 2018)

Relying on these four conditions – freedom to act, informed loyalty, ethical diversity, and judicial impartiality – it is possible to win the allegiance of citizens and all political communities to a joint political project. In a liberal democracy, allegiance cannot be imposed. Instead, it must be voluntary and negotiated continuously if the constitutional order is to be renewed and sustained.

As Anne Legaré points out, "The state derives its legitimacy from the consent of society" (Legaré 2020, 141). Similarly, whether within the Canadian federation or a liberal democracy of a pluralist nature, the multinational state must derive its legitimacy from the consent of its constituent nations, given that each possesses *equal democratic legitimacy* compared to the central state, which cannot claim a monopoly on representation and, by extension, an exclusivity of moral and political power (Whitaker 1991). The very existence of these legitimate national projects reminds us of the importance of adhering to democratic values that are increasingly stringent and sensitive to diversity.[9]

For this reason, as stated by sociologist Jean-François Laniel (2020, 243), it is important for "centres of knowledge and political centres [to be] asked to take into account the multiple modes of the aspiration to self-determination, and their equal democratic legitimacy." Among community-minded liberals, this is a reasonable and measured position to adopt in a democratic context, given the imperative of recognition and the need to accredit political communities. It is also the position I defend here.

A Fair Democracy

In the early twentieth century Max Weber proposed a highly relevant distinction between the fields of *Staatspolitik* and *Kulturpolitik*. The first concerns the elements that are connected with power, authority, and the integrity of the territory and state, while the second covers the cultural and societal aspects that are essential to the establishment and survival of a societal culture or, more specifically, a national culture. The two fields may be co-constructed, or may collide with each other. For Weber, *Kultur* plays an important role in the emergence of a national conscience (McCrone 1998, 20). The dynamic that interested Weber was primarily the relationship between the state and society. In his view, the state plays a key role by acting as both a shield and a nurturing hand to ensure the well-being of society (21).

The vision of the country generally held by the *Canadian political community* recalls the close relationship between the sovereign state and society imagined by Weber on the basis of a single national identity. However, the image of Canadian reality held by the political community in Quebec is more complex, first because it is involved in the edification of its own national construction project and its own collective identity, and second because its citizens tend to turn first to the representatives of the Quebec state in a crisis, whether constitutional, economic, social, or health-related (Gagnon and Iacovino 2007, 91–122; Noël 2013, 176; Gagnon 2020b).

The existence of projects for society that are often separate and specific either to Quebec or to the rest of Canada specifically raises the question of the legitimacy of power. Once again, it is to Weber that we must turn in order to clearly identify what is at issue. He refers to three typical ideals of "legitimate domination": the rational-legal, traditional, and charismatic authorities. For each of these forms of authority, the actors must perceive the relationships of authority and power as being fair and just. Similarly, to ensure full legitimacy, these relationships of authority must be fully recognized, consented to, and justified by all parties involved.

In more concrete terms, while summarizing slightly, the rational-legal authority ensures that the legitimacy of the laws passed is established and recognized by the members of the entirety of the political body. For this reason, there is no room for arbitrariness or an ad hoc decision-making process. The rational-legal legitimacy is both legal and political, but not necessarily immutable.

Traditional authority is, in contrast, based on customs and practices. It can be seen as an expression of an ancient constitutionalism in which customary rules prevail. In this context, "authority rests on the natural and continuous transmission of power, conferred by ancestral rules, customs, habits, and patriarchal or dynastic relations" (Meier 2019, 2). Authority relies on the long term. Here the repetition of a practice founds its legitimacy. Last, charismatic authority is based on an entirely different logic, in the sense that members owe total respect, devotion, and disproportionate obedience to the leader over time. Each form of authority expresses a specific type of legitimacy and it is never found in pure form.

Weber's contribution to the understanding of the sources of legitimacy is of great importance. However, it must be recognized that in light of various upheavals in history, it is difficult for people in power to retain full legitimacy. It is over time that we can measure the effective value of each authority. The most frequent criticism of Weber's analysis is that it lacks the normative considerations that are needed to assess the legitimacy of existing regimes. As a result, it does not offer a suitable approach to the political sphere, because it is necessary to consider the assessment of existing regimes and gauge the extent to which they still deserve the allegiance of the populations living under their authority. Robert Grafstein has identified this analytical gap with possibly the most lucidity, and he formulates the heart of his criticism as follows: "Weber distorts the essential meaning of legitimacy. The concept should properly signify a normative evaluation of a political regime: the correctness of its procedures, the justification for its decisions, and the fairness with which it treats its subjects. In Weber's hands, however, legitimacy no longer represents an evaluation of a regime; indeed, it no longer refers directly to the regime itself. Rather, it is defined as the belief of citizens that the regime is, to speak in circles, legitimate" (Grafstein 1981, 456). Grafstein's observation reminds us of the importance of distinguishing properly between "representation/perception" and "lived world/real condition." The way in which legitimacy is presented by Weber moves us further away from the four normative conditions that are essential to political stability, described at the beginning of this chapter. Weber's analysis of legitimacy has little to do with political freedom, informed loyalty, ethical diversity, and judicial impartiality. In fact, it can even be suggested that it bypasses them, meaning that the four principles appear as blind spots in his analysis.

I have already discussed the question of fair democracy – in other words, democracy accompanied by fair and equitable practices – in some of my work, and I will not spend much time on it here. Examples include, in particular, the essays that Brian Tanguay and I assembled and published (Gagnon and Tanguay 1992), in which we identified several shortcomings in the exercise of democracy in Canada. Similarly, in a research project with Guy Lachapelle just after the October 1995 referendum in Quebec, we discussed the failures of the Canadian federation in democratic practices. Our conclusion was that the Quebec government and federal government were seeking to ensure the allegiance of their respective populations by proposing separate societal projects based either on individual rights (the Canadian position) or community and individual rights (the Quebec position) (see Gagnon and Lachapelle 1996).

It is important to understand that the rise of independence movements in liberal democracies can be explained in large part by "the decline [at least in perception] in legitimacy of central states, resulting from their incapacity to adapt to new socio-economic problems (in particular the crisis of the welfare state), and the reconfiguration of political space resulting from continental integration and globalization" (Turgeon 2004, 63). These phenomena helped distance the "stateless" nations from the sovereign states in which they are embedded. The political representatives of several of these nations are convinced that they can do better, both nationally and internationally, by promoting their own know-how (Katzenstein 1985; Rioux 2020) while highlighting their contribution to the development of knowledge. With regard to the current context for a form of governance better adapted to the needs of national communities, Michael Keating states that "nationalist discourse is modernist and concerned with development and adaptation rather than antiquarianism and looking to the past. It accepts the limits of sovereignty and searches for ways in which self-government may be made effective and a project for national self-assertion mounted, in the absence of the classical nation-state" (Keating 2001a, 63–4).

Not all national communities have the same potential. Some achieve better results alone, while others appear to have more need of sustained assistance from the central state in order to earn a place on the glo-balized world stage. However, the ability to intervene at a finer scale appears to be a systematic advantage for cooperative actions between economic, political, and social actors. This cooperation promotes dis-cussions and trust among the actors and makes it possible to quickly establish strategies for targeted, calibrated actions. In the words of Keating, "Conditions for the viability of the new nationalisms are not a mere checklist of discrete items. They are elements in a stateless na-tionalist project which can sustain each other to create a system of ter-ritorial autonomy within the new framework of the changing state and international order.... On a more modest scale, they may hope partially to reconcile the imperatives of culture, identity, economic competitive-ness, social integration and democracy" (Keating 2001a, 75).

Recent years have seen considerable progress in the para-diplomacy of minority nations, as they have opted for increasingly innovative strategies to acquire access to international markets and gain, or regain, recognition without going through the intermediary of the sovereign state. These nations do not need to withdraw into themselves – at the economic level both Scotland and Quebec, for instance, have used ven-ture capital to consolidate their economic growth and their place in the international economy (Rioux 2020). The economic breakthroughs made by Scotland and Quebec have raised confidence, in their respec-tive populations, in good governance and the greater effectiveness of the programs put in place to conquer new markets. The same can be said of Bavaria, Flanders, and the Basque Country (Massie and La-montagne 2019). In each of these examples, there is a clear intention to participate fully in economic networks at the regional, continental, and international levels.

For this reason, fair democracy cannot be achieved if the majority nation remains impervious to the legitimate demands made by the mi-nority nations and political communities that form the backbone of the plurinational sovereign state (Parent 2011). In other words, it is not by imposing only the norms desired by the majority nation that nation states will be able to build an equitable relationship between the consti-tutional partners (Chouinard 2020).

It is therefore important to recognize the elements that can bring about change, since they are essential in order to avoid collective, identity-centred episodes of tension. Among the elements that have potential for making the constituent communities of plurinational democracies aware of the needs and demands of others is an equitable sharing of power among political communities, citizenship education to achieve strong social cohesion in each community, the establishment of constitutional asymmetry to better reflect community diversity, cultural socialization through the acquisition of a common language, and the creation of bridges to promote awareness of other political communities and the creation of places for shared decision-making (Burelle 2005, 2020, 524).

Redefining Markers

The sociological reality is that there are several nations in Canada (Langlois 2018), explaining the increasingly frequent use of the term of multinational or plurinational federalism to describe the Canadian condition (Secrétariat aux affaires intergouvernementales canadiennes 2017). However, this reality is not taken into account by many political actors, and this leads inevitably to dissatisfaction with the existing political institutions among a growing proportion of the Quebec population. During the intense constitutional debates of the early 1990s, Maude Barlow and Bruce Campbell stated, "We must redefine our concepts of sovereignty and nationhood in order to establish institutional relations among members of the three founding nations of Canada: aboriginal, French-, English-speaking. To do so, we will need to reverse our one-dimensional definition of a single nation. Our survival and emancipation will depend on our ability to build on well-defined aboriginal, French-, and multicultural English-speaking national identities and to channel the creative energies of those parts into a cohesive entity called Canada. (Barlow and Campbell 1991, 144; quoted in Jenson 1995, 108)

This criticism of the monist approach represents a trend that is slowly gaining momentum in Canada. Today, among academics, senior civil servants in central government, and the general population there is significant recognition for national diversity in Canada. The sustained contribution by what has been called the Quebec school of diversity and federalism (Gagnon 2011, 2015a; Mathieu 2020b)[10] and the meaningful additions by numerous Indigenous colleagues (Ladner 2019; Borrows 2016) have clearly played a part in this shift in the way in which Canadians see each other and the political communities they form at various territorial levels.

It is important, as established by Barlow and Campbell, to redefine how we think about the political community, nation, and state. Each concept has several possible meanings, and the way in which they are defined has significant repercussions for our understanding of citizenship, sovereignty, political authority, and the legitimate exercise of power. A balance must be struck between the political (state, nation, citizenship) and the cultural (nation, language, heritage, memory, identity).[11] The balance will be hard to achieve, but this is where one of the greatest challenges for liberal and democratic societies in the twenty-first century lies: the peaceful cohabitation of political communities within political spaces undergoing perpetual transformation (see Gagnon and Tremblay 2020).

The goal of my analysis here is to make readers aware of the importance of thinking of political relationships not as a zero-sum (or negative-sum) game but as a positive-sum game in which everyone can benefit. Sovereignty should not be presented as something that can be parcelled out or viewed as a competition in which each political force tries to subjugate its adversaries. Rather, sovereignty should be seen as relational, interdependent, and shared (Coyle 2019; Ladner 2019). This text seeks to establish to what extent "inclusive governance" – a system in which multiple voices are taken into account – contributes to the consolidation of democracies (IDEA 2017).[12]

There are countless cases of majority nations attempting to impose their own wishes. Of course territorial integrity remains important to sovereign states created following victory in war or the sharing of land after armed conflict. Democracies need political stability, but it cannot be maintained without ensuring the dignity of its political communities and in keeping with the highest international standards.

The federal formula has vast potential for the establishment of the essential conditions needed to ensure respect for national diversity in large territorial units. However, as legal and constitutional expert Stephen Tierney points out in connection with federalism, "Since federalism is a distinct order of rule for the modern state, it follows that it must be understood as transforming political power into legal authority *for a particular purpose* and one that differs from default or monist constitutionalism" (Tierney 2019, 1; emphasis in the original). This conclusion is not shared by other political actors, who would rather level down the meaning of the federal ideal, in particular by failing to take into account the multinational vision of federalism and the demoi that give full legitimacy to the resulting whole. Again according to Tierney, "A federal constitution … is premised upon territorial constituent power which prioritizes the constitutional status, symbolically and substantively, of its constituent territories. It is the consent of these territories that gives the constitution its foundational and ongoing legitimacy and which operates within the constitution to condition fundamentally, the constitution's pattern of authority" (2).

What makes the federal formula even more effective, in democratic terms, in national pluralism is its ability to pay serious and ongoing consideration to the claims made by territorially established political communities. Each territory requires the sovereign state to give it a decisive voice in the shared governance of the federation. This can be done, for example, by agreeing to a co-decisional process (Burelle 2020), governmental autonomy (Tremblay 2000; Nimni 2005), or significant representation in the central institutions (Popelier and Sahadžić 2019: see also Burgess and Gagnon 1993, 2010a; Gagnon and Burgess 2018a).

It is indeed the question of legitimacy that makes it possible to conceive of the political order as being the result of the federal traditions leading to the Canadian constitutional compact, rather than the expression of a monist vision overriding all others. The political aspect must express both the power relationship and an ethical approach based on what is fair and equitable. This quest for balance will be a focus throughout this work.

The question of legitimacy – whether through a deepening of the bond of trust or reciprocal recognition of the political communities involved – must be at the heart of inter-community relations. The key issue at the centre of constitutional negotiations in Canada since the start of the Quiet Revolution in the 1960s in Quebec has been recognition for several demoi and for several political subjects. This has led to struggles between the defenders of Canada as the single constituent power and those who could only conceive of the country as the expression of multiple constituent powers (Loranger 1884; Iacovino and Erk 2012, 211, 216–17). The Supreme Court of Canada leaned in the latter direction, in particular in paragraph 150 of Reference re Secession of Quebec (1998), where it invoked democratic legitimacy as the cornerstone of the entire Canadian constitutional edifice (I will come back to this in chapter 4), by endorsing the notion of *original sovereignty* as formulated by Claude Ryan, the former editor of *Le Devoir* and at the time leader of the Quebec Liberal Party.[13]

Some Conceptual Clarifications

Before looking more closely at the evolution of the Canadian constitutional order, it is important to specify how several concepts will be applied, including nation, state, national sovereignty, territorial federalism, plurinational federalism, and plurinational/multinational federal state – five key concepts that will be used here.

First, the concept of nation refers to a perpetually evolving political subject – connected to other political subjects, also evolving – that aspires to full emancipation through the advent of a traditional state or a state with a plurinational foundation. The objectives targeted vary naturally from one nation to the next but can be summarized essentially as: (1) recognition for a specific political identity – although one that is undergoing constant transformation and adaptation; (2) establishment of a recognized territorial presence in a specific political whole; and (3) establishment of conditions to ensure longevity and sustainability. As a result, a nation must be able to rely on the essential resources that guarantee its continuity within the existing constitutional order and in the wider concert of nations at the international level. The concrete implementation of a nation-building project requires effective political mobilization through the elaboration of shared historical referents, joint projects, and a feeling of belonging that promotes cohabitation and social cohesion. The depth and intensity of the sense of allegiance within a nation will provide a clear indication of the political objectives that can be achieved. The concept of nation suggests that the equal dignity of national cultures must be prevalent. In its weakest form, a nation may be a political community while still, for example, existing within a looser political framework that promotes the establishment of multicultural or intercultural practices.

The concept of nation state suggests concordance between a fully sovereign state and a culturally and sociologically formed nation. France and Germany come immediately to mind. The formation of both nation states often involved the use of coercion, although in some cases the political communities living in the territory joined voluntarily. In this chapter, the concept of a national state refers to a sovereign state recognized by international organizations and having a specific voice within them. In general, there is a strong match between a feeling of belonging and the presence of a sovereign state. Depending on how power is shared, a national state may be monist/unitary or pluralist/federal. Another possibility is the multinational sovereign state, where the state entity is made up of more than one national political community.

The notion of popular sovereignty in some ways confirms the democratic quality underlying state-building. Each nation can aspire to set up its own state if it possesses the resources to do so. Various formulas have been proposed to meet the needs of these nations or, in some cases, to force them to accept the rules imposed by the majority nation. The most frequent formulas in a democratic context are territorial federalism and multinational/plurinational federalism.

Sovereignty can be seen as the political expression of the constituting power or powers of the political authority. It gives substance to the demos as the institutional expression of the political entity. Inspired by the work of Bodin and Hobbes in the version current in the sixteenth and seventeenth centuries, the concept of sovereignty expressed the indivisibility of power, which is what gave it its absolute character. In its contemporary form, sovereignty is generally seen as fragmented and having the function of delimiting the responsibilities of the political institutions in place. This introduces the idea of shared sovereignty (generally associated with a federal regime), relational sovereignty[14] (Crown – member states – First Peoples), and totalizing sovereignty (generally associated with a unitary regime). The political actors in each configuration hope to occupy their jurisdictional fields and sometimes to assert their powers through coercion. The central government's quest for greater scope of action, to the detriment of the cantons, provinces, autonomous communities, or *Länder* appears to be an increasingly generalized trend,[15] although globalization has significantly mitigated the impact of the state's decisions. We should also note that the concept of sovereignty – at least for several Indigenous nations (Alfred 1999) and Quebec where it concerns the *original sovereignty* forming the foundation for the Canadian federation (Brouillet, Gagnon, and Laforest 2018, 3–25; Seymour 2016; Laforest and Gagnon 2020) – is used interchangeably with peoples' capacity for self-determination.

The concept of territorial federalism does not focus on the constituent nations or national political communities forming the federal compact, but instead advocates the implementation of public policies with no regard for community considerations. The territorial federalism formula is most often applied by centralizing political forces and is largely dominant in the field of federal studies (Requejo 2005; Requejo and Nagel 2011).[16] This can be explained, in large part, by the fact that the American model used to set up many different federal systems has come to be seen as the self-evident form of government. A US-style institutional rationale has often led to the imposition, by force, of a political mode that aims to merge all communities into a single nation based on the single principle of unity, thereby undermining and discrediting any other "pole of identification" that could have formed a basis from which a new context of choice might have emerged (Taylor 1992, 54, 55, 58).

The American model has spread to several countries engaged in territorial consolidation or cultural homogenization. Countries in Latin America have tended to apply this model when gaining independence as their political authorities pursued two objectives: to emancipate themselves from colonial tutelage, and to focus all political communities on a single point of cultural and political allegiance. The same applies in several national political communities attempting to free themselves from colonial forces in Africa and Asia. India and Nigeria, for example, opted for territorial federal regimes. Australia and Canada are also examples where the establishment of territorial federalism was favoured by the political elites and economic powers, even though calls for greater national diversity were expressed at various times.

Federalism is known to have had considerable success in keeping large states together. A prime example is India, but the group includes Brazil, Canada, the United States, and Mexico.[17] These states surprise us through their ability to renew themselves and endure, despite the political tensions that have marked their history. As federations, however, they have displayed an obsessive interest in unity, while they could have avoided serious political and social tension by adopting an approach better able to recognize and highlight the national diversity that characterizes their populations. Other federations have attempted to impose a territorial model and unity while ignoring the most elementary democratic requirements, and nobody can forget the drama of Yugoslavia (see Gatti 2017). Because tension is created when the territorial model is imposed, new scenarios must be found, and this will be discussed in chapters 5 and 6. For now, we will turn to the notion of multinational federalism.

Multinational (or plurinational) federalism offers the possibility of addressing community-to-community relationships by sharing sovereignty between the constituent entities of the plurinational state. This involves recognizing not one, but several constituent powers. This type of federalism balances the forces at play, but above all the competing claims of the nations living in interrelation within a complex democratic state (Gagnon and Keating 2012; Seymour and Gagnon 2012a). The intention underlying the establishment of multinational federalism is threefold: (1) to promote the democratic emergence of a range of choices allowing national political communities to achieve full emancipation, (2) to endorse the existence of plural loyalties within a complex democratic state, and (3) to slow significantly the homogeneization of culture and identity that continues to impoverish the planet.

This type of multinational federalism generally results from an alliance of political partners, which is why I will refer to it later as *pactist federalism*. In this way, the prevalence of multinational federalism helps justify the legitimacy of the right to recognition that is lacking in so many countries that claim an attachment to freedom and justice.

According to jurist Christophe Parent who, in my opinion, has produced the most complete analysis of the concept of a plurinational federal state, "Imagining a multinational federal state involves considering the possibility of a federation of juxtaposed nations and, from there, the coexistence of several national sovereignties within a single state. It means imagining federalism as sovereignty divided and shared" (Parent 2011, 25). The multinational federal state discussed by Parent offers a compelling response to the shortcomings of the modern state – a state that, instead of benefitting from the potential of its constituent nations, seeks to silence them in the name of the so-called superior interest of the unifying, homogenizing, and integrating nation (Schmitt 2016).

Having made these conceptual clarifications, I would like to conclude this chapter by describing how multinational federalism could provide a better response than any other federal formula to the democratic requirements existing in a context of national pluralism. I associate the establishment of a multinational federal state characterized by *deep diversity*[18] with three goals: harmonious cohabitation, political stability, and a reasoned balance between individual and collective rights.

First, harmonious cohabitation must be promoted. Multinational federalism promises a specific *political project*: to invite, in a complex democracy, both the majority nation and the minority nations to coexist within a federal state. This requires the majority nation to agree to share power by subscribing to principles other than those that rely on "the power of the state" (Beaud 1994). For this purpose, it is important, first, to devise institutional arrangements that promote the reciprocal recognition of nations (in the case of a plurinational federation) and ethnocultural groups (in the case of a plurilingual or pluriethnic federation) – or both – and second, to ensure that the communities can participate fully not only in collective decision-making – the principle of shared sovereignty – but also in their own decision-making – the principle of autonomy (Elazar 1979a, 1979b, 1991).

The adoption of the multinational formula still appears to me to offer the most promise of political stability in a federation that is a complex liberal democracy. The aim is not to promote the emergence of a nation-people – a *Staatsvolk* (O'Leary 2001)[19] – or the emancipation of the majority nation alone. Instead, the political project is to create conditions conducive to the representation of each nation within the multinational state and to promote, as I mentioned earlier in this chapter, its full emancipation in the name of democratic fairness. This is the second major goal underlying the establishment of a multinational federal state.

The third major goal in adopting the multinational federal state formula is to require liberal theorists to reconsider, in light of the theoretical advances of the last forty years, the endlessly recurring idea that individual rights must inevitably take precedence over other considerations. In short, I posit that the advancement of individual rights can, in fact, be achieved through the creation of political institutions better able to defend the political communities within a complex state. This way of conceiving the political arena will (1) give a prominent voice to the legitimate claims made by the minority nations, and (2) promote a political climate favourable to the establishment of a political culture associated with a community of belonging.

In the next chapters I will review the potential of multinational federalism for complex democratic states, while seeking to redefine power relations in light of the theoretical advances and academic work in Canada and Europe that I believe are the most promising.

Chapter Two

Foundations of and Changes to the Federal Project in Canada

The Canadian National Project

The Canadian federation was originally established in 1867 by two main political communities: French Canada, majoritarily Catholic, and English Canada, majoritarily Protestant (Paquin 1999; Brouillet 2005). To these communities we must also add the First Peoples, who were present throughout the land north of the forty-ninth parallel. Over the following decades, in response to both economic opportunities and social and military conflicts, other major waves of immigrants came to join the bold project to build a new state to the north of the United States.

The creation of this new state was a major challenge. First, two rival European traditions – one French, one British – had to coexist (Brouillet, Gagnon, and Laforest 2018). Second, a way had to be found to cohabit with the Indigenous peoples, who had occupied the land since time immemorial (Tully 1995b). The establishment of the new political regime caused the Indigenous nations grave injustice and untold harm, often by isolating them and invariably by depriving them of their resources.

Religion played a critical role in the creation of the country's political institutions as Protestants and Catholics jostled for position, with Protestants gaining the upper hand and enjoying access to the highest spheres of economic and political power. For almost the first century of Confederation, religion exerted an enormous influence over all sectors of society and created a significant divide between Catholics and Protestants. Language, however, gradually emerged as a more important factor for political mobilization and, beginning in the 1960s, became the most significant divide, and the transition was one of the underlying causes for the Quiet Revolution in Quebec.

French-speaking communities in the early 1960s, with newfound pride, were insistent in denouncing the historical inequities they had suffered.

With my colleague Richard Simeon, I have highlighted how the injustice faced by French speakers from the earliest years of the Canadian state was one of the main historical reasons for, first, their desire for cultural, political, and economic emancipation and, second, the transformation of Quebec's French-Canadian identity into an identity that is truly Quebec-centred – civic and territorial. It should be noted here that "following Confederation, Ontario and the newly created provinces of Manitoba, Saskatchewan, and Alberta, and the Northwest Territories, all enacted policies limiting the linguistic rights of French Canadians. This was a major historical cause of the eventual shift of national identity within Quebec from French Canadians to Québécois" (Gagnon and Simeon 2010, 7:115).

The many obstacles placed in the way of French Canadians as citizens of equal dignity within the Canadian federation generated major political disruption. Examples include the foundation of several political parties, both in Quebec and in Ottawa, to call for fairer and more equitable treatment (Bickerton, Gagnon, and Smith 1999), and the establishment of several commissions of inquiry, the most prominent of which in the field of French-English relations was the Royal Commission on Bilingualism and Biculturalism, known as the Laurendeau-Dunton Commission (Lapointe-Gagnon 2018). The goal of the next section is to highlight the monist logic that characterizes the functioning of the Canadian federation.

The Main "National" Policies

As the late Donald V. Smiley has shown, the central government took steps to impose its vision on all the political players. Taking advantage of the political situation at various times, it was able to reinterpret the foundations of the Canadian federation to its own advantage and to redefine its founding myths. For example, the central government deployed a series of pan-Canadian policies to leave its mark on the evolution of Canadian society as a whole. Five of these policies had a significant effect on nation-building and the transformation of the federal state in favour of the central government. These were: (1) the well-known National Policy of John A. Macdonald in 1879, (2) the national policy adopted during the Great Depression of the 1930s, (3) the national policy to establish Canadian citizenship in 1947, (4) the coming into force of the *Official Languages Act* in 1969, providing a formal framework for linguistic duality, and (5) the adoption of a new Canadian constitutional order in 1982.

However, in connection with these policies, it is also important to mention the White Paper on Indian Policy tabled in 1969 by Minister of Justice Jean Chrétien, designed to extinguish the rights of the First

Peoples with the "official" objective of making them citizens like any others. It was quickly withdrawn following the swift mobilization of Indigenous communities across the country. This apparently progressive policy, hiding behind a discourse of openness and the fight against discrimination directed at the First Peoples, in fact led directly to assimilation. The previous approach to managing the Indigenous issue, based on the creation of reserves, would have been dropped completely (Rodon 2019, 54–5). Opposing the White Paper in 1970, newly emerged Indigenous organizations rallied around the two documents they produced in response (the Red Paper and the Brown Paper). The Red Paper demanded compliance with the treaties signed and called for land essential to the development of their communities to be protected and reserved for their use. It also contained elements that recalled some of the objectives pursued by the Quiet Revolution in Quebec, which were presented to the federal Parliament in the spring of 1970 by the Indian Association of Alberta (such as to be master of one's own destiny, governmental autonomy, and access to education). The Brown Paper endorsed the idea of differentiated citizenship (*citizenship+*), a notion put forward in the report of the Hawthorn-Tremblay Commission on the Economic and Social Situation of First Peoples in Canada (1964–70) and specified that Canada's Indigenous peoples have Aboriginal rights (Mejia Mesa 2020, 118–19). In short, the reaction was so immediate that the central government had no choice but to end this new attempt at assimilation. We will come back to this in chapter 5. For now, we will look in turn at each of the five pan-Canadian policies that were energetically promoted by Ottawa to give concrete form to its centralizing vision.

The main objective of the National Policy of 1879 was to extend Canada's boundaries to include the vast territory located north of the forty-ninth parallel, from the Atlantic to the Pacific. In addition, the project called for the construction of a transcontinental railway to supply future inhabitants and bring the natural resources of Western Canada to Canadian and international markets. Last, it aimed to create the conditions needed to support settlement in the extensive lands west of Ontario and Manitoba. To achieve all of this, the central government introduced an immigration policy that, over the long term, would change the balance between Canada's French-speaking and English-speaking communities. This first true national policy also put protectionist measures in place to favour an East-West market using tariff barriers.[1] On the basis of this policy, the economic and political elites created a state based on the development of human resources, raw materials, and infrastructure, while the United States had to go through the torment of a civil war in its state-building process. The economic framework put in place at this time allowed Canada to develop a common project, even though it did not share a common language, culture, or religion.[2]

The second national policy we will examine here was more political than economic, although it was adopted because of the need to respond effectively to the economic problems of the time. The Great Depression of the 1930s had highlighted the difficulty for the member states of the Canadian federation of dealing with their accumulated deficit, given that their fiscal resources were no match for their obligations. Instead of seeking to replenish the provincial coffers by providing additional resources, the solution chosen was to centralize fiscal resources and give the central government responsibility for allocating them suitably. Because of the binational nature of the federation at the time, this would obviously create major political tension between Ottawa and Quebec. It was during the implementation of this second national policy that, in 1935, Canada created its own central bank following the work of the Royal Commission on Banking and Currency (the Macmillan Commission) in 1933, which looked at the operation of Canada's financial system. After taking this initiative, but still facing a difficult financial situation, the central government set up the Royal Commission on Dominion–Provincial Relations (the Rowell-Sirois Commission) in 1937 to investigate the balance of power between the central government and member states of the federation. The commission's work contributed to a review of the sharing of powers in Ottawa's favour in the area of social programs (unemployment insurance, the old age pension) and later to the introduction of an equalization program. The overall result of these initiatives was to give the central government control over some of the powers most likely to directly affect the lives of citizens, significantly increasing its legitimacy for all Canadians.

A decade later, more specifically on 1 January 1947, the government established its own policy on citizenship to continue Canada's emancipation from the British Empire. The new policy was part of a nation-building process and gave the Canadian identity a new symbolic anchor of key importance. Canadians from all backgrounds were invited to leave behind their previous identity (Indigenous, French, British, Irish, or other) and take up a new, shared identity. The *Canadian Citizenship Act* changed significantly over time as new challenges arose. They included, in 1977, the abolition of the criterion that gave special treatment to British subjects and the statement that it was a privilege to obtain and maintain Canadian citizenship. In 1977, when the Parti Québécois had been in power in Quebec for less than a year, the central government planned to "emphasize the responsibilities associated with Canadian citizenship, the symbolic value of the passport, and the need to help maintain Canadian unity and Canada's territorial and political integrity. Saying that one was Canadian meant, first and foremost, being accountable and loyal to the Canadian state" (Labelle and Rocher 2008, 159). The citizenship policy has been revised several times since 1977, but the essentially minor changes made have simply updated standards and criteria and reminded citizens that their commitment to Canada prevails over all other commitments.

The coming into force on 7 September 1969 of the *Official Languages Act* was another key moment in Canada's nation-building project. It ensured access to federal government services in French and English[3] across the country – at least where numbers warranted. The objective, for the central government, was to take the initiative in the language arena just as increasing numbers of Quebecers were identifying with the positions of the autonomist, sovereigntist, and independentist parties in Quebec, and when the Royal Commission on Bilingualism and Biculturalism (Laurendeau-Dunton Commission 1963–71) was continuing its vast project to draw up an overview of linguistic realities in the country. The goal was also to ensure that French speakers and English speakers would henceforth turn to Ottawa to defend their language rights and to short-circuit the decisive role that the Quebec government intended to play in defending the French fact in Canada. This gave rise to significant tension, and even legal battles, between Ottawa and Quebec.[4] And in fact, despite the way in which the mandate of the Laurendeau-Dunton Commission was worded, in its first term (1968–72) the government of Pierre Trudeau chose to ignore the contribution made by biculturalism to social cohesion country-wide and to substitute multiculturalism as its main point of reference. In this way Canada was no longer seen as an alliance between two main cultures but as a plurality of cultures placed in a bilingual framework that gave the central government freedom to take action in the language field.[5] The effect of this policy could only make Quebec's francophone community more fragile over time (Mathieu 2020c) – and perhaps foreshadowed the description of Canada by Prime Minister Justin Trudeau as neither binational nor multinational, but post-national. I will come back to this point in chapter 4.

The fifth national policy, and clearly the one with the most impact, was the fundamental review of the operation of the Canadian federation during the repatriation of the constitution in 1981–2. The substitution of a new formula to replace unanimous consent by the parties to the federative compact deprived the only French-speaking province of its historic veto. Similarly, the adoption in 1982 of the *Canadian Charter of Rights and Freedoms* created a situation in which, in Quebec, the *Charter of Human Rights and Freedoms*, passed on 27 June 1975, had to be interpreted in light of the norms imposed by the new "national" (meaning pan-Canadian) charter. The creation of the new constitutional order gave Canada additional tools for its nation-building project, but introduced conditions that could potentially lead to a breakdown of the Canadian federation.[6] The new constitutional order also generated a political dynamic that endorsed the principle of strict equality between the provinces (despite their substantial differences) and equality between individuals, and, last, gave the judicial power a quasi-hegemony over the Canadian political regime. These transformations resulted in the balance between competing claims (Quebec versus the rest of the federation, or the Indigenous nations versus the other nations within the federal compact) becoming a conflict of preferences (centralization versus decentralization, or tensions between state control over certain areas and the privatization of public services) (see Banting and Simeon 1983; Simeon and Minz 1982).

With the support of these national policies, the central government was able to impose its key aims and its own preferences on the Canadian federation. Even before the repatriation in 1982 and the weakening of the role of the provinces within the federal dynamic, Claude Ryan, the then leader of the Quebec Liberal Party, wrote in the "Beige Paper," "In the history of Canadian federalism, unilateral powers [disallowance power, reserve power, declaratory power, spending power, residual powers, general taxation powers, judicial appointment power, etc.] have been used frequently and have often been a source of contestation and crisis. They introduce into our institutions a dimension of unitarism that constantly risks unbalancing the division of powers in favour of the central government. They violate the basic principle of federalism, which is the absence of subordination of one level of government to another."[7]

In this way, the central government gradually imposed a monist form of logic on the Canadian federal system, with repercussions on the relationships between Canadians in different regions, and on the nations that form the basis for the state. The members of the Research Group on Plurinational Societies have been extremely active in this area in recent years and have highlighted the consequences of the change for the quality of democratic debate in Canada. They are concerned about the lack of interest in holding a constitutional discussion[8] in the form of a healthy, public debate (Karmis and Rocher 2012; Laforest 2014; Gagnon and Poirier 2020a, 2020b).

The Centralization of Power

In scholarly work on federalism there is a belief that all federal systems tend to favour the decentralization of power, and in Canada several authors have gone even further and claimed that the Canadian federation is the most decentralized federation in the world. The argument generally advanced is quite simple: decentralization is measured by the percentage of transfer payments to which conditions attach. In the United States, almost all transfer payments are subject to conditions governing their use, and therefore the American federation is, by this measure, more centralized. The same applies to Germany and Australia, where between 50 and 65 per cent of transfer payments are accompanied by conditions (Simeon 2002, 410).

This type of monocausal interpretation hides a serious lack of nuance. What about changes in the division of power, the role played by the courts, and the possibility for the central government of taking significant action in crisis, whether commercial, economic, societal, military, health-related, or other?

Although I will look at this in more detail later, my goal for now is not to reopen the debate between a Canadian and a Quebec school of thought on federal practices. However, the work published in Gagnon (2006b),[9] and in particular the contributions by Linda Cardinal, Joseph Facal, Andrée Lajoie, Alain Noël, Benoît Pelletier, François Rocher, Michel Seymour, and José Woehrling, is worth studying for the analyses that demonstrate the centralizing tendencies of the Canadian federation.

In a book that has not received sufficient attention, my former colleague from the Université de Montréal, Edmond Orban, has formulated and validated the thesis that even federal states have a tendency towards centralization, whereas common sense suggests that they should favour decentralization. Any decentralization that exists is simply administrative and does not call into question the true exercise of power and governance. This occurs, according to Orban, for two main reasons: the desire of states to remain competitive in the international economy, and their desire to create conditions conducive to economic growth. This leads the central state to take a range of initiatives to stimulate the economy and, above all, make it as efficient as possible (Orban 1984a, 1984b).

However this may be, the centralizing actions taken by Ottawa tend to discourage cooperation between the member states and the centre. This is reminiscent of an extreme case, the situation in Spain, where the autonomous communities cannot even sign inter-community agreements on pain of being accused of contravening and even undermining the constitutional order.

The successive introduction of the five national policies I outlined at the start of this chapter led to an impoverishment of the federal spirit in Canada, by setting aside the very reasons that were at the heart of the confederative project in 1867. This process has helped to de-federalize Canada's political culture, with the central government seeking to either circumvent the powers of the federation's member states, or to impose decisions on them using the spending power it has created for itself.[10]

The policies adopted by the central government form part of a long process of standardization across the country. This can be seen, for example, in several legislative measures behind central government initiatives to create and consolidate the welfare state and increase its own legitimacy in the eyes of citizens of all cultures and backgrounds. The most influential initiatives concerned unemployment insurance in 1940, the family allowance in 1945, hospital insurance and a transfer payments program in 1957, two pension plans in 1965 (including one just for Quebec), and a universal health-care plan and public assistance plan in 1966. Each program has been updated over the years to mirror political and economic events. For example, in 1984 the central government strengthened the public health-care plan by recognizing five fundamental principles: (1) universality, (2) public administration, (3) accessibility, (4) portability, and (5) comprehensiveness (see figure 1). Each principle helps ensure that, in the vast field of public health care, all Canadian citizens have access to comparable levels of services and care, whatever their province of residence.

Figure 1: The *Canada Health Act*, 1984

1. Universality: all residents are entitled to receive insured services under the plan on uniform terms and conditions.
2. Public administration: a provincial or territorial health insurance plan must be operated on a non-profit basis by a public authority.
3. Accessibility: there must be no financial or other barriers to access for insured persons to required hospital and physician services.
4. Portability: payment for the cost of health services is covered when an insured person moves or travels to another part of Canada, or outside Canada.
5. Comprehensiveness: all necessary medical services offered by hospitals and physicians must be covered.

Source: *Canada Health Act* (1985).

All of these initiatives have, to a large extent, transformed the Canadian federal state into a "social state," to use the formula of Peter Graefe (2014). In this way, over a period of around seventy years from the end of the Second World War to the present, the central government was able to impose its presence in several areas under the exclusive jurisdiction of the federated states.

Each initiative in the field of social policy helped, first, to strengthen the national project for the country as a whole and, second, to create a genuine national sentiment. In short, once again in the words of Peter Graefe (2014, 49), "The defenders of Canadian nationalism pressured the central government to implement new social programs and ensure that the citizenship rights connected with the programs be shared by all Canadians, whatever their province of residence. In return, the creation of new pan-Canadian programs strengthened the idea of a community of solidarity that spanned the country."

The Canadian federation gradually imposed a monist position in the drafting of its government policies, helping to reduce the role of the other political communities. There are several reasons for this. I will look briefly at the three that I believe are the most influential: (1) the struggle for power and legitimacy between the central government and the federated states, (2) the rise of the nationalist movement in Quebec, beginning in the 1960s, and the emergence of the provinces as leading players, beginning in the 1970s, and (3) the international economy.

The Struggle for Power between the Central Government and the Federated States

The field of federal-provincial relations is one of the main arenas for power struggles between the country's political actors. Federal-provincial relations have evolved significantly over time, depending on the period concerned, the quality of the actors present, and the resources available.

The years 1867 to 1949 saw phases in the judicial interpretation of the powers of each level of government, although throughout the period the central government attempted to impose its hegemony (Peleg 2007). A wide range of studies show that, until 1949 – the year in which the Supreme Court of Canada was established as the country's highest court – the Judicial Committee of the Privy Council in London favoured Canada's member states in several of its decisions. Jurist Andrée Lajoie (2006) has shown this convincingly in her work.[11] She writes of the Judicial Committee,

Constitutional scholars generally agree that the jurisprudence of this colonial court is the most decentralizing in the history of our Constitution.... This is precisely because of the court's foreign status: London was not at risk of losing the powers that the Council confirmed to the provinces, unlike the Canadian government, which also appoints Supreme Court judges. Throughout this period, therefore, the Privy Council asserted the legal autonomy of the provinces from any federal trusteeship, and even more so a strict compartmentalization of the division of powers: there was a broadening of the listed provincial powers and a parallel narrowing of federal powers that might intrude upon them, such as those relating to peace, order and good government and trade. (Lajoie 2005, 3)

By giving the provinces a voice in the construction of the Canadian federation, the Privy Council decisions helped (1) counteract the centralization of power, (2) energize federal-provincial relations, and (3) recognize the role played by the member states in the construction of the country.

The first decades in Alberta's existence involved numerous political struggles and significant constitutional tensions with the central government. The most influential work to have been published on this topic is by my former colleague at McGill University, James R. Mallory. He highlights the tug-of-war that played out in Alberta when the Social Credit Party wanted to give the province a political and economic boost (Mallory 1954). He demonstrates how, between 1937 and 1942 in particular, Ottawa moved to force the hand of the government of William Aberhart by repeatedly using its power to disallow provincial laws to subordinate the province (and by extension all outlying provinces) to its own ambitions and the needs of the Laurentian corridor.

Mallory (1954) emphasizes the importance of Ontario and Quebec within the Canadian federation and demonstrates how the provinces are, in fact, unequal:

> The inequalities in size and population of the provinces of Canada have been recognized tacitly in a constitution which to a large extent embraces two levels of federalism. The superior size and bargaining position of Ontario and Quebec give them a status and an autonomy which are different in kind to those of the rest of the provinces.... The outlying provinces are still Canada's empire and Canada is still, for many purposes, little more than the original area which it encompassed at Confederation.... These circumstances have tended to make of the disallowance power an imperial device for holding other provinces under the sway of the predominant economic interests of the central provinces. (176)

Mallory's analysis (followed by that of other authors and research institutes)[12] helped provide arguments for the promoters of equality between the provinces (Morton 2005).[13] This position, however fair in appearance, has weakened the dualist and, by extension, the plurinational vision of Canada. We will come back to this in chapter 7.

The Nationalist Movement in Quebec and the Parallel Rise
of the Provinces

In the 1960s and 1970s in particular, two processes for affirmation by the member states of the Canadian federation came to the fore: nationalism and regionalism. On the one hand, they involved recognizing a strong voice for Quebec within the Canadian "confederation" and, on the other, promoting a strategic association of provinces able to resist the pressures of the central government and stand up to the other political and economic players on the Canadian and international stage.

These two affirmation processes balanced, influenced, and inspired each other (Bickerton and Gagnon 2020; Gagnon 2002). However, it was the rise of nationalism in Quebec that did the most to energize federal-provincial relations and ensure that Quebecers enjoyed a period of economic, cultural, institutional, and political levelling up that was unprecedented in Canada.[14]

During a lengthy Quiet Revolution (Gagnon and Montcalm 1990), the affirmation movement in Quebec took the form of a cultural, economic, and political nationalism that could be combined with clearly independentist goals. Although in New Brunswick there were also expressions of cultural and economic nationalism – the political dimension being less evident – there was basically no drive for independence. In this way, the provincial state[15] became a key instrument for promoting the emergence of societies seeking collective emancipation.

Quebec gradually developed an increasingly effective state apparatus, able to support the work of the emerging elites in Canadian, continental, and international networks. In 1965 the creation of Quebec's Caisse de dépôt et placement (Quebec Pension Fund) caused a period of tension with the central government, since it had the potential to play an influential role in economic exchanges within Canada. One of the most intense episodes in this dynamic relationship occurred in the early 1980s, when the Caisse wanted to increase its stake in Canadian Pacific and play a key role in the destiny of what was, at the time, Canada's largest private enterprise. Instead of seeing this as a sign that the Quebec government wanted to take an active stance in the Canadian economy, the central government interpreted the move as economic aggression and an attempt to unduly influence the Canadian economy.

Against this background, and at a time when the governments in Quebec and Ottawa were at odds over the 1982 repatriation of the Constitution, the government of Pierre Trudeau tried to pass Bill S-31 (Corporate Shareholder Limitation Act) to undermine Quebec's initiative.

The bill set a 10 per cent limit on provincial ownership of private enterprises in transportation (Brooks and Tanguay 1985).

André Ouellet, the minister of transport at the time, decried the Quebec plan as an instrument of "socialism" (Bernier 2013). This led to a major conflict between the political and economic elites in Ottawa, Toronto, and Quebec. The bill never received royal assent but, like the sword of Damocles, could be brought back to the political foreground at a moment's notice.

Allan Tupper suggested a revealing interpretation of this incident, describing the bill as a strategic initiative to counter the power of the provincial governments. He saw "S-31 as resulting from a confluence of corporate and state interests. For corporations, the Bill provided a bulwark against provincial government influence in profitable, nationally significant firms. For the federal government, S-31 promised to curb provincial government investment strategies, enhance federal control over such strategies, and strengthen federal jurisdiction over transportation. In this alliance, corporations were defending themselves against threatening provincial interventions while Ottawa was once again on the offensive in its continuing struggle with the provinces" (Tupper 1983, 19). The central government's fear of provincial state-building[16] had reached its paroxysm, and the federal election in 1984 was very much about the role that the provinces – and Quebec in particular – should be able to play in Canada. The election of a Conservative government led by Brian Mulroney in September 1984 can be explained, in large part, by a desire to end the simmering resentment of the provinces over their economic and institutional ambitions. Naturally Quebec was first in line to demand compensation following the repatriation of the Constitution and claim a greater role within La Francophonie and its international networks.

The International Economy

The monist position of the central government has been portrayed as a necessary response designed to give Canada an effective place in the international economy. It gave Ottawa the ability to act without having to worry about the provinces, by adopting an economic strategy that was as coherent as possible and could dominate all the economic actions taken by the various levels of government in Canada.

Initially with Mary Beth Montcalm (Gagnon and Montcalm 1990) and then with Alain Noël (Noël and Gagnon 1995). I have had an opportunity to discuss the key role that the central government, especially under Pierre Elliott Trudeau and later Jean Chrétien,[17] played to the detriment of the member states of the federation. The central issue remained competition between the member states in the race to obtain contracts in all economic sectors and to attract enterprises able to create well-paid jobs with potential for added value.

In an increasingly liberalized economic world, states have access to a decreasing number of tools to influence economic decision-makers and attract private corporations. The rules have changed significantly since the introduction of various free trade agreements, including the North American Free Trade Agreement (NAFTA) – which became the Canada-United States-Mexico Agreement (CUSMA) in 2020 – but also the policies introduced by the World Trade Organization (WTO) and under the Canada-European Union Comprehensive Economic and Trade Agreement (CETA).

Each step involves states in the creation of constitutions, invisible to the average person but with enormous influence over the actions taken by the political leaders. As a result, "instead of taking over a company through nationalization or providing a loan at a preferential rate, governments are increasingly using fiscal policies to attract or encourage the creation of companies. The state subsidizes through the creation of infrastructure or on the basis of jobs created in a national territory" (Paquin 2005, 103).

The state can also encourage economic players to work together more regularly. This goes some way towards explaining, according to Peter Katzenstein (1985), the success of small states (Austria, Belgium, Denmark, Norway, the Netherlands, Sweden, Switzerland) that have been able to swiftly modify their economic strategies to adapt to the changes in international markets. He also notes that the countries that relied on democratic corporatism (see Schmitter 1974) were better equipped than others to make changes to their economic strategies.

The situation in Canada is all the more instructive in that various strategies are in competition with each other. The central government has sought to impose its presence as a leading economic player; however, its actions have not always been accepted by the member states, and the Quebec government in particular, which has often seen them as attempts to intrude on its jurisdiction. In addition, from the early 1960s to the present day, the main socio-economic players (Tanguay 1990; Lévesque and Bourque 2013; Rioux 2020)[18] have accepted the leadership role that the Quebec government previously played in the drafting of economic strategies.

In short, for each of the three reasons used to justify its often intrusive actions in areas of exclusive provincial jurisdiction, the central government had a twofold objective. First, and in the spirit of long-standing national policies, it was implementing initiatives to promote the building and consolidation of the state (state-building); second, it was attempting to create a pan-Canadian identity that incorporated all others (nation-building). It is important now to consider more consensus-based ways to share power and ensure better representation for the political partners within the Canadian federation (Royal Commission on Aboriginal Peoples 1993). In my view, this will require practices to institutionalize multinationality, and in particular an affirmation of the principle of democracy, the principle of federalism, and, last but not least, the principle of co-responsibility in the area of sovereignty.

Conceptual Advances in Multinationality and the Definition of Shared Sovereignty

It is important to separate the notions of "state" and "nation" in order to gain a better understanding of the field of study and the nature of the constitutional and political changes that can be promoted within liberal democracies. To begin, the notion of "state" describes the concordance of a territory, a population, and a government that has generally received international recognition. Applying the formula of Max Weber, such a state is said to hold a monopoly on the legitimate use of force and violence. The state is a representation of all the political institutions (executive and legislative powers), judicial institutions (courts), and coercive institutions (police, army) in a generally undisputed territory. In contrast, and as emphasized above, the notion of nation refers more generally to a proximate political community – although it may have a diaspora – with which "nationals" develop an affinity based on history. It is nourished by shared myths and sustained by a specific language and may be projected over the long term as a shared destiny in a recognized territory (Anderson 1996; Bouchard 2019). After making this distinction, I can now turn to the definition of "multi-nation" – a concept that I believe could become the foundation for the democracies of the twenty-first century.

The concept of "multi-nation" refers to political communities that cohabit in a given territory in order to create the conditions needed to ensure their own continuity.[1] In order to renew themselves, these constituent nations must create a constitutional order that is *negotiated, shared, and freely consented to*. These are the conditions sine qua non for the establishment of a democracy whose moral authority – or overall legitimacy – cannot be questioned by any of the partners to the constitutional compact[2] because it derives, specifically, from participation as well as their non-subordination.

Under this way of looking at the metes and bounds of the constitutional order (a central aspect that I will discuss in chapter 4), sovereignty cannot and should not be exercised in an absolute fashion by a single political authority. This was established by Lord Acton in his treatise on "nationality," when he stated that the theory of unity – which he contrasted with the theory of liberty – led to despotism and revolution and that self-government should be considered instead. Lord Acton (1949, 160) also recognized that "the presence of different nations in a given state ... protects against the servility which flourishes under the shadow of a single authority, by balancing interests, multiplying associations, and giving the subject the restraint and support of a combined opinion." In this way, the multinational approach, like the separation of powers, can guarantee a deeper form of democracy.[3]

Currently, sovereignty must first be relational and then shared. A fair sharing of sovereignty makes it possible for the political authorities, acting at various levels, to have a genuine voice in the decision-making process and in the choices made by the different political communities developing within the state's territory. This analysis will use the notion of relational sovereignty to refer to the exercise of democratic power within spheres of activity and within political institutions.

This chapter has four parts. The first part is devoted to the problematization of the concepts of territorial federalism and multinational federalism in light of the main schools of thought that coexist in the contemporary academic world. The second part offers a review of the federal traditions that coexist and sometimes clash in Canada. The third part explores *treaty-based federalism* as a possible way to achieve democracy with enhanced legitimacy, while mitigating the country's federal deficit. The chapter ends with an analysis of the relationship to be developed between Quebec and the First Peoples who originally occupied the land.

From Territorial Federalism to Multinational Federalism

Since the early 1990s, in the wake of the Royal Commission on Aboriginal Peoples (Erasmus-Dussault Commission), several authors have published scholarly studies of the relationship between French speakers and English speakers and the members of Indigenous communities.[4] However, we are simply at the start of a long process of unveiling, as James Tully would say, of one nation to another. The road will be long and the obstacles numerous, so embedded are the relationships of mistrust that have resulted from broken promises or incomplete discussions leading to negotiated agreements that are then postponed sine die, to the great disappointment of the First Peoples.

The history of Canada is a tale told differently, depending on the political community to which the author belongs, involving the discovery of new lands, conquests, the surrender of territory, or forced occupation. It is said that history is written by the victors, who then set themselves up as the new cultural, economic, or numerical majority. This serves their interest when it comes time to justify legal decisions or political, societal, economic, and institutional choices made in their favour. Stéphanie Chouinard points out, accurately, that "law, far from being an objective instrument, always bears the norms of the person who states it, in other words, in a democratic context, the majority – to the detriment of the minorities who question it" (Chouinard 2020, 175). The same can be said of the power dynamic in the political, societal, economic, and institutional fields, since "once again it is the majority that sets the contours of the law and the range of possible responses to the claims of minorities in the current legal context" (173).

My intention here is not to rewrite or reinterpret history. Instead, I plan to gauge the potential that was not exploited by political authorities and leaders at the time in order to imagine a way for actors of the present and future to join together to create institutions based on national pluralism as a force of emancipation. This would help remove the significant obstacles that remain to fully exercised democracy and the deployment of a well-founded political legitimacy foundation.

The federation set up in 1867 faced a series of challenges. Its first architects hesitated between the building of a new state – the fruit of a convergence of European cultures and traditions – and the creation of a state based point by point on the United Kingdom. It was not until 1982, with the repatriation of the Constitution, that the imperial (umbilical) connection with Britain was completed cut[5] after being so deeply embedded in Canada's constitutional culture.

The federation had little in common with the models proposed by the leading theorists of federalism, whether Johannes Althusius (1557–1638), Pierre-Joseph Proudhon (1809–65) or, on this side of the Atlantic, Thomas Jefferson (1743–1826) and James Madison (1751–1836), who were openly critical of unitary government and the exacerbated centralization of power. At the time of the discussions that led to Confederation – when the First Peoples were kept firmly out of any constitutional negotiation – only Canada East really hoped to see the creation of a federal union (Laforest et al. 2015), failing which there could be no possible constitutional agreement.

Nevertheless, the principle of federalism was adopted in 1867, despite the fact that a multinational federation was not formally institutionalized. As my colleague Guy Laforest and I noted,

> The principle of federalism was chosen in 1867 primarily to preserve Quebec's identity, since it could not consent to the dissolution of its nationhood. For this reason, a bi-juridic civil law system was created, recognizing the equivalence between the *Civil Code of Lower Canada* and the British common law practised in the other Canadian provinces.[6] Similarly, in the sharing of powers, the federated entities were given responsibility for most so-called local matters associated with cultural and community identity – in other words social, civil, family, school and municipal organization. The regime also gave strong legal guarantees to the English-speaking, Protestant minority living in Quebec. It was a regime of complex diversity for Canada, and also for Quebec. (Laforest and Gagnon 2017, 19)

The challenge of creating a new state was met, but without satisfying all partners. Over the decades that followed, Acadians, Quebecers, and, more recently, minority French-speaking communities expressed their disappointment and their desire to review the terms of the pact that joins them to the Canadian political project. As I mentioned above, a political project was imposed in 1982 following failed attempts at constitutional negotiation (Gagnon and Montcalm 1990), leading to the adoption of a new constitutional order.[7] This failed to settle all the problems, and I firmly believe that one day we will have to go back to the drawing board, applying our imagination and resilience in order to respond suitably to the legitimate claims of the First Peoples, the Acadian nation, and the Quebec nation.

Key Federal Traditions

It is relevant here to return briefly to two key federal traditions[8] that compete with each other in Canada. The first, espoused by most Anglo-Canadian researchers, is strongly influenced by the American model, which – since the atrocities of the US Civil War (1861–5) – has promoted the idea of a united and indivisible nation. The second, generally encountered in Quebec, is inspired and influenced mainly by the Swiss tradition, which involves recognizing and promoting national diversity, subsidiarity, political autonomy, and the non-subordination of powers.

The American tradition of territorial aggregation and a balance between the executive, legislative, and judicial powers currently dominates the field of federal studies. This can be explained in large part by the disproportionate role played by Americans on the world stage. Although the American tradition refutes an absolutist view of power, it ignores the national diversity that underlies the federal compact and proposes the creation of a homogenous, uniform society whose overarching goal is to preserve political stability. This tradition recognizes a single constituent power, a single political entity, and a single, unifying nation, and was constructed, at least in the United States, through armed conflict, and in particular by denying the Indigenous nations their most basic rights of representation and self-representation (Day 2018).

Specialists generally describe the US tradition as being the most highly developed expression of territorial federalism, and it clearly influences the direction in which the majority nation in Spain, for example, would like to move the power relationship, even after the departure of Franco and the creation of the state of autonomies (see Requejo 2005).

Fundamentally, the Swiss tradition of federalism differs from the American tradition in two ways. First, it is built on the principle of the political autonomy of the member states that founded the (con)federation; and second, it stipulates the non-subordination of powers between the different levels of government. This tradition has often proved successful in complex democratic societies, by recognizing the founding nations as separate constituent powers (Whitaker 1991; Iacovino and Erk 2012). The greatest challenge in this school of thought has been to reinvent the power relationship on an ongoing and evolving basis, without harming the political communities and historic nations behind the founding compact. The tradition has taken various forms over the years and is generally recognized as being the most advanced expression of *pluralist federalism* (Caminal 2002; Karmis 2009).

However, this pattern becomes more complex when applied to the situation in Quebec. Not only is there a demarcation between the American and the helvetic traditions, but another school of thought has emerged – one to which I have belonged since my early-career work at Queen's University – and become increasingly influential. It proposes the de jure establishment of a multinational type of federalism as a response to the lack of recognition and empowerment, which is a necessary step in order to achieve fair relationships among all the political partners within the federation. To do otherwise can only contribute, with no compensation for the minority nations, "to the legitimacy of the dominant order by addressing [for example] the law and judicial institutions of the majority" (Chouinard 2020, 172).

Viewing demands for recognition from Quebec and the First Peoples as concessions to be made by the central government is to say that the power dynamic is limited to the simple interplay of competing interests where success is largely dependent on the sum of the resources mobilized (Gagnon and Iacovino 2007, 24–5). In this approach, the political communities on which the original compact was based become mere participants, among many other participants, with no regard for their responsibilities and fiduciary obligations. The constitutional order becomes less attuned to the preferences of the founding political communities. This state of affairs allows the central power to consolidate the constitutional order in its favour, taking political realignments of varying intensity into account.

As the balance of power between the Quebec government and the central government shifted at the start of the 1980s during constitutional negotiations on the future of the Canadian federation, several Indigenous groups made their voices heard and began to state their claims with more precision. They included the Attikamek-Montagnais Council, which addressed the Special Joint Committee of the Senate and of the House of Commons on the Constitution of Canada looking at the "Proposed resolution for a joint address to Her Majesty the Queen respecting the Constitution of Canada" in 1980–1. René Simon, president of the council, argued that the Indigenous peoples should at last be definitively recognized as founding peoples with a voice equal to that of the two other founding peoples: "As independent peoples before the arrival of the Europeans, we wish to be recognized as the founding peoples on an equal basis with the English and the French" (Simon 1980; quoted in Savard, forthcoming). This claim added an important historical depth to the call for Canada to present itself, going forward, as a multinational federation.

In Canada outside Quebec, following the constitutional failures of Meech Lake and Charlottetown but prior to the October 1995 referendum in Quebec, a growing number of academics called for the institutionalization of constitutional practices based on a multinational process. The key intervention was clearly the *Toronto Manifesto, Three Nations* in March 1992, signed by Christina McCall, Frank Cunningham, Mel Watkins, Abraham Rotstein, Stephen Clarkson, Pat Armstrong, Roberto Perin, Kenneth McRoberts, Leo Panitch, Daniel Drache, and Reg Whitaker, all academics and public figures from the most progressive circles in Canada (McCall et al. 1992). This public statement helped make the vision of Canada as a multinational federation more popular. Other authors, as we will see in this book, have added highly relevant theoretical precisions, by distinguishing territorial federations from multinational federations (see Gagnon and Laforest 1993; Resnick 1994; Kymlicka 1998, 136–41) or by identifying the major challenges that needed to be met in order to set up multinational institutions in Canada. The Centre de recherche interdisciplinaire sur la diversité et la démocratie (CRIDAQ) held a symposium at Université du Quebec à Montréal in 2009 that brought together a large number of specialists in federal studies, including Michael Burgess, Hugues Dumont, Montserrat Guibernau, Ferran Requejo, Michel Seymour, who first launched the idea and design for the project, and myself, as the director of the centre (see the result in Seymour and Gagnon 2012a). Other research centres following this lead, including the Centre d'analyse politique: constitution et fédéralisme (CAPCF), which published *Federalism and National Diversity in the 21st Century* (Gagnon and Tremblay 2020), and the Centre on Constitutional Change in Edinburgh, directed by Michael Keating, which published *State and Majority Nationalism in Plurinational States* (Cetrà and Brown Swan 2020).

The multinational approach is increasingly attractive to minority nations within liberal democracies (Gagnon 2014; Gagnon and Mathieu 2020). It has certain intrinsic qualities, the most important of which are the ability to create conditions conducive to the establishment of a bond of trust between the partners in the federation, to deepen the democratic experience, and to refine the notion of sovereignty. Each quality helps give more legitimacy to all political forces and their interactions.

The outbreaks of political and constitutional tension in recent decades in Canada have clearly demonstrated the need to devise mechanisms to manage national diversity that are more ambitious and, above all, more respectful of the essential principles for the emergence of a healthy democracy: justice, legitimacy, recognition, hospitality, and empowerment. Only *respect* for and *adhesion* to these principles can allow federal democracies[9] to renew themselves and remain viable over the long term. Reconciliation between the main partners in a pluralist and plurinational state can occur only if the nations are not only recognized and respected but also, in deep diversity, empowered to strengthen and promote their own language, culture, traditions, and institutions.

Only too often, the majority nation seeks to dictate the agenda or ignores the legitimate claims made by the representatives of the minority nations, generating inter-community tensions of varying intensity, depending on the issues involved and the ability of the antagonists to mobilize.[10] It is important, in this age of uncertainty, to promote inter-community discussions and to engage in dialogue to ensure that the terms and conditions of federalism are not imposed but freely negotiated. As pointed out by sociologist Joseph Yvon Thériault, this is all the more necessary because this option may have "a political future in the wake of a stalled sovereigntist project, while the population remains strongly involved in a national intention to create a distinctly French society in North America" (Thériault 2019, 215). His analysis can easily be extended to the situations experienced by the First Peoples, who would also like to embody their own *national intention* while forming a society in their own way within the Americas. This is the approach to multinational federalism formulated here.

Pactism, or Treaty-Based Federalism

When the first volume of this triptych, *The Case for Multinational Federalism: Beyond the All-Encompassing Nation*,[11] was published in 2008, Louis Cornellier (2008) described my vision of federalism for Canada as utopian. Writing for *Le Devoir*, he claimed that Canadian federalism, from the point of view of the majority nation and the dominant forces, could not be viewed in the same way as a multinational federation. Cornellier could not see, in the post-repatriation and post-referendum Canadian world, how and when multinational federalism could be expected to take the place of, or simply cohabit with, territorial federalism, given how unwelcoming the political spheres outside Quebec (and even some élites in Quebec) were to the idea of re-examining the new constitutional order imposed on Quebec in 1982. More recently, in 2019 and 2020, Cornellier mentioned that, at least in theory, it had become possible to think about the development of Canada, as for example in the work of political scientist Félix Mathieu (2020a),[12] from the standpoint of multinational federalism (Cornellier 2019, 2020).

In fact, since the mid-2010s, support for multinational federalism has progressed substantially in academic circles and government offices. The Quebec government even promoted this approach when on 1 June 2017 it published its new constitutional policy, *Quebecers, Our Way of Being Canadian: Policy on Quebec Affirmation and Canadian Relations*. This document mentions that "on several occasions during the last 150 years, the Government of Quebec has stated a vision of federalism that makes it possible for it to affirm its national identity while participating in Canada. This vision is supported by history, and also by contemporary political thought, which sees federalism as the best way to manage cohabitation of various communities within a single state" (Québec 2017, 93).

The first of June 2017 marked a key date in the evolution of federal-provincial and intergovernmental relations in Canada, with the publication of this new statement of constitutional policy. The year was also important for Quebec because the Liberal government of Philippe Couillard wanted to guarantee fair, respectful relations with the First Peoples and to establish nation-to-nation relations within the Canadian federation. This approach *could*, if it had been sincerely promoted, have had significant repercussions for the development of an authentically federal culture. In addition, the Quebec government stated its goal of adopting a policy of inter-culturalism to promote inter-community discussions, while promoting principles designed to bring all citizens together around shared goals and common values.

In light of the progress made by the Quebec school of diversity[13] in contacts with the scholarly community and leaders of minority nations living in a democratic context, as well as senior administrators working at international organizations (see chapter 6), it is possible to state that multinational federalism has become a political option that is more than credible in the deliberations of the committees that address the issue. This federal formula is now taken into consideration for its potential for democratizing institutions, revitalizing political communities only too often barred from negotiations, and renewing the bonds of trust between political partners.

Multinational federalism is generally presented as being based on a freely negotiated compact or treaty. The formula relies on shared sovereignty for the establishment of fair, egalitarian relations between political partners (Burelle 2020). However, such conditions seldom occur spontaneously, given that the competing forces do not all have the same resources, willingness, and ability to change the course of history. This can be seen easily in the Canadian context, for example, when the central government or the provincial governments say that they want to negotiate in good faith with the representatives of the First Peoples, claiming to seek their free, prior, and informed consent in order to launch "development projects." It quickly becomes clear that despite demands from the spokespersons for the First Peoples that the government authorities conduct supplementary studies, assess the feasibility of other scenarios, and increase the environmental requirements, none of the people responsible for the negotiations are willing to sacrifice economic growth in response to those demands.

The pactist tradition requires the political partners to adhere to a federal culture (Burgess 2012, 2015a) that is able to recognize and value the national diversity that forms the basis for inter-community relations. The tradition emphasizes, for example in the case of the First Peoples, the requirement to obtain their free, prior, and informed consent, as formulated in the United Nations Declaration on the Rights of Indigenous Peoples (UNDRIP: United Nations 2007; Webber and Macleod 2011).

Another illustration of the situation was provided, in early 2020, when the hereditary chiefs of the Wet'suwet'en nation in British Columbia opposed the proposal to build the Coastal GasLink pipeline across their ancestral lands.[14] The confrontation lasted several weeks, before the hereditary chiefs agreed, on certain conditions (Picard 2020), to accept the proposals of the political authorities in Ottawa.

It should be specified here that the more the consent is robust, the more the actions taken by various parties will be legitimate. It is important to focus on the political arrangements that should be given priority to establish a form of governance that is legitimate and respectful of the communities involved. This approach makes it possible to adopt the essential conditions that will ensure a return to political stability.

The representatives of the colonial forces saw the treaties they signed with the chiefs of the Indigenous nations as a way to guarantee access to land at a low cost. Political scientist Simon Dabin (2020, 300) notes, "The numbered treaties (those signed between 1871 and 1921) can be considered as the clearest example of the colonial practice" of gradual dispossession, given that the colonizing power could, in fact, impose its presence both militarily and demographically across the entire territory (Bacon 2020).

The pactist tradition underlying treaty-based federalism subscribes to the idea at the heart of this book that conditions conducive to the interrelations between sovereignties must be promoted (Hoehn 2012). Jurist Felix Hoehn observes major flaws in the "doctrine of discovery" used to justify the occupation of Indigenous lands by colonial states[15] and develops an argument to suggest that the Supreme Court of Canada has, in recent years, shifted its interpretation in a way that is of great value to Indigenous nations, moving from negotiations allowing access to their land to the free exercise of sovereignty over specific territories. As a result, sovereignty no longer resides solely in the hands of the colonial states, but in several locations, erasing the idea that the rights of Indigenous nations can be extinguished by constraint, ruse, or force. In this way, treaty-based federalism opens the way to ongoing negotiations between the representatives of various political communities, ensuring an effective method for the emergence of a healthy multinational democracy. It is too soon to confirm such a significant change of attitude by the political authorities,[16] but this pactist variant of federalism brings the idea of pluralist federalism, discussed above in connection with Swiss federal tradition, back into the spotlight. Pluralist federalism has the properties needed for the institutional expression of cultural and national diversity.

Although it specifically incorporates the policy of recognition, the pactist tradition is not always well received (see Dabin 2020; J.-O. Roy 2020). The most critical authors consider it as a continuation, and even an institutionalization, of colonial power by the central government. The analyses by Taiaiake Alfred (1999, 2005) and, more recently, Glen Sean Coulthard (2018) are part of this trend. In *Red Skin, White Masks: Rejecting the Colonial Politics of Recognition*, inspired by Franz Fanon,

Coulthard states, "Without conflict and struggle the terms of recognition tend to remain in the possession of those in power to bestow on their inferiors in ways that they deem appropriate" (Coulthard 2014, 39). It is clear that the possibility that representatives of the First Peoples may be co-opted during the negotiations is a concern that harms all egalitarian-type relations between political partners. The pactist tradition has evident qualities, but also requires the good faith of all players and the establishment of a climate of reciprocal and conditional trust (Gagnon and Poirier 2020a, 2020b).

Quebec and the First Peoples

In Quebec the years 1867–1960 were characterized by a general lack of understanding of Indigenous issues (Rodon 2019, 210–11). It was only during the Quiet Revolution that Indigenous questions began to emerge, while Quebec itself was experiencing economic, cultural, political, and institutional growth of unprecedented speed and scope (Gagnon and Montcalm 1990). The most serious conflict affecting relations between the Quebec government and the Indigenous community concerned the James Bay hydroelectric project in the early 1970s (Gagnon and Rocher 2002). It highlighted the systemic unfairness to which Indigenous people were subjected, setting the stage for an intense struggle and leading to the outlining of the first practices based on the pactist tradition.

The James Bay and Northern Quebec Agreement had its faults but constituted the foundation for building a less unequal relationship between Indigenous and non-Indigenous people living in Quebec (Trudel 2009; Rodon 2019). The agreement was updated when the *Paix des Braves* [Peace of the Brave] was signed in 2002. During this period, when relations were sometimes far from cordial,[17] the Quebec government, more aware of the need to create suitable conditions for a climate of trust and for a contribution by Northern Quebec to its own economic development strategy, adopted a "resolution concerning recognition for Aboriginal rights" (see figure 2) on 20 March 1985 and endorsed a comprehensive plan for a new approach to relations with the Indigenous peoples (Gourdeau 1993, 349–50).

Éric Gourdeau, who was closely involved in Indigenous claims and the first director of the Direction générale du Nouveau-Québec in Quebec's Department of Natural Resources in 1963, has commented on the resolution: "Like the policy toward Inuit, Crees, and Naskapis, the official policy as expressed in the 1985 resolution centres on the signing of negotiated agreements and the legal protection to be given. But it differs in that it is not limited to negotiating when development projects urge settlement of land claims, and in that it is not premised on the extinguishing of aboriginal rights. Rather, the policy is based on the recognition by Quebec of the special status of the Amerindians and the Inuit through [the National] Assembly legislation" (Gourdeau 1993, 354).

Figure 2: Resolution of the National Assembly

That this Assembly:

RECOGNIZES the existence of the Abenaki, Algonquin, Attikamek, Cree, Huron, Micmac, Mohawk, Montagnais, Naskapi and Inuit nations in Quebec;

RECOGNIZES existing aboriginal rights and those set forth in the James Bay and Northern Quebec Agreement and the Northeastern Quebec Agreement;

CONSIDERS these agreements and all future agreements and accords of the same nature to have the same value as treaties;

SUBSCRIBES to the process whereby the Government has committed itself with the aboriginal peoples to better identifying and defining their rights – a process which rests upon historical legitimacy and the importance for Quebec society to establish harmonious relations with the native peoples, based on mutual trust and a respect for rights;

URGES the Government to pursue negotiations with the aboriginal nations based on, but not limited to, the fifteen principles it approved on 9 February 1983, subsequent to proposals submitted to it on 30 November 1982, and to conclude with willing nations, or any of their constituent communities, agreements guaranteeing them the exercise of:

(a) the right to self-government within Quebec;

(b) the right to their own language, culture and traditions;

(c) the right to own and control land;

(d) the right to hunt, fish, trap, harvest and participate in wildlife management;

(e) the right to participate in, and benefit from, the economic development of Quebec,

So as to enable them to develop as distinct nations having their own identity and exercising their rights within Quebec;

DECLARES that the rights of aboriginal peoples apply equally to men and women;

AFFIRMS its will to protect, in its fundamental laws, the rights included in the agreements concluded with the aboriginal nations of Quebec; and

AGREES that a permanent parliamentary forum be established to enable the aboriginal peoples to express their rights, needs and aspirations.

Source: Quebec National Assembly, 30 March 1985.

Although some progress was made in the relationship between Indigenous and non-Indigenous people in Quebec, it was important – as it still is – to continue on the path to closer contact by offering the Indigenous communities guarantees of a constitutional or quasi-constitutional nature. Institutional or political recognition, subject to the hazards of politics, had to be converted into constitutional recognition in order to improve the living conditions of the First Peoples as effectively as possible and help promote the growth of true multinational federalism in Canada.

A negotiation-based culture has gradually, but all too slowly, been introduced in Quebec between Indigenous and non-Indigenous people over the last half-century. The adoption in the summer of 2000 of the government policy *L'Approche commune* marked a decisive step by suggesting, in particular, that relations between the two communities should be more conciliatory and open to dialogue, for the greater benefit of all. However, once again it will be necessary to move to a higher level and create conditions conducive to the signing of genuine treaties in order to contribute to bringing the communities closer together.

Major steps have been taken by signing freely negotiated agreements with representatives of the First Peoples. These include the signing, on 7 February 2002, of the Peace of the Brave in Waskaganish[18] between the Quebec government and the Grand Council of the Crees, respectively represented by Premier Bernard Landry and Grand Chief Ted Moses.

This way of seeing the situation confirmed that inter-community relations could be viewed as a positive-sum game.[19]

The policy document *L'Approche commune* received a favourable response in several regions of Quebec and, in particular, in the Lac-Saint-Jean region. An analysis by Étienne Rivard (2013) in connection with territorial co-management emphasizes the importance of a process based on dialogue and inter-community/inter-ethnic relations to ensure economic, political, and cultural progress for the groups living on and occupying the land. Rivard speaks of an "active cultural dialogue," a "more effective decentralization of the means of development," and "local empowerment" (32) and describes the implementation of a joint approach and the creation of a partnership-based strategy for representatives of the business community, government authorities, and Indigenous leaders in the region. I would like to quote at length from his enlightening analysis:

> Not only are decision-makers strongly supportive of the agreement [*L'Approche commune*], they also go further by taking concrete action to demonstrate their open-mindedness, joining with the Innu community of

Mashteuiatsh for development and land-use projects and for certain public consultations resulting from provincial policies, and in particular the new forestry regime implemented in the spring of 2013 [CRÉ Saguenay–Lac-Saint-Jean and Conseil des Montagnais du Lac-Saint-Jean 2008]. Examples of partnerships of an institutional nature include the creation in 2009 of the Agence de développement des communautés forestières ilnu et jeannoise, a non-profit organization to promote sustainable development in local, Indigenous, and non-Indigenous communities, which depend largely on forestry. The inclusion in 2009 of the Conseil des Montagnais du Lac-Saint-Jean in the Société de l'énergie communautaire du Lac-Saint-Jean (which, at the time, included the regional county municipalities of Domaine-du-Roy and Maria-Chapdelaine) is another concrete example of a partnership with a clear influence over land use and development. The Société is behind two projects for small-scale hydroelectric plants (in Val-Jalbert and on the Rivière Mistassini) as part of an electricity purchase program launched by the Quebec government for generating plants of less than fifty megawatts. The Entente is one of the reasons given for the partnership, a sign of its impact for regional decision-makers, even though it still does not have the power of a treaty. (Rivard 2013, 31–2)

This empowering way of viewing the relationship between, on the one hand, the Quebec government and the regional authorities and, on the other, the First Peoples, is at the heart of Quebec's *Approche commune* agreement. There are, of course, some shortcomings, but overall progress was made and bridges were built to deepen and encourage inter-community discussions, helping to strengthen the link of trust based on more, and more extensive, joint projects and on the governmental autonomy of the First Peoples while bringing the communities concerned closer together.

In Canada, the Supreme Court has recognized the expression of Indigenous sovereignty in the case of the Haida nation, although state sovereignty remains the keystone of the political system. In contrast to the situation in certain US states, the Supreme Court of Canada is still hesitant to support the discourse of Indigenous sovereignty. As jurist Geneviève Motard recognizes, "There is a form of autonomy that results from the case law concerning the application of section 35 of the Canadian Constitution, but it is limited and gradual – in other words established case by case – even when Aboriginal title has been confirmed. The Court has not, however, specified the scope of the management powers this authorizes" (personal communication, 8 January 2021). Essentially the political actions taken are based on the obligation to negotiate in good faith and do not guarantee that the

First Peoples will be able to exercise (full) sovereignty. Major work remains to be done before the description of Indigenous sovereignty will genuinely apply.

Current challenges to the advancement of multinational federalism are substantial. Gradual convergence of the claims made by the First Peoples and by the representatives of the Quebec nation is a compulsory first step to building strong, durable, and respectful ties and for the definition of positions that can achieve a consensus on the future of the political communities. Concerted action, focused on shared sovereignty, is essential if any political progress is to be made, within the state of Quebec or the Canadian federation.

Several opportunities have already been missed in the relatively short history of the Canadian federation, so it is important now to create conditions that will allow the interests of the parties to converge, without asking any party to renounce its goal of achieving greater justice.

A few years ago I, along with colleagues from the Groupe de réflexion sur les institutions et la citoyenneté (GRIC), highlighted what we felt to be the key elements, starting with the right to self-determination, in devising and creating the conditions to establish a genuine partnership between the Quebec nation and the First Peoples. I reproduce here an excerpt from a text we published in Le Devoir: "To provide a solid foundation for the relationship between the Indigenous nations and the Quebec people based on an effective partnership, certain fundamental principles must be established. These include legal equality between the Indigenous peoples and the Quebec people. Their respective right to dispose of their own destiny, to freely select their political status, and to freely ensure their economic, social, and cultural development must be asserted with conviction and without reserve. This general principle of self-determination is essential and must structure the direction taken in relations between Quebecers and the First Nations" (GRIC 1994).

This position emphasizes that the nature of the relationship that should exist between the Quebec nation and the First Peoples is similar in all points to the relationship that the Quebec nation, as a minority nation, has demanded and continues to demand from the majority nation in Canada. The demand is not new – it can be traced back to the Quebec Act of 1774 and has not been extinguished by the constitutional reforms that have followed. Jurist and political scientist Peter H. Russell calls on the majority nation to make amends by dealing in an egalitarian way with the nations living on the land when the federative compact of 1867 was made. As he points out, "For many in both groups, their primary social identity and political loyalty attach to 'nations' or 'peoples' older than the Canada created by Confederation. These Canadians do not accept that the tide of history has somehow washed away these nations of their first allegiance or diluted their constitutional significance. Their enduring presence as 'nations within' Canada is fundamental to understanding Canada, as is the often troubled, uncomfortable accommodation of these 'nations within' by the country's English-speaking majority" (Russell 2017, 3).

This illuminating comment by Russell offers a living, up-to-date view of the direction of inter-community relations in Canada, while opening the way to the creation of a relationship of powers that match the historically multinational nature of Canadian federalism. The use of a term inspired by the multi-nation would make it possible, according to Russell, (1) to restore trust in the central institutions among the members of the minority nations; (2) to bring about a liberal democracy that would be more advanced in the sense that it would take nationalism of a liberal type more seriously into consideration; (3) to have a more accurate view of the identity issues and legitimate claims made by these nations; and (4) to de-couple the notions of "sovereign state" and "nation" – a nation of nations – to better highlight the characteristics of political association and the joint decision-making processes that must accompany it.

The emergence of a multinational federation – which is comparable in many respects to the well-known notion of *unionism* in the United Kingdom and consists of formally recognizing national identities in order to implement a joint political project – gives real meaning to the edification of a complex democratic state whose operating principles involve first naming, but also supporting, each of the political communities seeking freedom and justice.

However, the multi-nation can be distinguished from unionism in the sense that it allows sovereignty to be seen not as indivisible and singular, but as shared, relational, and plural. By recognizing from the outset the coexistence of several demoi as the foundation for the sovereign state, it becomes possible to think about the relationship between the original political communities on a solid foundation in a language that promotes deliberation and ongoing unveiling. In this context, depending on the situation, the national communities could implement policies to support multicultural practices, establish intercultural policies, or, in a more consociational tradition, promote a given language within a national territory. The first possibility matches the official policy that the central government adopted for Canada starting in 1971, while the second is more in harmony with the government policies established by successive Quebec governments since the late 1970s in response to the federal strategy to impose institutional bilingualism. The third possibility has been adopted in countries such as Belgium and Switzerland (Gagnon 1991b) and was the goal of several Indigenous nations in Canada to end the dismantling of their cultures and the impairment of their languages (Richez and Pandya 2020).

In return for their loyalty to the sovereign state, multinational federalism allows minority nations to re-establish – or revive – their original sovereignty, while taking into account the need for coordination, cooperation, and cohabitation with political partners in the federation. The exercise of shared, relational sovereignty between the constituent nations is not simple window-dressing. It is a genuinely existential question (Baker 2005), in the sense that its absence can jeopardize the future of the political community. The exercise of sovereignty is crucial if each political community – organized socially, economically, politically, and institutionally – is to achieve full emancipation, as suggested over fifty years ago in Quebec by Marcel Rioux (1969). When he provided an overview of the far-ranging changes in Quebec society that helped raised its profile on the international stage.

The spokespersons for the First Peoples and Indigenous authors often do not agree on the meaning to be given to the concept of sovereignty.[20] Some see it as the expression of a form of colonialism, some as the consecration of Western imperialism, while others believe that it is an essential instrument supporting the self-determination of Indigenous nations and, by extension, the recognition of their original sovereignty.

In summary, I have tried to show in this chapter that the legitimacy of the national projects pursued by the political communities in Canada remains intact. Similarly, the statement – heard so many times – that it is not possible to reopen the Constitution to make changes is nothing short of a denial of freedom for the nations making up the Canadian multinational federation. This position must be challenged vigorously, especially since the Canadian federation constitutes "an association of sovereign peoples" as stated by an increasing number of Indigenous authors and political thinkers in Canada[21] including John Borrows, Michael Coyle, Kiera Ladner, Joshua Nichols, Peter Russell, and Michel Seymour. In short, as my colleague Raffaele Iacovino and I have written, "Canadians do not constitute a sovereign people, they are a plurality of sovereign peoples" (Gagnon and Iacovino 2007, 28).

Chapter Four

The Canadian Political Order and Constitutional Nationalism

A constitution is a formal and institutional expression of the power relationships within a sovereign state. Of course these relationships can evolve, but the founding intentions generally act as safeguards, reminding everyone of the spirit and limits governing the players' actions and interactions. The same applies in multinational sovereign states where, in a similar context, it is possible for the dominant elites or dominant national group to establish constitutional arrangements that promote the harmonious cohabitation of the components that make up the political whole.

However, constitutions are never neutral. They apply parameters that may favour one societal culture, one world view, or one legal culture over another. Constitutions are drafted to introduce and sometimes impose a defined constitutional order, in particular to produce performative effects. Political stability is the central objective pursued – and sometimes the ultimate goal.

This chapter addresses four main topics.[1] First, I will focus on the competing historical narratives and the ways in which politicians seek to reconcile them or to disqualify the narratives that do not reflect the country's values. Second, I will discuss how present-day societies – including those of Canada and Quebec – are all marked by diversity, whether societal, ethnocultural, religious, linguistic, or national. Choosing how to respond to different expressions of diversity is one of the most important challenges facing contemporary societies. Third, I will discuss the adoption by the central government, led by Justin Trudeau, of a minimalist type of recognition policy inspired by constitutional patriotism, before offering some thoughts on how to move towards a deliberative form of constitutionalism in which relations between political communities are neither fixed nor marked by domination. To end the chapter, I will discuss the vision proposed by Trudeau's government and illustrated by his declaration that Canada is nothing less than the world's first post-national state. The vision promoted by Trudeau is consistent, albeit in a more muted form, with the national policies discussed in chapter 2.

Competing Historical Narratives

Canada, like other multinational states, is characterized by the presence of competing historical narratives. Some historians say that Canada does not have enough history, others that it ignores its history – it could even be said that it has too many histories – while yet others would like to write a new history to erase all traces of the past.

The battle for the hearts of Canadians often takes place in the classroom, at all educational levels. The best example is the debate among our fellow historians about whether or not there should be a single national history. Following in the footsteps of Donald Creighton and Frank Underhill[2] – renowned for their work celebrating the birth of Canada – Jack Granatstein has probably played the most prominent role, claiming that Canadian history and, by extension, its social cohesion and even its territorial integrity, are under threat.

It is important to take the time to read Granatstein's *Who Killed Canadian History?* (1998), a ferocious indictment of his fellow historians who, in his opinion, have lost interest in Canadian history and turned to subjects of secondary value. For him, the teaching of Canadian national history is not just another task; it is first and foremost a public duty to defend the national interest.[3] His way of thinking about Canadian society involves ignoring the tensions between social classes and between national communities. In short, he seeks to silence conflicts of a cultural, territorial, religious, gender-related, or other nature.

Fortunately, many voices have been raised against the monochromatic reading of the Canadian experience proposed by authors like Granatstein. Historian A. Brian McKillop has offered a strong and measured rejoinder to Granatstein's comments: "Younger historians, with little deep commitment to the monarchy or the empire-commonwealth, and who did not share the anglophilic sensibilities of those who often taught and wrote within such a framework, looked around them and began to write about the history of their own Canada: a multi-ethnic, multilingual, highly regionalized nation in which social and economic inequality was abundantly evident, entire groups within it were marginalized, and many voices remained silent" (McKillop 1999, 282).

Not only does Granatstein condemn historians' lack of interest in his view of national history, he also sees it as a clear lack of patriotism

(McKillop 1999, 285). He wants Canada to be thought of "as a nation, as a whole, as a society, and not as a collection of races, genders, regions and classes" (Granatstein 1998, 77). But surely finding a way to allow genders, political communities, cultural and social groups, regions, classes, and work environments to cohabit effectively is, in itself, a nation-building project.[4] Canada has never been characterized by unanimity, although this is clearly the heartfelt desire of Granatstein and, before him, Underhill and Creighton.

In Canada, for the entire decade from 1990 to 2000, we were treated to the *Heritage Minutes*,[5] a program generally stripped of any form of critical interpretation or consideration of historical misunderstandings. In fact, many pages of Canadian history have yet to be written and will have to discuss Canada in terms that take various historical sensitivities into account. In this area, the work of Micheline Dumont (2001) and Veronica Strong-Boag (2019) on women's history, John Borrows (2016) and George Sioui (1999) on the history of Indigenous nations and cultures, and Gérard Bouchard (2013, 2019), and Bettina Bradbury and Tamara Myers (2006) on collective identities will provide invaluable assistance.

It is important for history in Canada to discuss marginalized, ostracized, minoritized, gendered, and racialized groups, just as it is important to present and discuss the contributions of members of the majority nation. The task is as demanding as it is essential for the future of the country and has been undertaken by several contemporary historians aware of realities. Two books by John M. Bumsted (1992a, 1992b)[6] of the University of Manitoba have made a significant contribution and shed much-needed light by offering a far less indulgent history of the country. Both books, in which Bumsted has no hesitation in speaking of Canada as a land inhabited by several peoples, were published in the midst of the constitutional crisis of the early 1990s. He depicts a Canada made up of multiple nations, communities, regions, and cultural and gender identities. This very range of diversity has raised concerns and led to the emergence of a movement based on constitutional patriotism, as discussed in the next section.

Constitutional Patriotism

A bias in studies produced in the West generally supports formulas inspired by constitutional patriotism, at least among representatives of majority nations, with the main flag-bearer being the German philosopher Jürgen Habermas.

Constitutional patriotism can be of two types, depending on whether its supporters adhere to a watered-down version or to a more substantial vision of the political community. The first, "light" version simply involves recognizing the universal ideals of liberal democracies, while adopting the characteristics of a civic nation. This expression of constitutional patriotism assumes a low level of solidarity among citizens and, for this reason, does not adequately meet the expectations of the majority nation. A relatively superficial level of support among citizens is generally not well regarded by the members and representatives of the dominant group in a sovereign state operating in a context of national pluralism. Gradually, the majority group tends to demand renunciation of membership arrangements directed first and foremost towards *non-sovereign national entities*,[7] and a transfer of their support to the majority nation to further societal cohesion and political integration.

The more substantial version of constitutional patriotism places the defence of liberal values and rights on a long-term historical footing. Supporters of this approach add depth to the defence of universal values by declaring that they are acting to uphold the values and rights of the majority nation. This leads to a conflation of the values of the dominant group with the values to be defended and promoted by the institutions put in place, where any deviation is seen as a lack of loyalty to the encompassing state (Schwartz 2011, 506). These actions contribute to the transformation of constitutional patriotism into a new form of nationalism, which can be depicted as "constitutional nationalism." The consequences of this transformation from constitutional patriotism to constitutional nationalism can be significant for minority nations and cultural groups as they are forced to give way before the dominant group.

Will Kymlicka has accurately identified the challenge for federal states of a plurinational type. Like the philosopher Charles Taylor (1993, 61–84), who aptly identified the issue during the constitutional debates on the Meech Lake constitutional accord (1987–90), Kymlicka states, "What is clear, I think, is that if there is a viable way to promote a sense of solidarity and common purpose in a multination state, it will involve accommodating, rather than subordinating, national identities. People from different national groups will only share an allegiance to the larger polity if they see it as the context within which their national identity is nurtured, rather than subordinated" (Kymlicka 1996, 189).

For good reason, constitutional patriotism was popular after the Second World War. The work of Jürgen Habermas (1991, 1998) on the subject offers a good example and has had a major influence in academic and political circles. However, in a context of national pluralism, any success enjoyed by the formula can only be temporary, since both the light and substantial versions contain the seeds of their own undoing. In Canada, requiring members of the minority nations to give their primary allegiance to the political community defined by the borders of the sovereign state is tantamount to putting an end to the vision proposed at the time the federal pact for Canada was concluded (Brouillet, Gagnon, and Laforest 2018). It should also be remembered that the Canadian federation was founded by communities of distinct cultures who agreed on the terms that gave the federal pact its full legitimacy. It is important to go back to this founding moment to identify and name "the partners at the origin of the confederative pact" (10).

Reflecting on the federal pact of 1867, jurist Jean-Charles Bonenfant of Université Laval pointed out, a few years before the centenary of the Canadian federation, "Most nations were formed not by people who had an intense desire to live together, but rather by people who could not live separately. This was the spirit of 1867: it may yet be the spirit of 1967" (Bonenfant 1963, 38). Canada has been through several episodes that have inflicted damage on its political communities, and today it is important to ensure that the societal and cultural projects of minority nations are not sacrificed on the altar of the constitutional nationalism that some elites may wish to adopt, without regard or consideration for the national diversity that is at the heart of the original political project.

Constitutional Deliberation

Complex democratic states such as Canada's multinational federation cannot sidestep the need for an ongoing constitutional discussion that respects the principles on which its political institutions were originally built. The same is true of every attempt to renew the federal compact. Similarly, these states cannot avoid their duty to empower minority nations to create contexts of choice that contribute to their full development. In Canada, this means fostering the development of political institutions likely to support the realization of a federal ideal whose scope is crucial to an affirmation of the constituent forces of the multinational nation, including in particular the First Peoples and the Quebec nation.

Whenever there is a proposal to discuss the constitutional question in Canada, the political stakeholders say that the time is not right, or that the fruit is not ripe, or that everything is for the best in the best of all possible worlds. Meanwhile, power relations are being strengthened and structured, and their effects are becoming more permanent. In this regard, and before going any further, a few comments are in order regarding Indigenous claims.

Since the early 1980s, the First Peoples have increasingly caught the attention of political figures in Ottawa, thanks to ongoing constitutional tension. In short, the more constitutional issues are in the spotlight (the 1980 referendum, the 1982 repatriation of the Constitution, the 1987–90 Meech Lake Accord, the 1992 Charlottetown Agreement, the 1995 referendum), the more politicians are willing to listen to First Peoples' claims. In addition, media coverage of discussions at international organizations, and particularly at the United Nations, has made it impossible to ignore demands from the First Peoples. We will return to the contribution of international organizations in this area in chapter 6. To give one example, the creation of the Royal Commission on Aboriginal Peoples (known as the Erasmus-Dussault Commission) in August 1991 came in the midst of a constitutional crisis between the Quebec government and the central government.

The mandate of the commissioners was to map relations between Indigenous and non-Indigenous people, between Indigenous authorities and central government institutions, and between members of Indigenous nations and Canadian society as a whole. The commissioners made no fewer than 440 recommendations, many of which sought to foster respect for Indigenous cultures and traditions and the establishment of a new relationship to take into account the First Peoples' right to internal self-determination, building on the concept of self-government. A proposal for the creation of an Indigenous Parliament and a third order of government has also been put forward (Courchene 2018). This Parliament would be given the responsibility of making proposals prior to the adoption of government policies by the Canadian Parliament. The central idea behind the work conducted by the commissioners was to establish a *relationship of equals*, which was already present in the days of the *coureurs de bois* and the first settlements in North America.

The crucial question concerns the exercise of sovereignty itself. It is possible to imagine, in the context of a multinational federation, that sovereignty can be fragmented or shared between equal partners. However, Canada describes itself as a constitutional monarchy, although it also promotes federalism[8] as a quasi-universal panacea for fragmented societies on every available tribune.[9]

The time has come to think differently about Canada. With Raffaele Iacovino, I was able to open up a field that we still find promising for the future history of the Canadian federation (Gagnon and Iacovino 2007). Félix Mathieu and Dave Guénette have brilliantly continued and enriched the process in *Re-imagining Canada: Towards a Multinational Canada?*, in which they flesh out the proposal with around fifteen other researchers (Mathieu and Guénette 2019).

At the heart of the debate is the divisibility of state sovereignty, which can be inferred from the very existence of a plurinational democracy

(Gagnon and Tully 2001) or plurinational federation (Burgess and Gagnon 2010a). However, as Geneviève Nootens points out, "Even in federations, a constitutional *demos*, a single constituent power, is usually assumed; this is the case in the 1998 *Reference* [*Re the Secession of Quebec*]…, in particular because of the majority bias, the fact that Quebec is reduced to a cultural and linguistic minority, and the absence of any challenge to the existing constitutional rules that ultimately benefit the majority, despite the emphasis on constitutional dialogue" (Nootens 2019, 128).

The central objective of these aspirations is clearly to achieve a position of equality, based on non-domination[10] among the constituent nations of a complex federal democracy. To return briefly to Nootens's analysis, this is a significant challenge "when the application of the majority principle systematically perpetuates the sidelining of minority nations in certain decisions or fields of decision, or when it is time to determine who should vote on certain particularly important issues in a referendum" (Nootens 2019, 128). It was clear, for example, in the months following the 2018 election of Coalition avenir Quebec, that the application of the majority principle is socially and politically unhealthy and cannot guarantee the full exercise of a participatory and deliberative democracy. To put it another way, the fact that it constitutes a majority (in this case, a parliamentary majority) does not give the Quebec government all necessary rights and legitimacy to act in the area of school organization or to adopt several measures using the parliamentary guillotine. I am thinking here of the *Act respecting the laicity of the State*[11] and the new immigration measures. The majority principle alone is insufficient and can be attacked from various angles. To reiterate an idea that I have put forward elsewhere, the moral greatness of a democracy can be measured in the treatment it reserves for its minorities.

The fact that the federal institutions under Ottawa's control have, since the imposition of the *Constitution Act, 1982*,[12] lost their legitimacy in the eyes of several groups does nothing to change the Quebec government's obligation to act in a moderate, responsible, and hospitable fashion towards all the components and all the communities that define it as a political entity. In fact, this is an essential part of its project to continue to exist as a distinct French-speaking nation in North America.

Deliberative Constitutionalism

One main requirement of the democratic exercise is that the future of plurinational federations be left "open" to ongoing negotiation or renegotiation as social, political, and economic conditions change and the positions of the actors are formed and transformed.

State representatives of the Quebec nation and spokespersons for the First Peoples question the norm that sovereignty is not divisible. This, in my view, is where new energy must be directed, by returning to practices inspired by deliberative constitutionalism. Instead of thinking of an authority-based relationship as having been imposed through (a definitive) victory on the battlefield, or through the preferences agreed upon by members of the majority nation, it is important to ensure that all communities living in the same sovereign state can enjoy the same opportunities for emancipation and fulfilment and benefit from the ability to make their own choices. This is what I refer to as *pactist federalism*.

In so doing, it is important not to be bound by constitutional texts alone. This approach leads, as James Tully has shown with regard to Canada's 1982 Constitution, to the establishment of a "structure of domination" (Tully 1999, 35), which undermines national minorities and minority nations. The situation in Spain reflects this kind of unfortunate slippage, as the Spanish constitution has become an expression of "*constitutional fundamentalism*" (Bossacoma i Busquets 2020, 275), in the sense that nothing is considered permissible or legitimate if it lies outside the legal order.

It is crucial to be able to debate constitutional issues, and even to question past political arrangements that received the support of the political communities called upon to cohabit within a specific political space. Indeed, this support should not be understood as irrevocable or unconditional. In Reference re Secession of Quebec (1998), the Supreme Court of Canada states at paragraph 150,

> The Constitution is not a straitjacket. Even a brief review of our constitutional history demonstrates periods of momentous and dramatic change. Our democratic institutions necessarily accommodate a continuous process of discussion and evolution, which is reflected in the constitutional right of each participant in the federation to initiate constitutional change. This right implies a reciprocal duty on the other participants to engage in discussions to address any legitimate initiative to change the constitutional order. While it is true that some attempts at constitutional amendment in recent years have faltered, a clear majority vote in Quebec on a clear question in favour of secession would confer democratic legitimacy on the secession initiative which all of the other participants in Confederation would have to recognize.

Kiera Ladner's work invites us to imagine pathways to intercommunity reconciliation and suggests the adoption of a transformative political reconciliation (Ladner 2017), the foundation of which would be a form of "relational sovereignty" (see also Stacy 2005).[13] This new approach suggests that it is completely legitimate to apply both a legalistic reading of the sharing of sovereignty and a pragmatic or even programmatic reading that allows communities to challenge the established order in the name of a set of fundamental principles. At this point, sovereignty is seen as the expression a positive-sum rather than a zero-sum game. This way of thinking about politics promotes trade-offs between legality and legitimacy, which is precisely what is missing from both constitutional patriotism and constitutional nationalism. This relational sovereignty echoes what I refer to in my own work as pactist federalism, in which the partners are called upon to interrelate and engage in constitutional negotiations on a fair and equitable foundation.

This is where deliberative constitutionalism[14] takes on its full meaning and prescriptive force. Quebec in the 1970s, 1980s, 1990s, and since the turn of the century has been ahead of the other members of the Canadian federation, in the sense that it organized commissions of inquiry, task forces, and socio-economic summits to take stock of the needs and expectations of its citizens. For this purpose, it had to go beyond the legal system to make its demands known and defend its causes. It is in this spirit of openness to inter-community exchanges that Quebec interculturalism has produced its best results.

In light of this analysis, it is important to scrutinize Prime Minister Justin Trudeau's statement in December 2015, just after coming to power in Ottawa, that Canada did not have a primary identity and was in fact the first post-national state in human history.[15] He explained this by the fact that Canadians share the same values, and in particular "openness, respect, compassion, willingness to work hard, to be there for each other, to search for equality and justice" (Lawson 2015).

Looking closely at Trudeau's words, it is clear that he has an undying love for the *Canadian nation*. Nothing is more revelatory than his public speech marking the centenary of the battle of Vimy Ridge: "The battle of Vimy Ridge, which took place during the First World War, shaped our nation." And quoting from Brigadier General Alexander Ross, on the subject of what was accomplished that day, "I witnessed the birth of a nation" (Trudeau 2016). In fact, for Trudeau, there is nothing more "national," in Canada's collective imagination, than a post-national state. Everything is quickly brought back to the nation, and this is where the difficulty lies.

I agree with the position that the presence of several constituent nations in the Canadian multinational federation must be recognized (Gagnon 2011, 2014, 2020a). Rather than silencing diversity, as we will see in the next chapter, it is important to value and empower diversity at the political and constitutional levels. This approach will help ensure that the members of these diverse nations can achieve full emancipation.

To conclude, I give the final word to Peter Russell, who takes the claims of the First Peoples and the Quebec nation very seriously. He states, "Multinational, multicultural Canada might offer more useful guidance for what lies ahead for the peoples of this planet than the tidy model of the single-nation sovereign state. Indeed, Canada might be more like a civilization than a nation-state. As an example of how diverse peoples can live together in freedom and peace, this loose, never settled alliance of peoples called Canada could replace empire and nation-state as the most attractive model in the twenty-first century" (Russell 2017, 19).

Chapter Five

Diversity in Advanced Liberal Democracies[1]

In this chapter I will assess the clear symbolic value of diversity in advanced liberal democracies and review the arguments presented on the basis of their ability to persuade and convince, rather than on the domination and powers of each player involved.

The Canadian context is very instructive on *first-degree diversity*, namely the *multiple origins* of different Canadians. However, it is much less instructive on *second-degree diversity*, namely the *cultural trajectories of the founding peoples*. When formulating government policy and identifying and engaging with cultural, social, and political references, political leaders in Ottawa have rarely taken second-degree diversity into account in their proposals for constitutional reform.

Like a sovereign state that portrays itself as "one and indivisible," the government of Canada has gradually attempted to impose its conditions on the federation's member states, acting as if it were the only relevant player and able to freely impose its political will. This attitude had led several Indigenous leaders, as well as all of Quebec's political parties, to take frequent action and to propose major political changes to the operation of the Canadian federation in order to find workable solutions at the constitutional, economic, and political levels. The constitutional policy released by the Quebec government on 1 June 2017 is part of this historical process (Secrétariat aux affaires intergouvernementales canadiennes 2017).

In Canada, as discussed in chapter 2, analysts generally agree to distinguish two main federal traditions: territorial federalism and multinational federalism. The former, which might more accurately be called "mononational" federalism, is well established in Canada outside Quebec and consists in uniformly applying government policies across the land – in particular by using "national standards" to support the homogenous application of pan-Canadian policies – thereby implying that the country was built on the basis of a single political nation. This vision suggests that member states are interchangeable, including their historical obligations and the agreements that led to the initial constitutional arrangements.

It is difficult to imagine a fully honourable outcome to the Canadian question unless the focus of the discussion returns to the treaty federalism approach proposed by the First Nations or to the multinational federalism advanced by deep diversity thinkers – or by members of the Quebec school diversity (Mathieu 2020b). In short, I question whether the goals of standardization and homogenization are not obsolete in complex political settings. The Belgian, British, Indian, and Swiss examples merit greater attention to ensure that the ties uniting Canadians do not deprive national founding communities of their freedom to act and to self-determine internally.

To discuss these issues in more detail, I will proceed here in four stages.

First, I will examine what is meant by the concept of diversity in the Canadian context and assess to what extent some forms of diversity seem to matter more than others.

Second, I will highlight how the models that prove most attractive for political leaders tend to attenuate, rather than encourage, diversity.

Third, I will evaluate the work of some federalist thinkers who have spent their academic careers identifying ways to accommodate cultural and national diversity.

Last, I will draw some lessons from their teaching and examine the paths it opens up for the future.

The Concept of Diversity

There are many types of minority and many forms of diversity. They can be culturally, ethically, ideologically, ethnically, racially, or religiously driven, as well as gender-based. These different types of diversity matter to the extent that they can mobilize (political) support at the level of the civil society as well as within the state. As a result, groups need to be in a position to transform such support into political resources in order to influence the policy process.

The biggest challenge in a country such as Canada is the *political obligation to strike a balance* between claims made by the founding nations (English, French, Aboriginals, Acadians) and by the many emerging cultural minorities that have settled in the country since its establishment in 1867 (Brouillet, Gagnon, and Laforest 2018). This *strange multiplicity* (to use James Tully's expression) has often been neglected, when not simply ignored (Coakley 2011), by the central state, which has sought to advance a single national project founded on particular juridical premises.

In some ways we can say that deep diversity was initially sacrificed to advance a model that feeds procedural liberalism. This was Pierre Trudeau's solution for the coexistence of diverse collective identities within a single state. At least three key policies with a connection to identity-(re)building were initiated under his leadership: the White Paper on Indian Policy (1969), the policy on multiculturalism (1971, revisited in 1988 under Mulroney), and the constitutional entrenchment of the *Canadian Charter of Rights and Freedoms* (1982). Together with an identity discourse that was said to be sensitive to Canada's compounded diversity, these political initiatives led to unprecedented mobilizations of Aboriginals and the Quebec nation.

The White Paper on Indian Policy was quickly abandoned in 1970, but it became a lightning rod for Aboriginals, who became increasingly vocal and politicized. In the same year the Trudeau government adopted a policy on multiculturalism in order to challenge the then-dominant view of Canada – at least if we take seriously the mandate given by Lester B. Pearson to the 1963–71 Royal Commission on Bilingualism and Biculturalism – as being constituted principally by the two founding nations.

This attempt to abandon a bicultural definition of the country in favour of a multicultural mindset led to several moments of political tension, including the 1980 and 1995 Quebec referendums. Since then, francophone Quebecers and Indigenous peoples have pursued, with varying degrees of success, their attempt to reshape Canada as a "three-nation"[2] political community.

According to Alan C. Cairns, writing in the aftermath of the failed Charlottetown Accord, "Canadian identities, however, are no longer adequately accommodated by the coexisting provincial and country-wide identities natural to a federal people. They are supplemented and challenged by various internal national identities – Québécois, Aboriginal, and, haltingly, ROC" (Cairns 1994, 26).

This connects particularly well with a crucial point made by Charles Taylor (1993) that first-level diversity – founded on social markers based on gender, region, religion, first- or second-generation multicultural background – is not sufficient to tackle the existential challenges faced by Canada.

Writing at the same time as Cairns, Taylor noted that the Canadian duality had lost its relevance for many citizens considering that their own experience has taken place within a multicultural political environment. This has led to the emergence of a form of *constitutional nationalism*, as I noted in the previous chapter – in other words a monolithic sense of belonging without which, apparently, the country could not survive (Taylor 1993, 93–4). Taylor responded to this mononationalist claim that what is needed is to be much more accommodating in our way of being Canadians.

To quote Taylor, "To build a country for everyone, Canada would have to allow second-level or 'deep diversity,' where a plurality of ways of belonging would also be acknowledged and accepted. Someone of, let's say, Italian extraction in Toronto, or Ukrainian extraction in Edmonton, might indeed feel Canadian as a bearer of individual rights, in a multicultural mosaic. His/her belonging would not 'pass through' some other community, although the ethnic identity might be important to him/her in various ways" (Taylor 1993, 94).

This portrayal of the polity north of the forty-ninth parallel allows us to draw a demarcating line between the approaches to diversity advanced in American and Canadian scholarship. In Taylor's opinion, the United States advances a citizenship model that is uniform[3] but of no help for societies that are traversed by deep diversity, with Belgium, Canada, Spain, and the United Kingdom coming to mind.

In contrast with many other societies, it is worth stressing that Canadians have continued to openly debate their differences. Examples of this ongoing discussion include the Royal Commission on Bilingualism and Biculturalism (Laurendeau-Dunton Commission, 1963–71) and the Task Force on Canadian Unity (Pepin-Robarts Commission, 1977–9) at the federal level and, in Quebec, the Consultation Commission on Accommodation Practices Related to Cultural Differences (Bouchard-Taylor Commission, 2007–8). As shown by Reference re Secession of Quebec (1998), even the possibility that one constituent unit (Quebec) might secede from the country has been openly debated.[4] It ought to be added that, contrary to the United States, Canada can be depicted as "an ongoing negotiated country rather than a country of revolution or a single-majority nation" (Gagnon and Simeon 2010, 111).

A caveat should be added on the imposition of a new constitutional order in Canada in 1982 – when the Canadian conversation between Canadians outside Quebec and Quebecers came to a standstill – as the majority nation imposed its political will.

It was considered by some political actors that ongoing negotiations between partners might exacerbate tension at times but, in the long haul, I argue that it is these very tensions that have helped guarantee political stability and give democracy its full strength in Canada (Gagnon and Tully 2001).

In other words – and this is the main paradox of democratic federalism – federal institutions might feed political tension in some cases, but they also provide mechanisms that help give a voice to political communities and, as a result, act as crucial safety valves.[5]

This reflection provides an interesting link with the influential work of Hans Kelsen.[6] In his theory of democracy, Kelsen makes the point that neither the majority nor the minority can claim to have the full truth, but need to pay attention to arguments made by (relevant) others. In the end, Kelsen advances a culture of compromise that will be shaped by the push and pull of democratic deliberation and lead to concrete forms of *"dynamic integration,"*[7] at which time the views of all are taken seriously.

Diversity as a Primary Characteristic of Modern Societies

Several studies have already been devoted to the emergence of diversity as an essential reference for modern societies. I am thinking here of the scholarly contributions of Kraus (2008), May (2016), Mathieu (2017), Vézina (2018), and Carbonneau (2019). Each clearly highlights the centrality of cultural and linguistic diversity to the consolidation of contemporary democracies. The authors also show how standardization-focused models of the Westphalian type, like other more cosmopolitan models, tend to promote the most powerful national groups.

In Canada it is important to note from the outset that, despite the presence of an official discourse that is generally supportive of multiculturalism, there has been a significant decline in the actual influence of multiculturalism in public policy.[8] Abu-Laban and Stasiulis were among the first academics to notice this phenomenon in the early 1990s (Abu-Laban and Stasiulis 1992; Abu-Laban 1994; see also Bouchard 2019), even though the central government updated its multiculturalism policy in 1988 to combat all forms of discrimination against members of ethnocultural communities (*Canadian Multiculturalism Act* 1988). Here, the recent work of Arjun Tremblay is of key importance (especially Tremblay 2019). Tremblay notes the Canadian paradox where the public discourse suggests that the politics of multiculturalism is increasingly present in people's lives, while in fact the opposite holds true.

This can be seen, for example, in the public pronouncements of the main political families active on the federal scene, whose representatives confine themselves to making fine-sounding statements in support of an official policy of multiculturalism (Abu-Laban and Gabriel 2002; Abu-Laban 2020). The same political parties in fact clearly give precedence to the defence of individual rights and freedoms over the collective protection of ethnocultural minorities. For them, the priority is to promote public policies designed to develop a shared citizenship for the country.

In Quebec, the work produced in the wake of the Consultation Commission on Accommodation Practices Related to Cultural Differences (Bouchard-Taylor Commission), which was set up in 2007 in response to identity-related concerns in welcoming and finding a place for immigrants (B. Gagnon 2010), is proving to be highly relevant to the discussion about cohabitation. In response to Canada's multiculturalism policy, the commissioners proposed that the Quebec government introduce a bill or statement of principle on interculturalism. But what is interculturalism? How does it differ from the Canadian policy on multiculturalism?

Much has been written about Canada's multiculturalism policy as a symbol of identification, a public policy, an ideology, or an expression of sociological reality (see Kallen 1982; Stevenson 2014). In reality, interculturalism and multiculturalism are two forms of identity-based pluralism. These two types of pluralism have not evolved in a vacuum and, in the case of Canada, it is important to note that the evolution of multiculturalism, since its adoption as public policy in 1971, has been strongly influenced and inspired by the Quebec model of interculturalism.

Quebec's interculturalism model was proposed in response to the central government's tendency to present Canada, officially, as the sum of all its ethnocultural components moving forward within a formally bilingual framework. My main interest here is to clarify how Quebec's model of pluralism has come to transform the model of multiculturalism in Canada.

The Bouchard-Taylor report[9] defined the five main components of interculturalism, stating that it "a) institutes French as the common language of intercultural relations; b) cultivates a pluralistic orientation that is concerned with the protection of rights; c) preserves the necessary creative tension between diversity, on the one hand, and the continuity of the French-speaking core and the social link, on the other hand; d) places special emphasis on integration and participation; and e) advocates interaction" (Bouchard and Taylor 2008, 121). This definition of interculturalism results from a back-and-forth between the ways in which theorists and practitioners think about cultural and national diversity in Quebec and Canada. The objectives of the promoters of interculturalism and multiculturalism converge on several fronts. Both groups want to propose models for society that promote both integration and social cohesion. As events have unfolded, these objectives have evolved and even drawn closer together to the point that in 2020 the Canadian model of multiculturalism took on the main characteristics of the Quebec model.

I would like to come back to multiculturalism as a policy. It is a real success in the official image that Canada projects on the international stage, and it presents Canada as a land that welcomes all people, a place open to foreign influences, and an unequalled space for freedom and cultural diversity.

However, the actual definition of multiculturalism has changed significantly over the past half-century, and Fleras (2009) has identified four main stages in the development of the Canadian model of multiculturalism before it emerged in its current form. After an initial phase based on the valorization of ethnocultural differences in the 1970s, Canada went through a period of equality of conditions from the mid-1980s onwards, before arriving at the civic phase, and then, from the mid-1990s onwards, the promotion of an engaged form of civic citizenship. Last, the current period is characterized by multiculturalism of an integrationist nature that relegates ethnocultural identity to the background in favour of a Canadian identity. Increasingly, Canada wants to shift the emphasis from a country of immigrants to a country of interchangeable citizens, with cultural heritages that are certainly diverse, but who are all moving forward under a single umbrella as the basis for their national identity.

This reformulation of Canada's policy of multiculturalism bears a striking resemblance to the policy of interculturalism put forward by Quebec institutions, except that the Canadian model is closer to the image of the American melting pot: a community in which all citizens are equal in status and have the same rights and obligations (Stevenson 2014, 209). However, unlike interculturalism, the Canadian model does not officially recognize a majority, but only minorities.

In some ways, the current formula for multiculturalism is reminiscent of former prime minister John Diefenbaker's idea of Canada. For Diefenbaker, multiculturalism could only be an expression of a transition towards a common Canadian identity. Referring to the immigrants who arrived in the aftermath of the Second World War, he said, "Their coming has enriched the mosaic of Canada and I firmly believe that our strength is based partly on the great diversity of culture. Definitely we have a new blend of Canadianism.… In Canada we encourage the new citizens to be proud of their heritage and to as quickly as possible absorb themselves in the ways of this country" (quoted in Stevenson 2014, 201).[10]

The model of identity-based pluralism found in interculturalism is viable in a multinational democracy or a consociational democracy, but much more difficult in a federal democracy of the territorial type, which has a centralized rights regime. The adoption of the interculturalism model aims to foster contexts of choice and to respond to the particular needs formulated by the national communities that make up Canadian society.

However, Canada's homogenizing vision,[11] associated with the introduction of a type of undifferentiated, unitary citizenship, makes it difficult to establish Quebec's intercultural project, even though Quebec openly and legitimately projects itself as a fully constituted political entity. This quest for a single type of citizenship for Canada has also had major repercussions for the components of Canadian society. This was noted in the late 1990s by sociologist Micheline Labelle and political scientist Daniel Salée in a hard-hitting article that has lost none of its relevance. It is worth including an excerpt here:

> Canadian citizenship is currently at stake in an ongoing tug-of-war over the meaning and content of cohabitation in Canada between, on the one hand, individuals and minority groups who demand that the design of the public sphere more accurately reflect their economic, political and identity concerns and allow them to enjoy the available resources more equitably and, on the other hand, all those who benefit from a position of strength in the social power dynamic, but feel besieged and under pressure because the image they have of Canada – an image in which they figure prominently – is being attacked. In short, the current redefining of Canadian citizenship is essentially part of a complex and multifaceted movement that is reflected in the political quest of Quebec sovereignists, in the socio-economic demands of racialized groups across the country, in the demands of Indigenous nations for self-government, and finally, in the anxiety of the majority, which is disconcerted to see the traditional vision of Canada, which it uses to define its own identity, undergo the potentially destructive assaults of political and identity movements that are directed against the canons of *Canadianness*. (Labelle and Salée 1999, 140)

Labelle and Salée note the perceived fragility of the social bond among the political elites of the majority nation and their desire to see all citizens adopt specific lifestyles, norms, and ways of thinking within a well-defined political framework. This is what Brubaker (1992, 23–9) rightly referred to as *social closure*, which seeks to impose specific boundaries on the whole of the body politic.

The Danger of Being Blind to Deep Diversity

Ilan Peleg (2007) invites us to reconsider majority-minority relations in divided societies. The prevailing hegemonic model in the Western world, which I have just discussed, is openly promoted by the United States, as well as by countries such as Spain, France, Italy, and, more recently, Germany (following the refugee crisis and the concomitant rise of Alternative for Germany), which all advocate practices close to the Bourbon and Jacobin tradition. These models all celebrate uniformity and unity, as it is assumed that what is lost in diversity and legitimacy is gained in social cohesion, effectiveness, and performance.

I have identified some particularly strong opposition in American scholarship on the need to accommodate deep diversity. This is especially true in "ethnic federations" and, by extension, multinational federations. Among the authors whose work is often cited are Snyder (2000), Bunce (1999a, 1999b), and Brubaker (2004, 2011). They argue that "ethno-federalism" leads to the emergence of local ethnic entrepreneurs and fuels secessionist goals.[12] In contrast to Canadian authors such as Kymlicka, McGarry, Taylor, and James Tully, American authors Snyder and Bunce, along with other members of the same school, which dominates the field, are unwilling to imagine pathways to accommodate deep diversity, even if the ultimate goal is to better integrate political communities to the larger political community.

Taylor's work on cultural and national diversity and, in its wake, research by Kymlicka (1996), Seymour (2017), Tamir (1993, 2019), and Tully (1995b) has, however, significantly influenced the writing of many other scholars, although the United States remains largely closed to these ideas. For example, Tully's pioneering work on ancient and modern constitutionalism seems to me to offer a promising interpretation for cohabitation. He discusses at length the extent to which modern constitutionalism imposes "a uniform and comprehensive legal and political association" (Tully 1995b, 55), making it impossible to diverge from the norm. "The sovereign people in modern societies … establish a constitution that is legally and politically uniform: a constitution of equal citizens who are treated identically rather than equitably, of one national system of institutionalized legal and political authority rather than many, and a constitutional nation equal in status to all the others. This feature of legal and political monism is perfectly understandable. It emerged out of the one hundred years of wars in Europe which ended with the Thirty Years' War of 1618–1648" (Tully 1995b, 66).

The fundamental ideas that emerged from this profoundly violent period, and the decades that followed, denied the existence of competing constituent powers that could weaken the newly acquired power of the mononational state and also challenge the legitimacy of empires on the basis that they constituted an undesirable form of domination. Tully contrasts this modern constitutionalism, with its uniformity and homogenization, with ancient constitutionalism, which emphasized in particular the notions of historical continuity, (prior) consent, and reciprocity.

The federal traditions most conducive to cohabitation are those inspired by Western Europe, and Switzerland in particular. These federal experiments have been very successful, thanks to their ability to embody the principles underlying ancient constitutionalism. It is important to find the right balance between the political communities present in a particular case.

Alain Noël stressed that for the practitioners of federalism in Canada, "federalism is more likely to be established soundly if there is a clear winner" in a post-conflict situation. However, he continued his exposé by reminding his audience that "when one side prevails, usually the majority, it may be enlightened enough to make concessions and share power in a federal arrangement. Otherwise the underlying conflict is likely to continue and to undermine the global promise of federalism" (Noël 2013, 179).

The irresistible desire to impose an all-encompassing vision has often been detrimental to the rapprochement of political communities. To continue with the Canadian case, under Pierre Trudeau there has been a strong inclination to build a pan-Canadian nation and to develop a single centre of national allegiance. With the goal of unifying Canadians, Trudeau appealed, strangely enough, more and more to nationalism and emotion, as I have emphasized (Gagnon 2014).

His program was focused on the development of the individual and sought to foster allegiance to what he described as a juridical nation. In short, any allegiance to a particularistic, collective status founded on historical, cultural, or territorial legitimacy was rejected.

The ideal of individual autonomy was to be guaranteed from coast-to-coast-to-coast by the central state imbued with a sense of moral righteousness in the framing of citizenship status (Bickerton, Brooks, and Gagnon 2006). National identity in Quebec, according to Trudeau, and in sharp contrast with Taylor's approach, was to be relegated to the same formal space in the federation as other ethno-cultural groupings (Gagnon 2000), thus reducing Quebec identity to an ethnic identity.

Policymakers in Ottawa justified this stance using the language of individual rights, in the hope that it would foster more universal grounds for allegiance and act as a countervailing force to undermine Quebec and Indigenous allegiances. It was indeed an antagonistic vision of society.

Pierre Trudeau's intention was to oppose the recognition of deep diversity at all costs. In many ways he shared the assimilationist goals pursued in the United States and their quest for the homogenization of identity, albeit with a certain cultural relativism.

However, in contrast to the United States, the Canadian strategy devised by Pierre Trudeau was not to raze identities, but to augment the status of the cultural communities to the same level as that of the minority nations. This strategy was aimed at not recognizing group-differentiated rights as a founding federal principle. The effects of the policy have been counter-productive.

By forging a common identity throughout the country, it was hoped that the identity marker for unity could be universal – equal recognition of all cultures, within a regime of individual rights and institutional bilingualism. In proceeding in this way, adherence to particular cultural attachments could be voluntary for all individuals, while Canada's symbolic order could be based on the negation of any particular cultural definition.

I need to say a few words about the *Canadian Charter of Rights and Freedoms* that was entrenched in the Canadian Constitution at the time of the 1982 repatriation from Britain. This was a powerful act taken to establish a significant basis for pan-Canadian identity but, at the same time, it helped create new tensions between Quebec and the central government as well as between the central government and Indigenous nations.

The Quebec government, as we have been reminded by Claude Ryan, has always resisted a philosophy that posits "an abstract and doctrinaire equality of individuals and provinces" and an approach that "denies any form of asymmetry in our federal system" (Ryan 2000, 222). Many similar passages can be found in the *Policy on Quebec Affirmation and Canadian Relations Quebecers, Our Way of Being Canadian* (Santafé and Mathieu 2019).

But, as we will see in the next section, Quebec's main political forces rejected a blanket application of the principle of individual rights on a pan-Canadian basis, as it would, in effect, override the prerogatives of the Quebec National Assembly and potentially undermine the rights of territorially based sociocultural collectivities (Brouillet and Lampron 2013), one of the main pillars of Quebec's interpretation of federalism.[13]

Reclaiming the Spirit of Ancient Constitutionalism and Advancing an Authentic Federal Project

The most appropriate instrument to give meaning to diversity in complex political settings (see Gagnon and Keating 2012) remains the concept of federalism defined as *a political ideology* capable of accommodating deep diversity. It is worth pointing out that a federation is not identical to a unitary state, since it is "a state based upon the constitutional recognition of difference and diversity in their many different forms and which derives essentially from the seventeenth and eighteenth century European Protestant Reformist and Enlightenment traditions that produced the compelling idea of European constitutionalism rooted in shared notions of divided and limited government" (Burgess 2015b, 18–19). Federalism constitutes a political principle that can be validly used for the establishment of viable institutions to encourage interstate relations, intrastate linkages, inter-community relations, and internal self-determination. In short, federalism fragments (and democratizes) power by ensuring that political responsibilities are shared.

Daniel Elazar is particularly well known for his outstanding contribution to the study of federalism. He has best understood the need to combine autonomy, diversity, and solidarity in liberal democracies. Elazar's description of the autonomous and joint exercise of responsibility as the optimal way to manage diversity is highly relevant in countries built on ethnic, linguistic, religious, or cultural foundations. This is especially true in democratic multinational federations, where political tensions can be mitigated through a balanced use of autonomy and shared responsibility.[14]

The main challenge for political actors is to find the right balance between the two so as (1) to prevent communities from being alienated or estranged from each other and (2) to encourage collaborative initiatives between communities sharing the same territory (see the excellent contribution by Henders 2010).

Elazar considers the federal principle to be both a pillar of modern democratic states and an insurance policy that allows communities to further develop their democratic practices. Elazar (1991) points out that the federal goal is *not centralization* but rather *non-centralization*. He is of the view that powers need to be distributed between centres of political authority to ensure that no centre can dominate the agenda and permanently impose its views on the others. According to Elazar, the pursuit of this objective will help contribute to building trust among the partners and lead to the development of an evolving compact that guarantees respect among all members. Such an understanding of the political dynamics confirms that non-domination,[15] as a political ideal, constitutes a key objective to be constantly pursued, especially in divided polities.

The advent of a new constitutional order in Canada in 1982 has, in my view, led to a weakening of the federal compact and contributed to an undermining of trust between Quebec and the other partners in the federation.[16] Is it any surprise that Quebec has become more protective of its political institutions and its principal language of education, employment, communication, and creation?

Canada and several other federal countries have adopted different strategies to respond to the conflicts of claims and conflicts of taste[17] emerging from the political communities that give them a unique expression. The types of federation have a significant impact on the expected outcomes – it matters if a federation has a territorial, mononational, multinational, and asymmetrical form. The two main types being territorial and multinational federalism as we discussed earlier.

To synthesize, territorial federalism corresponds to the situation in Germany, the United States, Austria, and Australia; generally this form of federation is also mononational. The division of powers matches technical considerations without serious concern for ethnocultural groups or national minorities, and with an assumption of the existence of a single nation. All of the member states are conceptualized as identical legal entities. In contrast, multinational federalism is found in nation states marked by national pluralism: Belgium and Canada are two clear examples. The constituent communities make the argument that the sharing of powers ought to proceed from community claims.

The asymmetrical form allows diverse communities to offer their citizens the possibility of self-realization by emphasizing the enrichment of additional contexts of choice so that each major community, at the origin of a political covenant – to use Daniel Elazar's concept – can find a strong match with its claims.

Asymmetry in the implementation of public policies does not entail unfair treatment, but instead is a way to guarantee that everyone is treated equally: "But equality for individual citizens does not require equal powers for federal units. On the contrary, asymmetrical status for nationality-based units can be seen as promoting this underlying moral equality since it ensures that the national identity of minorities receives the same concern and respect as that of the majority nation" (Kymlicka 1998, 141).

The federal spirit calls on political actors to respect legitimate claims made by their political partners rather than attempting to make gains at their expense so as to avoid unnecessary political tensions and strains. This is not an easy task, considering that federations generally exhibit a propensity to centralize powers. This trend has been particularly well documented by Edmond Orban (1984a) in what he describes as the "inevitable process of centralization." He notes that, in federations said to be the most inclined towards decentralization – Canada, Germany, Switzerland, and the United States – the long-term trend has favoured the central state in the economic domains and has been accompanied by administrative decentralization in the four federations.

In the words of Jorge Cagiao y Conde (2012, 113), "Everything that, in a federal constitution, comes under the free and sovereign will of the federated parties seems to disappear in favour of the free and sovereign will of the federal state or federation alone, making the Constitution a straitjacket for the federated parties."

It ought to be pointed out at this point that political actors in a position of authority are often more interested in grabbing additional powers than in searching for avenues to accommodate the political communities of their nation state, even though this might help increase political stability in fragmented polities. In other words, the emergence of a more altruistic class of politician is urgently needed.

In order to reclaim and re-establish the federal spirit in fragmented and differentiated societies it seems, as I pointed out (2014), that we need to mobilize three moral considerations: (1) self-restraint, (2) constitutional morality, and (3) binding loyalty. The pursuit and concretization of these considerations constitute nothing less than an ambitious political program that ought to be encouraged and valued as highly desirable.

The first of these considerations, *self-restraint*, has been advanced by Burgess, who summarizes it as follows: "The duty and obligation of both the federal and constituent unit governments to take into account each other's interests when exercising their respective constitutional powers" (Burgess 2012, 20). In other words, central to the discussion *is the extent to which* and *the manner in which* all parties are being equally accommodated in the pursuit of their respective legitimate goals.

Constitutional morality is the second of our ethical considerations. Often the toolkit of federalism is called upon simply to identify the most efficient ways to deliver services or the most practical manners to implement public policies. Too little concern is given to the presence of deep diversity in these processes.

This was true more than half a century ago; it is still true today.

The third ethical consideration, assuming the first two considerations have been met, is *the importance of obtaining binding loyalty from all protagonists*. To the extent that majority nations are willing and do everything in their power to accommodate minority nations in complex democratic settings, it is expected that the latter will show their loyalty and engage in trust-building at the level of the state (a form of consociational democracy) that extends to civil society.

To return to Hans Kelsen's influential work, it is essential to remember that these three ethical considerations (self-restraint, constitutional morality, and binding loyalty) are necessary to the existence of a dynamic integration in which the majority and the minorities gradually commit to each other. In sum, these three ethical considerations are necessary conditions for the advent of a democratic state that will be able to resist the test of time to the extent that it is founded on "a renewable compromise between the different actors in the plurality" (Baume 2012, 29).

Chapter Six

The International Context and the All-Important Question of Rights

The central objective of this chapter is to assess the interest of international organizations in the claims of national minorities, minority nations, and, more recently, Indigenous nations. More than 100 years after the declaration of American president Woodrow Wilson on 11 February 1918[1] that referred to the right of self-determination, it is worth asking what progress has been made by nations seeking recognition. How, and with what degree of energy, have minority nations taken action in response to the power and, in many cases, the selfishness of "unifying nationalisms" (Rupnik 1995) in the West, India, the former Soviet Union, and the Arab world?

Following the collapse of the Soviet empire, new sovereign states were created on a smaller scale. Once again, composite states proved attractive to political players as a way to respond to national diversity and promote the emancipation of individuals and political communities. The creation of these states offered a strong contrast to the indifference of some states to cultural and national diversity.

Has the development of the international system enhanced, delayed, or hindered the recognition of these nations? What measures have been introduced to support the exercise of democracy, ensure the establishment of equal citizenship, and guarantee the representation of segments of society within institutions? What measures have been implemented to promote the internal self-determination of minority nations within plurinational settings and thus ensure a fairer democracy?

It is important to assess formal declarations made by the international community as well as the policies it has adopted to establish norms for the proper functioning of democracies and the protection of minorities. Here Antje Wiener's (2007, 2014) work on "norm contestation" has opened the way to a re-examination of the principles adopted by international organizations to ensure a fair balance of power and the protection of the most vulnerable communities.

I begin this chapter by briefly exploring the period from the Second World War to the fall of the Berlin Wall in 1989. Next, I look at the period from the creation of the Organization for Security and Cooperation in Europe in 1989 to the adoption of the Ljubljana Guidelines on Integration of Diverse Societies in 2012. Finally, I will comment on the United Nations Declaration on the Rights of Indigenous Peoples, adopted in 2007, as a promising way to advance debate within international institutions and also to foster more egalitarian relations between peoples.

From the Yalta Conference to the Fall of the Berlin Wall

The Yalta Conference of February 1945 preceded the victory of the Allied forces against the Axis powers. The conference was designed to advantage the Soviet Union, the United States, England, and even France, which was gradually regaining its influence and power after the occupation years; the goal of the participating powers was to agree among themselves on a new world order.

The post-war years saw a new focus on human rights in international forums, culminating in the adoption by the United Nations of the Universal Declaration of Human Rights on 10 December 1948 in Paris. The formula chosen reflected the will of the forty-three signatory states[2] not to adopt binding measures, but rather incentives to encourage UN member countries to stand up for individual rights by implementing non-discriminatory policies, as stated in article 2 of the declaration: "Everyone is entitled to all the rights and freedoms set forth in this Declaration, without distinction of any kind, such as race, colour, sex, language, religion, political or other opinion, national or social origin, property, birth or other status. Furthermore, no distinction shall be made on the basis of the political, jurisdictional or international status of the country or territory to which a person belongs, whether it be independent, trust, non-self-governing or under any other limitation of sovereignty." It is important to note that this prominent declaration contains no reference to the existence of special rights for national minorities, minority nations, or Indigenous Peoples. Indeed, Eide (2014) notes that, although several European states lobbied hard to include rights that guaranteed the protection of minorities, their efforts were unsuccessful.

Marko et al. (2019, 79–80) emphasize that the same scenario played out when European states agreed on their own Convention for the Protection of Human Rights and Fundamental Freedoms, also known as the European Convention on Human Rights (ECHR). The convention was adopted in 1950 and came into force in 1953. The ECHR added no extra consideration for national minorities and minority nations and was silent on the rights of communities that had inhabited or occupied the territory before the formation of the European states.

Marko et al. (2019, 80–1) point out, however, that despite this lack of recognition of community rights by the European institutions, the focus being on individual rights, some states chose to recognize certain rights for the minorities living in "their" territory. As an illustration, they point to South Tyrol,[3] at the heart of a major dispute between Austria and Italy. The Gruber–De Gasperi Agreement, signed in 1946 in the aftermath of the Second World War, determined specific rights for German and Ladin-speaking nationals, which paved the way for the recognition of a right of territorial autonomy for these communities.[4] Territorialized community rights were also recognized at the time for certain provinces in Yugoslavia, such as the Kosovo region (Bieber 2005). The same holds true for the region of Transylvania in Romania, which enjoyed a degree of territorial autonomy (Keating 2004).

The end of the 1950s and the decade that began with the 1960s saw a vast movement to create new sovereign states, as the colonizing states (Belgium, Spain, France, Italy, Portugal, the United Kingdom, etc.) withdrew more or less willingly or were forced to leave. The creation of new states gathered pace, particularly in Africa and Asia, where boundaries were modelled on the colonial borders drawn decades earlier in European chancelleries (Coquery-Vidrovitch 2016, 187). This, however, required that more attention be paid to the presence of ethnic groups, clans, or national groups in the same areas that wanted their voices to be heard and their presence recognized.

Somewhat surprisingly, few secessionist efforts have succeeded in an African continent undergoing rapid change. Attempts at secession for Katanga in Congo (1960) and Biafra in Nigeria (1967–70) failed. The successful secession of Eritrea, a former territory of Ethiopia, after years of war, is an exception if one excludes the case of the negotiated secession of Sudan between the North, with its dominant Arab-Muslim culture, and the South, which is more animist and Catholic.[5] The right of a people to self-determination, however, has remained at the centre of the international debate, as several minority nations are still unable to gain recognition for their cultural particularities and identities.

I should reiterate here that the main goal of this chapter is not to produce a study of the right to self-determination;[6] rather, it is to identify the issues surrounding the legitimacy of the claims made by national minorities, minority nations, and Indigenous Peoples. Although some nuances have been introduced (see Cassese 1995; Crawford 2006), a people's right to self-determination has been established as fundamental, for example in the international covenants on human rights adopted in 1966 – namely the

International Covenant on Civil and Political Rights (ICCPR) and the International Covenant on Economic, Social and Cultural Rights (ICESCR). Article 1 of the ICESCR states, "All peoples have the right of self-determination. By virtue of that right they freely determine their political status and freely pursue their economic, social and cultural development."

Internationally the 1970s were important for recognition of the rights of national minorities and Indigenous peoples. It was also a period of advancing rights for minority cultural groups. In Canada this resulted in the adoption of an official policy on multiculturalism in 1971 (Pal 1993; Cardinal and Couture 1998), and several other countries followed suit. The United Nations, too, launched a new approach to the recognition of human rights, shifting the focus to protection for minorities and Indigenous peoples (Eide 2014, 51; Marko et al. 2019, 80). It is important to note that demands for the empowerment of Indigenous peoples gradually took precedence over similar demands from minority groups at international organizations and were considered from the standpoint of comprehensive community rights rather than as strictly individual rights. This prompted some minority nations and national minorities to formulate their claims as the original occupants of historical territories (Kymlicka 2008; Gagnon 2014, 73–6).

Over the last half-century, UN committees have helped define benchmarks for coexistence in fragmented societies. The best example is the work of the Sub-Commission on Prevention of Discrimination and Protection of Minorities, which drafted the International Covenant on Civil and Political Rights (United Nations 1966). Article 27 of the covenant states, "In those States in which ethnic, religious or linguistic minorities exist, persons belonging to such minorities shall not be denied the right, in community with the other members of their group, to enjoy their own culture, to profess and practise their own religion, or to use their own language."

This was a statement of principle rather than a binding declaration, but it still invited all members of the international community to take a strong symbolic step. Strangely, and this needs to be emphasized, France, a powerful country that presents itself on the international stage as the natural home of human rights, has still not adhered to article 27 of the International Covenant on Civil and Political Rights. The reason given is that there are no such ethnic, religious, or linguistic minorities in France because every individual, according to the official discourse, gains identical rights on acquiring French citizenship.

Norwegian Asbjorn Eide is a senior official recognized for having advanced the demands of minority groups and Indigenous Peoples at the UN and, more generally, at international organizations. He was involved in the work of the Sub-Commission on Prevention of Discrimination and Protection of Minorities. Among other things, he proposed the creation in 1982–3 of a working group on the rights of Indigenous peoples, which he then chaired. This was the start of a period that saw many political events, including the end of the Cold War, followed a few years later by the fall of the Berlin Wall, the collapse of the Soviet Union, and the creation of several new states in Eastern Europe.[7]

As Will Kymlicka (2004a, 2004b) points out, from the post–Cold War period onwards, international organizations have become increasingly sensitive to recognition as a way to foster stability and security within regional blocs and sovereign states. In this context, however, it was important to imagine new governance formulas more likely to propose a fair distribution of resources instead of the coercive forces used by individual states to silence disagreements. This is what Kymlicka was trying to do in several of his works in the 1990s and more recently. Today it is important to look afresh at ways to accommodate and empower minority nations and minority groups. In the next section, we will see to what extent the gains made by minority nations have been threatened by central authorities worried about loss of hegemony and cracks in the structure of their states.

From the Collapse of the Soviet Union to the Failure of the Nationalist Project in Spain

When the Soviet Union was dismantled, the former republics chose to resume their previous existence as unitary states and often sought to move closer to the European Union in the hope of improving the living conditions of their citizens. This, according to the main actors involved, required the liberalization of trade (Soloch 2009). Several important authors have studied these major transformations across the European continent.[8]

The decade from 1990 to 2000 was pivotal for the affirmation of nations in search of statehood. However, the creation of new states, concerned as they were about community rights, did not always result in stronger individual rights. Reconciling recognition for community rights with recognition for individual rights remains a major challenge (see in this respect the work of Seymour 2017).

This is where the role of international organizations can make a difference by proposing targets to be achieved, standards to be met, and reforms to be undertaken. The policies endorsed by international organizations are not binding, but they do provide benchmarks against which the performance of states can be assessed.

Among the most prominent organizations are the committees operating within the United Nations, including the Commission on Human Rights,[9] the Organization for Security and Cooperation in Europe (OSCE), the Council of Europe,[10] and the European Commission for Democracy through Law (Venice Commission).[11] There are also prominent courts – including the European Court of Human Rights (ECHR) and, although it rarely makes decisions with major implications for member states, the Court of Justice of the European Union (CJEU) – that rule on a variety of cases and interpret treaties whose effects on the application of the law may be major once states have adhered to them.

The Commission on Human Rights and its sub-commissions play a significant role in recognition of rights by producing reports that often act as effective guides for the actions of sovereign states. Asbjørn Eide (1993) produced a report for the Sub-Commission on Prevention of Discrimination and Protection of Minorities that was highly sensitive to several international issues. It helped make Eide a key figure in international diplomacy.[12]

The commissions set up successively by international organizations have increasingly focused on identifying best practices in order to support and promote the accommodation of minority nations and national minorities within nation states, the main exception being Kosovo's unilateral declaration of independence in 2008 (Gagnon 2014, 81).

The European Commission of Human Rights has had an important influence on the way we think about state and community relations, but there are other bodies working in the same field. They include the committees and commissions working within the OSCE, which have made a key contribution. Since the establishment of the post of high commissioner on national minorities in 1992, several reports have been produced and important recommendations have been adopted. These include the 1996 Hague Recommendations Regarding the Education Rights of National Minorities, the 1998 Oslo Recommendations on the linguistic rights of national minorities, and the 1999 Lund recommendations on the effective participation of national minorities in public life (Gagnon 2014, 74; Palermo 2009). However, this period also saw opposition to demands for forms of territorial autonomy, while demands for personal autonomy for members of minority groups within constituted states were more favourably received.

Since 2005–6, the situation in Spain has confirmed the existence of a significant backlash against claims based on a specific territorial basis. A brief review of the Basque and Catalan cases reveals the failures of the state of autonomies, as the historical nations demand more power to foster the cultural, political, and societal development of their national communities.

As discussed in chapter 1, there has been an intense struggle between the government of the Basque Country and the government in Madrid, which refused to hold the referendum on sovereignty-association proposed in 2005 by the government of Juan Jose Ibarretxe. In 2008 the Constitutional Court of Spain unanimously declared the holding of such a referendum to be ultra vires, arguing that the autonomous region did not have the constitutional authority or the sovereignty needed to organize or consult the population of the autonomous region on its own political future. Similarly, the holding of the referendum was seen by the government in Madrid as a breach of the 1978 Constitution and an encroachment on the jurisdiction of the central power (Gagnon and Sanjaume-Calvet 2016, 153), meaning that the consultation could not be held under any pretext or in any form by the regional government of the Basque Country. From the point of view of the Spanish government, the referendum was an illegitimate act since it was unlawful. This decision of the Constitutional Court did not bode well for the referendum on political sovereignty in the autonomous region of Catalonia that was called for a few years later.

As the demands of civil society groups intensified and the political forces in Catalonia mobilized, it became clear that the Spanish territorial model – as established at the end of the Franco regime – could no longer meet the needs of the historic nations.[13] Given this fact, it was surprising to see the political authorities in Madrid turn a deaf ear to regional demands and take an intransigent position of non-negotiation, leaving it up to the judicial authorities, the police, and eventually the army to impose law and order, ignoring all possibilities for any form of public consultation or constitutional negotiation. In this way, the conflict between Barcelona and Madrid became a clash of legitimacies of enormous magnitude. No genuine and impartial arbiter could be identified and accepted by all, leading all the political actors into a blind alley. This is also the view of the Genevan constitutionalist Nicolas Levrat:

> This premeditated flight from the political to the legal terrain is not sustainable for a European democratic state. As the Council of Europe's Commission for Democracy through Law says in its opinion [of] March 13, 2017, "It would be desirable to review the assignment of direct general responsibility for the enforcement of the decisions of the Constitutional Court to the Court itself in order to promote the perception that the Court acts as an impartial arbiter and judges according to law." In very measured and diplomatic terms, the independent members of this respected Council of Europe commission say that this particular procedure casts doubt on

the impartiality of the Spanish Constitutional Court when it acts on the basis of these new provisions. This is serious and grave. (Levrat 2017)

As a result, a constitutional impasse has been created, with no way out in the short or medium term. Our understanding of the politics of the right to political self-determination is that sovereign states have the right to protect their own institutions, but it is just as legitimate for minority nations as for majority nations to aspire to self-government. The very integrity of the democratic exercise is at stake. In short, the sources of legitimacy of the Catalan and Spanish governments are incomplete in that Catalonia seeks to act outside the constitutional framework, while Spain stubbornly refuses to allow the free exercise of the democratic and fundamental rights of fully constituted political communities within the framework of the state of autonomies. This worst-case scenario clearly contradicts the advances in cohabitation that have been made in the countries of Western Europe, as Kymlicka points out when comparing these countries with those of Central and Eastern Europe: "There is no obvious way for a free and democratic country to prevent a self-governing minority from electing secessionist parties, and from holding referendums on secession. This, at any rate, appears to be the lesson from the Western multination[al] federations, all of whom have grudgingly accepted the legitimacy of secessionist political mobilization. The state can only prevent this by undemocratic and illiberal means" (Kymlicka 2004a, 163). This suggests that, although Spain is an old state, we are in fact dealing with a minimal democracy that has failed to obtain the free consent of its constituents. To this day, the government in Madrid refuses to call on international organizations or impartial observers for political and legal advice, simply claiming that it alone can impose the (its) law throughout Spain. This is a far cry from the adoption of recognition policies discussed in previous chapters.

The situation in Spain, in a so-called advanced liberal democracy, is surprising in its lack of openness to the demands made by the political representatives of the Basque and Catalan nations, among others. However, it has been established time and again that the most effective way to achieve social peace is not to criminalize opposition movements but to invite the people concerned to openly debate the issues that concern them within existing institutions and public forums in order to understand the expectations of all parties and find the most reasonable form of accommodation possible in the circumstances.

In the event of a systematic blockage, it is important to think about negotiated rather than imposed exit scenarios, as is the case in Spain

(Gagnon and Simeon 2010). Power and coercion cannot be the only vectors for political action.[14]

Rights of National Minorities, Minority Nations, and First Peoples

Since the creation of the position of high commissioner on national minorities in 1992, the reports issued have resonated with international organizations, senior officials, and academics. Among the most recent initiatives is the adoption in 2012 of the Ljubljana Guidelines on Integration of Diverse Societies. These guidelines have re-emphasized community law as a measure to protect national minorities, whereas many of the earlier recommendations focused on more equal access for members of national minorities to state services and health and education programs, and on facilitating their participation in public life[15] (see figure 3).

Figure 3: Major Initiatives Taken by the High Commissioner on National Minorities (Organization for Security and Cooperation in Europe), 1996–2021

2017: The Graz Recommendations on Access to Justice and National Minorities
2012: The Ljubljana Guidelines on Integration of Diverse Societies
2008: The Bolzen/Bolzano Recommendations on National Minorities in Inter-State Relations
2006: Recommendations on Policing in Multi-Ethnic Societies
2003: Guidelines on the Use of Minority Languages in the Broadcast Media
1999: The Lund Recommendations on Effective Participation of National Minorities in Public Life
1998: Oslo Recommendations regarding the Linguistic Rights of National (updated in 2021)
1996: The Hague Recommendations regarding Education Rights of National Minorities

---

The recommendations adopted by international organizations have helped draw a line between the claims of minority nations and national minorities, on the one hand, and those made by representatives of First Peoples, on the other. In general, the means available to the former group were limited to, for example, devising how best to advance the individual rights of members of national minorities and racialized groups through the adoption of anti-discrimination measures (Young

1990). In the case of First Peoples individuals, there was a pressing need to recognize their collective rights (Xanthaki 2014), and this was generally achieved by selecting well-delineated territories recognized by sovereign states (Eide 2014, 58), through the federal formula (Burgess and Gagnon 2010b; Seymour and Gagnon 2012b) and the consociational formula (McGarry and O'Leary 2004; Bieber and Bieber 2021). In short, states had to be encouraged to stop procrastinating and to recognize both minority nation and First Peoples' rights (Tully 1995b; Kymlicka 1996; Gagnon 2011, 2014).

Inspired by a stronger commitment to recognize the rights of First Peoples, on 13 September 2007, acting on a recommendation from the Human Rights Council, the United Nations General Assembly adopted UNDRIP. This declaration does not solve everything, of course, but it does provide an opportunity for sovereign states to make amends by adopting recognition policies, compensatory measures, and support programs to help communities achieve full emancipation and even reclaim territories whose use has been confiscated. In the introductory notes to the declaration, the members of the General Assembly emphasize that "Indigenous peoples have suffered from historic injustices as a result of, inter alia, their colonization and dispossession of their lands, territories and resources, thus preventing them from exercising, in particular, their right to development in accordance with their own needs and interests" (2007, 3). On the basis of this observation, the General Assembly endorsed forty-six articles for reparatory actions by the signatory states.

Fifteen years after the adoption of UNDRIP, in August 2022, the government of Canada has still not implemented it, despite frequent expressions of good faith by its political leaders.[16] According to Michael Hudson, a former senior civil servant at the Department of Justice in Ottawa, formal endorsement of the declaration would help in the reconciliation between the First Peoples and Canada's political authorities (Hudson 2020).[17] Actions, rather than words, are needed.

Ratification of UNDRIP has had a significant and positive effect on the evolution of relations between First Peoples and sovereign states. The same is true of the publication of the Ljubljana Guidelines on Integration of Diverse Societies by the Office of the High Commissioner for National Minorities. This document emphasizes that states should not discriminate between majorities and minorities, but rather should put in place policies to promote the full participation of all in the political life of society, in all its forms (economic, social, cultural, institutional) (Ljubljana 2012, 2–3). According to the authors of the guidelines it is important to move beyond the horizon of symbolic recognition, accommodation formulas, and promotion of participation for all, to adopt concrete measures conducive to the development of multi-ethnic societies that are diverse and cohesive, while aspiring to integrate members of minority groups – without assimilating them – into the social and political body of the state. In addition, the guidelines themselves "provide guidance on how States can work towards increasing integration and social cohesion while addressing the broad question of how to protect and promote human rights, including the rights of distinct communities to have their identities protected" (4).

The Ljubljana Guidelines focus on the participation of different groups in the functioning of the system through substantial representation in central institutions. They address effective equality, sustained participation, mutual accommodation, active inter-community relations, and shared public institutions:

> To achieve the effective involvement of all members of society, including organized groups, requires that both State structures and societal groups respect the principles of good governance, for instance, by selecting their representatives democratically and pluralistically.
>
> Mutual accommodation and active engagement are more effectively achieved through inclusive decision-making processes that enable all who want to be heard to participate directly or through legitimately designated representatives. These processes should also provide clear procedural channels for participation and effective remedies against unjust or arbitrary exclusion. (Ljubljana 2012, 23)

The primary intention is to find the most effective ways to avoid marginalization and ostracism of minority groups and facilitate their full participation in institutions. This approach can help to create solidarities previously considered unimaginable. However, one caveat is that the hope that the state will display benevolent neutrality is still more myth than reality (Dieckhoff 2004a, 31).

In the wake of Mitchell Cohen's (1995) pioneering work, Alain Dieckhoff understood, even before publication of the Ljubljana Guidelines, that complex sovereign states had to imagine the future of their fragmented societies by imposing new benchmarks on themselves. This could be done by relying on both "rooted cosmopolitanism" and the "legitimacy of plural loyalties" in order to realize a shared world (Dieckhoff 2004a, 31). It is by aspiring to bring such collective projects to fruition that sovereign states will be better equipped to ensure their political stability and see the emergence of a fairer democracy.

The Rise of the Majority

Majority nations must become more accommodating to minority nations and national minorities. At the pan-Canadian level, the Truth and Reconciliation Commission – created as a result of lawsuits seeking redress for abuse in residential schools – has given Aboriginal people an opportunity to come forward to discuss the abuse they suffered. In the opening lines of their report, the commissioners make a very serious statement: "For over a century, the central goals of Canada's Indigenous policy were to eliminate Indigenous governments; ignore Indigenous rights; terminate the Treaties; and, through a process of assimilation, cause Aboriginal peoples to cease to exist as distinct legal, social, cultural, religious, and racial entities in Canada. The establishment and operation of residential schools were a central element of this policy, which can best be described as 'cultural genocide'" (Truth and Reconciliation Commission of Canada 2015, 1). This direct, blunt statement is damaging for the image that Canada has of itself and wishes to project on the international stage. For decades, and even centuries, colonizers have attacked the First Peoples and their way of life in order to focus on their own well-being. The consequences have been severe and reconciliation will take a long time, especially since the power of the state was imposed without the agreement of the original inhabitants and their sovereign demand.

Today Canada's government authorities say that they want to reach out. However, it is clear that they are still struggling to put in place measures that promote the sharing of sovereignty and still maintain governance practices based on subordination.

The primary aim of multinational federalism is to establish and maintain egalitarian relations between nations. It also aims to put an end to the practices of domination, including primarily all the forms of colonialism so often repudiated by Indigenous and a growing number of non-Indigenous authors. In the first group, we should mention the ambitious works of Taiaiake Alfred (Mohawk Nation) (1999, 2005), Alexandre Bacon (Innu Nation) (2020), John Borrows (Anichinabe/Ojibwe Nation) (2015, 2016), Jeff Cornstassel (Cherokee Nation) (2012), Glen Sean Coulthard (Dene Nation) (2007), Val Napoleon (Saulteaux Nation) (2009), Georges Sioui (Huron-Wendat Nation) (1995), and Leanne Betasamosake Simpson (Nishnaabeg Nation) (2011). These authors have helped raise awareness among members of their own communities as well as the Canadian population at large of the grave injustices suffered, while putting forward proposals to end these inequities. In the second group of authors, some of the most important work has been done by Michael Coyle (2019), Carole Lévesque (2015a, 2015b), Rémi Savard (1985, 1996), and James Tully (1995b).[18]

At the level of relations between Indigenous and non-Indigenous people, reconciliation must first be achieved through the sharing of sovereignty (Hoehn 2012). Yet too few sovereign states are willing to act on this front. As Martin Papillon rightly reminds us about Canada, "Recent efforts by the federal government to rebuild the relationship with the Indigenous peoples on the principles of the UNDRIP and recognize their inherent rights, however, show that the obstacles remain considerable. Despite its openness to the principle of coexistence of Canadian and Indigenous legal and political systems, Ottawa still refuses to consider a true sharing of sovereignty that would go beyond the division of powers stemming from the colonial constitution of 1867" (Papillon 2019, 417).

The Canadian federation is grappling with the need to think about its future in light of the injustices of its colonial past, and repercussions can be foreseen if it takes seriously the multinational project discussed in this book. It is also important to note the work of emerging scholars whose scholarly contributions point in the same direction. Marc Woons concludes, after analysing the situation of several First Peoples, that there is an urgent need to develop substantial scientific analyses of the multi-nation (Woons 2020, 227). The challenge, he reminds us, is great, but so it was when states gradually took over from empires and new benchmarks had to be established to measure societal relationships in the new context.

Alexandre Germain takes stock of the territorial question and multinational federalism in Canada by looking more closely at Aboriginal territorial planning. He highlights two possible approaches to multinational federalism, depending on whether the federation is built from a founding moment (a form that Germain calls "initialist") or built over the long term, reflecting the evolution of power relations, through the transformation of practices and implementation of public policies (which he calls "incrementalist") (Germain 2015, 91–4). The second approach is mainly descriptive, while the first has the merit of being associated with the pactist tradition. By being faithful to this tradition, it will be possible for the partners to trust each other and show greater empathy.

I should also refer to the work of Felix Hoehn (2012). He highlights the need to reject the so-called discovery thesis (*terra nullius*), which suggests that no one owned the land, especially in the Americas, before the imposition of sovereignty by colonizers from Europe, and does not take into account the long-standing presence of the First Peoples on the land usurped by the colonizers. In short, we can now be glad that important work is being done thanks to the scientific contribution of a new generation (see Marceau Guimont, Roy, and Salée 2020) using analytical prisms, including law, history, sociology, and political science.

Multinational federalism, as formulated here, seeks to combine the democratic principle with the communities at the origin of the compact, while developing the grammar needed for reconciliation, without either party having to sacrifice its communal ideals, traditions, customs, or vernacular. The most daunting challenge arises from the possibility that constitutions may have to break away from sometimes centuries-old practices of domination (Tully 1995b; Borrows 2015; Ladner 2019; Bacon 2020). We will turn our attention to this dimension in the next chapter.

In the wake of the many commissions[19] that have studied the nature of the relationships between the members of the First Peoples and the components of Canadian society and institutions, the political advisor for the Innu Nation of Mashteuiatsh, Alexandre Bacon, makes some acute observations and lists the wishes that must be realized to give the First Peoples a future free of colonialism: "More is required than simply abolishing the *Indian Act* and ending all forms of discrimination against the Indigenous peoples, valuing their cultures and languages and instituting a policy of equal opportunity. Moving Canada out of colonialism means much more than giving Aboriginal people the same 'opportunities' as other Canadians. The logic of colonial domination is, to this day, fully operational not only within the national borders, but also in the country's international actions" (Bacon 2020, xx).

The multinational federalism that I propose consists of an "egalitarian federalism"[20] in which the nations involved can "cohabit with equal rights" as Albert Camus put it when, at the time of decolonization, he tried to imagine the future of a free Algeria in which French, Arabs, and Kabyles could cohabit in peace and with equal status. To exist in concrete terms, this egalitarian federalism must be able to count on the cooperation of the various components of society and of the cultural, economic, social, and political elites. This egalitarian federalism is a guarantee of justice and political stability. However, to achieve it, it must be nurtured by a culture of non-domination.

Throughout this book, I have tried to present several proposals in explicit terms to flesh out the concept of multinational federalism. The development of this approach to federalism will, in my view, help enrich our conception of sovereignty, which should be seen not as monolithic, but rather as the expression of the power relationships between communities that have agreed to pool substantial powers for certain matters, while retaining their original sovereignty on other issues. The concretization of multinational federalism corresponds to the advent of relational sovereignty, most often taking the form of a pact that can be updated with the consent of all parties to the political contract.

Chapter Seven

Multinational Federalism: Challenges, Shortcomings, and Promises

Recent decades have shown the extent to which the pursuit of a common nationality, seen in many multinational states, can be harmful to many national groups and can challenge and even imperil the continuation of the all-encompassing nation state.[1] Myanmar comes to mind, where the Bamar majority has sought to impose its will on other constitutive national groups (Bertrand 2012; Pelletier 2019). This case illustrates the extent to which majority nationalism can be an obstacle to achieving and sustaining a democratic, multinational federation. Meanwhile India – a country depicted in most textbooks as the most populous federal democracy in the world – has given serious signs of departing from the institutionalization of democratic federal practices (Adeney and Bhattacharyya 2018). The same goes for so many cases around the world, including Malaysia, Sri Lanka, and Iraq, that have experienced problems in this respect.[2]

After a period particularly favourable to the advancement of deep diversity, from the late 1980s until 2005 or so, liberal Western democracies have seen a backlash against this trend. Politicians, state managers, and political associations in those years were encouraged to rally behind policies favourable to diversity, adopting vigorous initiatives so that diversity could enter the public discourse while being legitimized from above. It was this policy drive that produced UNESCO's (2001) Universal Declaration on Cultural Diversity in November, which states in its article 2 that "cultural pluralism gives policy expression to the reality of cultural diversity. Indissociable from a democratic framework, cultural pluralism is conducive to cultural exchange and to the flourishing of creative capacities that sustain public life." This was followed in 2008, among many other policy initiatives, by the publication of a White Paper on Intercultural Dialogue entitled *Living Together as Equals with Dignity* (Council of Europe 2008), which stressed the combined core values of human rights, diversity, democratic citizenship, community engagement, and the rule of law, along with a strong policy posture in favour of intercultural dialogue. These two decades constituted the golden era for the advancement of public policies stressing cultural diversity as a rallying call at the international level. This favourable moment, however, was time limited.

Christian Joppke (2012, 1, 9) notes that states are now more inclined to take actions and adopt measures to secure or even fortify the majority culture and impose their authority at the expense of minorities. A kind of fatigue has settled in among majority groups in their response to claims made by minorities (Tremblay 2019). Joppke himself appears to be insensitive to the presence of distinctive political demoi as sources of legitimacy in the context of states composed of diverse political communities. For Joppke, "policies must protect the majority culture" (2012, 1). Such actions have in his telling become an imperative for states' stability and even for their survival. Along the same lines, Brian Barry – exploring the impact of multiculturalism on state policies – is concerned that cultural diversity can lead to state fragmentation and "reward ethnocultural political entrepreneurs who can exploit its potential for their own ends" (Barry 2001, 21). As a result, authors such as Joppke and Barry remain generally insensitive to minority claims.

Similarly, some students of federalism and nationalism have argued that for a multinational federation to be stable it is essential to have a *Staatsvolk* that can impose its political will, thanks to the fact that it is "demographically and electorally dominant" (O'Leary 2001, 285). In my view, this position is highly questionable and can lead to unfortunate consequences, as we have seen in Spain with the jailing of political leaders, and in Kashmir with the removal of the statute of political autonomy that had been granted to the Muslim population of the region at the time of India's foundation to then bring peace and political stability to the region.

The *Staatsvolk* argument is increasingly used by political leaders from majority communities, as well as by ancillary state managers whose main goals are based on efficacy and performance. Such a posture tends to undermine policies that were accommodating group-differentiated rights (Kymlicka 1998) during the diversity period and lead to the imposition of majority rule in the name of administrative efficiency, individual liberalism, and state stability, which trump all other policy objectives.

In this final chapter, I intend to focus mainly on experiences from Europe and Canada to make the discussion more manageable by limiting the number of cases under scrutiny.[3] My main focus is on a new distinctive form of political association – multinational federalism – which seeks to demarcate itself from the territorial form of federalism, associated with less heterogeneous countries such as Austria, Australia, and Germany, and to support the expression of national diversity within complex democratic settings. This chapter is divided into three sections. Section 1 pertains to the concept of multinational federalism itself, discussing ways in which it offers an alternative to the dominant literature on territorial/mononational federalism. Section 2 discusses ongoing nation-building processes and explains how multinational federalism can provide a democratic response to some of their excesses. Section 3 reviews the main reasons for adoption of multinational federalism in contexts characterized by national diversity.

Multinational Federalism: A Definition

The literature on federal democracies (Burgess and Gagnon 2010a) reveals two main schools of thought. The first and dominant school is based on the notion of territorial or mononational federalism. Here the authors simply ignore the federal complexity of a given polity, as their main research focus is the territorial division of powers and the implementation of public policies countrywide. Formulated differently, the cultural and societal characteristics of a given nation state are not reflected in its state institutions and political arrangements. With Michel Seymour I have made the point that "multinational federalism would among other things allow different peoples, occupying different territories, to each have access to distinct administrative units in which they constitute a majority. In contrast with territorial federalism, multinational federalism would reflect the diversity of the peoples in the diversity of its federated states" (Seymour and Gagnon 2012b, 4). The second school of thought – which has gradually taken hold in response to the lack of concern for deep diversity and, since the early 1990s, with the dissolution of some important federations – stresses (1) the political presence of more than one sociological nation within nation states and (2) its significance for the pursuit of political legitimacy and the maintenance of political stability (Gagnon and Laforest 1993).

Multinational federalism supports the advancement of nations – even when these nations are contested political communities – within the confines of an existing state. Multinational federalism is about the simultaneous development of nationhood and statehood within existing plural nation states (Keating 2001a). Multinational federalism recognizes the presence of multiple identities. Indeed, it is because of the existence of this plurality of identities that nation states are able to imagine political configurations that will contribute to the renewal and promotion of *group-related rights* (Marko 2019c, 112). Multinational federalism aims to sustain appropriate institutions capable of empowering political communities at the regional level and the centre so that state differentiation and state collaboration can be pursued simultaneously.

The notion of multinational federalism assumes the existence of several demoi, in contrast with the notion of ethnofederalism, which suggests that ethnicity is the main driving force. In the literature, the notion of ethnofederalism has been used to depict federations structured around ethnically distinct groups with the ultimate goal of forming their own homelands and, in some scenarios, seeking independence once they have gathered sufficient resources. So it is simply a question of time before political leaders will be in a position to galvanize political forces and demand secession for an ethnic community. Ethnofederalism is said to be potentially unstable, as narrow ethnic identities prevail over broad civic achievements. Philip Roeder came to the conclusion some years ago that "most destabilizing of all are the incentives established by ethnofederalism for homeland leaders to play the sovereignty card – that is, to privilege their claims to greater powers by linking these to the claim that their minority community, which is the basis of their state within a state, constitutes a sovereign nation" (Roeder 2009, 212). Other authors have pointed to institutions organized along ethnic lines to account for the unravelling of communist federations (Bunce 1999a; Bunce et al. 2005). Through multinational federalism, my aim is to take seriously the representation of political interests and their democratic expressions rather than assuming, like Bunce and her colleagues, that all political actions are motivated by self-centred ethnic aspirations and goals.

Democratic multinational federalism should not be seen as a panacea but rather as a concrete way to achieve three objectives that are essential for the management of conflicts: (1) decoupling and distinguishing the notions of "nation" and "state," (2) strengthening a sense of identity through implementation of a *politics of recognition*, and (3) developing a healthier equilibrium between self-rule and shared rule through the implementation of collaborative initiatives while respecting the principle of political autonomy. Nowadays, according to Arthur Benz and Jared Sonnicksen, this can also take the form of "multilevel 'collaborative' policy-making in a number of fields" (2017, 17), allowing for ongoing competition and mutual adjustments among members of a federal regime.

Nation-Building Processes

The last three decades have seen a succession of distinct processes that are taking place concurrently within and between nation states. These powerful forces are intended to bring the (central) *state* back in through re-nationalization (Evans, Rueschemeyer, and Skocpol 1985; Marko 2019a) and re-symmetrization (Requejo and Nagel 2011). In divided societies, the implementation of such processes has consequences and tends to pit one actor against the other as weaker groups gradually lose their hold on power. This can lead to distrust and mistrust among leaders of the political class and, as a result, have a negative impact on the relations between political communities.[4]

Belgium, Canada, Finland, Germany, Switzerland, and the United Kingdom in particular have been willing to provide support, to varying degrees, to regional state structures that provide linguistic minorities, cultural groups, and minority nations with broader control over their own destiny. This has occurred through a dynamic of push and pull that greatly benefited from a new sensitivity to cultural pluralism, national diversity, and linguistic diversity (McRae 1998, 2000, 2006; Lecours 2021). In other countries such as Spain, this lasted for a number of years before dominant political forces started to reverse that trend for reasons of efficiency, performance (Bakvis and Skogstad 2002, 2020; McRoberts 2017), and central state hegemony (Gagnon and Requejo 2010), as well as to uphold state stability in the name of the national interest (Nincic 1999; Roeder 2009; Brubaker 2011; Burg and Chernyha 2013).

Joseph Marko, a former international judge at the Constitutional Court of Bosnia and Herzegovina, has identified three key processes of re-nationalization applied in Europe since the end of the 1980s (Marko 2019b). These processes have varied in intensity and in their repercussions on the management of diversity in various political settings. However, all three reinforce each other and help strengthen central political authority at the expense of both minority nations and national minorities.

The first process of (re)nationalization identified by Marko has to do with the recurrence of violent conflicts in Central and Eastern Europe following the collapse of the Soviet Union. Similar political tensions had taken place concomitantly with the dismantlement of Yugoslavia in 1991 and Czechoslovakia in 1993 – two other multinational federations. Such failures by major states were viewed by several experts as evidence that multinational federalism could only lead to or feed political instability. In other words, these events suggested to some authors that multinational federations contained the seeds of their own failure due to their ethno-nationalist composition and therefore that such federal arrangements should not have been set up in the first place (Bunce 2007, 31). Such an argument, made by Valerie Bunce and some other authors active mainly in the field of international relations, does not hold for the simple reason that these failed multinational experiments were originally not the results of democratic arrangements.[5]

The second process of (re)nationalization has to do with the nationalist responses given by minority nations to nation-building strategies emanating from the central state. "In Western Europe, particularly in Great Britain, Spain, and Belgium, a nationalist paradox can be observed whereby sub-national, regional political parties mobilize against the dominant nation (Marko 2019b, 2). Here one sees that countercultural economic and political elites reply to central state initiatives by advancing their own nationalist projects. These nationalist movements state that their political communities ought to have equal status with the majority nation and claim to have the right both to internal and external self-determination (Seymour 2016). Quebec constitutes an important case in point, considering that, as early as the mid-1960s, important political forces mobilized behind the notion of "equality or independence" (Johnson 1965; Gagnon 1991a). Quebec was ripe for a major political transformation with the goal of rethinking Canada on the basis of a binational set of political institutions. Were this project to fail, the only avenue left would be to rally behind the secessionist option. Similar scenarios have emerged in Catalonia, the Basque Country, Scotland, Flanders, and beyond (Keating 2001a, 2001b; Cetrà 2019).

Efforts of minority nations to get *a better deal* within their existing political settings have seen central state actors advancing scenarios that were at times conciliatory (e.g., the 1987 Meech Lake proposal with respect to Quebec in Canada) or confrontational (e.g., the suspension of political institutions in Catalonia, in 2017, through the application of article 155, which imposed direct rule by Madrid). In both cases, what we see are attempts by the central state to use either the carrot (Canada) or the stick (Spain) to succeed with their state-building strategy and tame or silence the opposition (Coakley 2011 is highly relevant here).

The third process of (re)nationalization has been set in motion by right-wing populist forces in several Western countries. Cases in point include Austria, Greece, Hungary, Italy, and Spain (Pirro 2015; Medda-Windischer and Popelier 2016; Akkerman 2016). These movements are not simply Eurosceptic (FitzGibbon 2014) but clearly anti-immigration (Medda-Windischer and Popelier 2016). Joseph Marko notes that this re-nationalization is depicted by its adherents as aiming "to protect the national cultures of European countries against population flows of global migration" (Marko 2019b, 2) and to respond to "the challenges stemming from the need for immigrant integration into European societies" (2019b, 2). The last decade has witnessed a significant decline in support for immigrant accommodation throughout the Western world. Political leaders from France, Germany, and the United Kingdom have adopted a common posture by challenging the principle of "deep diversity,"[6] arguing that multiculturalism is detrimental to the maintenance of political and social cohesion. This posture of political leaders such as David Cameron, Angela Merkel, and Nicolas Sarkozy has contributed to undermining the diversity principle in Western democracies (Tremblay 2019).

To these three trends, we can add a fourth process of (re)nationalization, which consists of forcing federal members or regional units to adhere to the norms, standards, and objectives determined by the central state in the name of efficiency, performance, and rationality. The most obvious case is the situation prevailing in Spain, which, after having supported political asymmetry, has become particularly reticent – when not entirely opposed – to having autonomous regions adopt policies suited to their specific needs (Requejo and Nagel 2011; Payero-López 2020).

This phenomenon consists in backtracking from engagement in the recognition of deep diversity – that is no longer standing behind the rights of minority nations and their cultural as well as their political claims and rights. These re-nationalization processes produce major hurdles for implementation of an interactive dynamic that would bring about the development of trust between minority and majority nations.

Adopting a Multinational Federalism Stance: A Pressing Need

State managers, party leaders, and members of minority nations have been keen to respond to these processes of (re)nationalization and re-symmetrization by adopting a variety of strategies. In this chapter, as a response to these processes, I will focus on three main dimensions: (1) the importance of decoupling the notions of nation and state; (2) the importance of returning to a politics of recognition; and (3) the necessity of implementing competing multilevel state initiatives that can provide a much-needed balance between self-rule and shared rule.

Decoupling the Concepts of Nation and State

The literature about federalism owes a lot to the American model, which has been used as a yardstick in several other settings. Especially germane in this respect is the work of William Riker (1964) and Carl Friedrich (1968), who respectively see federalism as a political bargain or a political process. The United States has become a benchmark to which other federations can be compared. The US model is said to bring about political stability. What is not said though is that it came at a very high cost in human lives and that, in contrast with the Canadian experiment, it is a case of imposed federalism (Gagnon and Simeon 2010; Brouillet, Gagnon, and Laforest 2018).

Yet the US model ignores or opposes the political and juridical expression of national pluralism, which has become a common feature of several nation states. Multinational federalism suggests the need for countries to imagine political avenues that question the prevailing monist conception of the demos and, by extension, that affirm the constructive role to be played by several demoi in state-building and in the redefinition of the democratic exercise.

The emerging literature pertaining to multinational federalism stresses the importance of distinguishing the concept of nation/s as demos/demoi from the state as a *political institution*. Nation then corresponds to a cultural expression of a given political community and is characterized by specific features that carry a set of values as well as cultural and social attributes. This nation, in its full expression, can acquire a high degree of control over state instruments. Ferran Requejo has best encapsulated the nature of the theoretical problem that needs to be addressed by state managers and social scientists when addressing multinational democracies and, by extension, multinational federations. "In fact, theories of democracy have traditionally been theories of the democratic *state*, and they have usually been conceived as based on a uniform *demos*. Multinational democracies show the need to revise, for moral as well as for functional reasons, some of the traditional 'statist' assumptions that the hegemonic national groups have often imposed under some homogenizing versions of 'democratic citizenship' and 'popular sovereignty'" (Requejo 2005, 11).

The need to decouple the concepts of nation and state becomes even more obvious when looking at the way state nationalists act in diverse political settings. In the following section, my main focus will be on the challenge of adopting a politics of recognition and its expected impacts on the advancement of democracy.

Implementing a Genuine Politics of Recognition

Contrasting with arguments made by Karl Renner and Otto Bauer that we ought to depoliticize ethnic and cultural rights in multinational and multi-ethnic political settings (Nootens 2002), what I want to underscore here is the urgency of advancing the political rights of communities based on a territorially delineated space so that liberalism can take on a different and more performative expression that prompts state actors to go beyond the expression of individual political autonomy.

Following in the footsteps of Charles Taylor, the idea of implementing a politics of recognition, which could be either thin or thick,[7] has characterized the political situation prevailing in Western Europe over the last century. From my standpoint, the adoption of such a politics explains why secession remains rare. In fact, since 1921, with the exception of the partition of Northern Ireland from the Republic of Ireland, there have been no cases of secession. This needs to be contrasted with the situation prevailing in Eastern Europe, which has witnessed several cases of secession.

A politics of recognition has institutional requirements. In other words, if national pluralism really matters, it needs to be protected institutionally (Gagnon and Requejo 2010). The affirmation of a politics of recognition requires at least two institutional undertakings. First, it highlights the need for asymmetrical arrangements to account for the special needs and preferences of political communities living in a given nation state. Second, it generally requires a more decentralized political regime. Implementation of these two features, I argue, would tend to favour the political stability of multinational states. Such features provide no absolute guarantee that a given state will be able to avoid political conflicts. However, they put in place the necessary conditions to cope with inter-communal tensions in democratic political settings.

Some authors writing about Central and Eastern Europe have argued that asymmetrical arrangements and decentralization constitute major incentives for ethnic territorial interests to mobilize and organize their opposition against a central state. Cases in point include the successive collapses of the Soviet Union, Yugoslavia, and Czechoslovakia (Crocker, Hampson, and Aall 2004). The point to be made here is the extent to which what was at fault – in these tough and complex situations, which ended up in state break-ups – was the dependence of state continuity on the presence of "centralized dictatorships" (McGarry 2005, 11) and the fact that once they had been removed, little could stand in the way of a series of successful secessions.

Adhering to a politics of recognition contributes to strengthening trust between political partners and, without constituting a guarantee that a multinational state will last forever, it remains the best available democratic option for the maintenance of social peace and political stability. In other words, if they are to last, political arrangements cannot be imposed by the central state on member units, but need to be negotiated day-to-day.

In the midst of the failed renegotiation of the Catalan statute of autonomy in 2010, some Spanish authors were quick to suggest that to advocate political asymmetry among the autonomous communities would lead to the granting of privileges to Catalans (and by extension to the members of other historic nations) that would fuel political instability in Spain while encouraging autonomous regions to constantly ask for additional powers. On the subject of asymmetry at the time, political scientist Angustias Hombrado (2011, 480) wrote that it

> exacerbates inter-regional conflicts in a way that is likely to trigger diverging demands for territorial restructuring, in the form of constitutional reform or informal change, from regions respectively granted or denied differentiated status or powers. In many cases, these demands call the territorial design into question permanently, thus increasing the propensity for change. To the extent that they exist and that the central government is responsive to them, the system enters a pendulum-like process of reform, whereby each pro-asymmetry step is followed by a "re-symmetrizing" one. Alternatively, any reform attempt can be brought to an impasse as a result of those incompatible regional demands.

Asymmetrical transfer of central state powers and responsibilities in favour of regional state authorities in Western Europe has also been viewed by some authors in Eastern Europe – such as Sergii Tolstov from the National Academy of Sciences of Ukraine – as feeding political alienation and even secession in Catalonia and Scotland (Tolstov 2019).

In the following section, special attention is given to the importance of finding an adequate balance between self-rule and shared rule, with a view to properly managing the state and not estranging members of different political communities within the all-encompassing state (Gagnon 2010).

Developing a Fairer Balance between Self-Rule and Shared Rule

With Michael Burgess, I have stressed the idea that federalism can be instilled and prosper only in democratic political settings (Burgess and Gagnon 2010b; Gagnon and Burgess 2018b). Our understanding of federalism stands in sharp opposition to that advanced by authors such as Franz L. Neumann (1955), who claim that the two notions cannot be associated.

As a starting point, it is useful to bring in Pierre Trudeau's point that, for a federation like the Canadian one, which he depicted as a multinational federation, to last and gain prominence, it is crucial that "the advantages of the minority group [read Quebec] of staying integrated in the whole must on balance be greater than the gain to be reaped from separating" (Trudeau 1968, 192). The level of success will then depend on the capacity of the central state to accommodate deep diversity. This can be accomplished by sharing political power, encouraging political autonomy for the member states, and adopting collaborative initiatives to create bonds between the peoples, the regions, and the orders of government.

Philip Resnick has convincingly and lucidly analysed power dynamics between central state and member states within federal political settings. He made the point that "there is constant tension between federal and confederal/decentralizing constraints within multinational states. Both Catalan Socialists and the formerly governing Convergència i Unio (CiU) in Catalonia have pressed for recognition of the plurinational, pluricultural, plurilingual character of Spain, participation by the *Generalitat* in the EU in areas of its responsibility and direct Catalan representation in the European Parliament and UNESCO" (Resnick 2012, 72).[8]

A central challenge to be met by political actors, then, is the need to find a proper equilibrium between self-rule and shared rule. In complex political settings, some members desire a larger share of political powers. This is the case of Quebec within the Canadian federation. Other member states are often pleased to leave such powers to the central government, either for lack of expertise or limited interest or simply because they are of the view that the central state can assume full leadership in the name of the all-encompassing multination state. Adoption of this position can undermine minority nations, since guarantees they once had can easily start to unravel as the central state exercises its might.

A case in point is the situation prevailing in India, where the guaranteed rights of Jammu and Kashmir have been struck down by New Delhi in the name of individual equality and the equality of treatment of member states. Indeed, a constitutional change was adopted in early August 2019, through the abolition of article 370,[9] which guaranteed specific rights provisions to the Muslim majority when the region decided to stay with India at the moment of its foundation in 1947, while the northern segment of Kashmir was made part of the region administered by Pakistan. It is through this recently imposed constitutional reform that the region of Jammu and Kashmir was downgraded from a fully autonomous state to a union territory (A. Roy 2020).

It should serve as an important warning that in many cases where the central state has opted to remove or threaten regional state autonomy – cases in point include East Timor, Eritrea, Kosovo, Montenegro, and South Sudan – the regions affected have since gained their independence (McGarry 2005, 18; Muro and Woertz 2018).

Finding an equilibrium between self-rule and shared rule is not the only challenge to be addressed since, above and beyond it, guarantees need to be offered to minorities in multinational contexts on language protection, hiring practices in the civil service, and the provision of fair representation in the legislative assembly and upper house (Wheare

1962; Turgeon and Gagnon 2013). Today we can add the powerful role exercised by the adoption of a charter of human rights and political freedoms in various countries. In order to retain legitimacy in the eyes of minorities, member states and the central state must entrench such charters of rights and freedoms and make them part of their own constitutional dispositions.

Resistance to recognition of deep diversity has been documented in unitary and federal states. Ultimately what matters most is the extent to which reciprocal consent between majority and minority nations has been (or can be) put in place. The main advantage of the federal model over a unitary model is that it can develop the institutions essential for the recognition of nations as constituting political communities.

Multinational federalism has the potential to institutionalize a politics of recognition and lead the way in developing policy instruments that can limit domination of the majority nation over other national groups. To the extent that minority nations are treated fairly, one can expect that state stability will be greatly augmented and that constitutional loyalty will gain prominence. In sum, self-restraint of the majority nation is more of a guarantee of success than the imposition of norms without due respect to the aspirations expressed by minority nations.

In this chapter I have sought to highlight the importance of taking the federal formula seriously in complex political settings (Keating and Gagnon 2012; Mathieu and Gagnon 2021). Multinational federalism is not a panacea in all cases where several nations cohabit, but of the available options, it is the most likely to fulfil democratic principles and give voice to a larger number of political communities. At the same time, multinational federalism has the capacity to give added value to the principle of self-government in complex democratic settings through the potential to implant innovative political practices while maintaining the benefits of multinational unity.

Conclusion

In this book I have expanded on several themes connected with sovereignty in national pluralism, while highlighting the democratic requirements that plurinational states must respect in response to the lessons of pluralist federalism. Throughout I have identified and assessed the issues connected with the sharing of powers, as well as the obligations that must be addressed by political actors in order to act in a responsible and measured way. Similarly, I have reviewed the necessary contributions by institutions and actors to maintain a political balance within democratic states.

While it is possible to be aware of another party's claims, the principles on which political gestures are made and evaluated still need to be determined. Here we must appeal directly to the concept of legitimacy. As Hélène Hatzfeld (2013, 2) points out, "Claims of legitimacy refer back not simply to a given situation, but to the place where the discourse on legitimacy is produced; they question its values, norms, institutions, attributes of representation, and superior attitude." The impartiality of institutions and judicial bodies is paramount in ensuring substantive – rather than procedural – equality between competing societal projects. It becomes clear from this analysis that the authorities of central government, in a federal context, cannot claim a monopoly of legitimacy for themselves. It is natural that these clashes of legitimacy give rise to conflicts of varying degrees, depending on the forces involved and the historical, economic, and international context.

In a plurinational democracy, legitimacy also depends on a nation's capacity to gain recognition for the validity of the principles on which its political projects are based. Insofar as these principles are endorsed by the other, they can be institutionalized through the usual democratic channels. As James Bickerton reminds us, the very existence of "the 'deep diversity' found within multination states requires an approach to national unity that focuses on the management of 'legitimacy deficits'" (Bickerton 2019).

The situation becomes more complex when mistrust between political authorities grows as a result of broken promises or fundamental disagreements about the goals pursued by political communities within states. It is often when reforms are made to introduce changes to the constitutional pact that the actors seek to impose their preferences, while challenging the relevance and sometimes the very legitimacy of the positions advanced by their political partners.

Hannah Arendt (1958, 178–9, 184–6) was right to insist on the central role of interactions when projects are developed by actors in the political arena. These interactions are also essential to the unveiling of positions, without which it is difficult to act in full knowledge of the facts. The fewer the challenges to the legitimacy of the forces involved, the greater their ability to adopt binding decisions. Thus the advantages of the federal formula are clear: on the one hand, it helps to fragment political authority and, on the other, it provides the constituent elements of a multinational democracy with ways to give formal expression to their expectations and demands.

Legitimacy

Pierre Calame correctly reminds us that political actors do not always act in a morally satisfactory way and sometimes even intervene in a way that is detrimental to the well-being of the differentiated communities within complex states: "In democratic regimes, it is assumed that the legality of the exercise of power, i.e. its conformity to laws, is sufficient to ensure its legitimacy. However, legitimacy is a much more subjective notion and expresses the deep adherence of the population to the way it is governed – and almost everywhere in the world we can see that the gap is widening between the legality and legitimacy of power" (Calame 2003, see also 2002).

The chapters that make up this book have highlighted an important interpretive shift in comparative politics. In the work of several contemporary authors, the focus is less on legitimacy – which is not always easy to measure – and more on the process of legitimization to gain the support of partners within a given state. In short, the concern is more with how the actors go about legitimizing those who hold political power, and with the emergence of new concepts that shield them from criticism and questions. It is interesting to note the energy expended by political actors in positions of authority on the use of new formulas, which reproduce the same power relationships but under a new name (Gagnon 2015b). In Canada, for example, federalism has been described as cooperative, consensual, coordinated, efficient, inter-state, infra-state, effective, profitable, and territorial.

Over the last two decades, during debates within the European Union, there has been much talk of good governance (Gagnon 2015b). Yet each of these variations (in which federalism is described as cooperative, executive, coordinated, etc.) confirms an underlying trend to reduce federalism to a hierarchical and technical way of organizing power relations, rather than a way to imagine equitable relations between the political communities at the very origin of federations. The work of Jorge Cagiao y Conde is timely, as he identifies blind spots in the federal studies: "The dominant approach neglects the legitimizing sociological substratum in federative systems and thus tends to depoliticize the relations between the federal and federated levels.… [T]he question arises whether the logic of federalism does not, in contrast to the dominant theses, require a return to a sociological approach, more attentive to the tension and sources of legitimization that underlie and animate the federation" (Cagiao y Conde 2015, 114).

Throughout this political essay I have answered the question raised by Cagiao y Conde in the affirmative, mainly to shed more light on the decisive role of the political communities that are at the origin of the federal pact and therefore must also be at the origin of any legitimate constitutional reform. He has shown, as I have tried to establish in my own work, that "by reintroducing the notion of political legitimacy specific to contexts of political [and national] pluralism, the sociological snapshot makes it possible to better understand the resistance naturally found at the federated level with respect to the powers it wants to keep, and to avoid the hasty judgments that only too often criticize the so-called conservative or retrograde character of resistance movements in federative contexts" (127). In short, before addressing institutional issues, it is important to think about inter-community relations and the needs of the political communities that underlie and precede the same federal institutions.

Aspirations and Constraints

We live in a world that is increasingly inclined to reject identity politics and political demands at the supranational level in order to impose projects of an integrative and uniform nature. On a smaller scale, however, we are seeing the emergence of social movements for the recognition of minority (racialized, gendered, intersectional) identities.[1]

Frequently, at the level of the central state, political leaders want to impose the same rules on everyone, regardless of the living conditions and legitimate aspirations of members of the political communities forming the body politic.

In Canada the most frequently used expression is, "A province, is a province, is a province" – which means that special status for Quebec is viewed with suspicion and discomfort. In Spain, the expression is *Café para todos* also reveals a discomfort with regions and communities that insist on advancing a specific model of governance with respect to culture, language, territory and citizen engagement.

In Spain, following the introduction of measures to accommodate deeper diversity (based on national pluralism) in the second half of the 1970s, we have seen central institutions reintroducing programs that help tilt the balance in favour of symmetrical treatment (Requejo and Nagel 2011). As a consequence, sensitivity to the desire of minority nations to implement more advanced self-government methods and practices has been reduced significantly, to the point where members of the majority nation feel that they can legitimately deny political autonomy in the name of the political stability of the nationalizing state. This is then used to justify opposition of the policymakers to political and social reforms and to transform the constitution into a once-and-for-all set of arrangements.

On 12 November 2018 Nicolas Sartorius stated, "The right to decide is reactionary." He made a circular argument on the right of a historic nation or an autonomous community to legally consult its constituents. He mused rhetorically, "It is that the legal and agreed referendum is neither legal nor agreed. It is an impossibility. It is not legal because the Constitution does not allow it because it changes the subject of national sovereignty. And there is no agreement because nothing has been negotiated, and the question is predetermined" (quoted in Mendez 2018).[2]

This kind of shock statement does nothing to bring the parties to the dispute closer together. As a result, such political thinking means that the law, imposed by the majority nation, loses all its legitimacy with a large proportion of the members of minority nations.

Historically, and contrary to a widely held view, the Spanish state has been unwilling to adopt federal practices and has opposed confederal initiatives. For example, in article 145.1, the 1978 Constitution states, "Under no circumstances shall a federation of Autonomous Communities be allowed." From a Canadian perspective, it is difficult to understand why, in a so-called advanced liberal democracy, bilateral relations between autonomous communities are discouraged or, in this case, prohibited.

At this point in the conclusion, I would like to return to four issues. First, and in opposition to the view expressed by people of influence, I urge political actors to take advantage of the analytical tools offered by specialists of conflict management. Second, we need to identify the necessary conditions to hold democratic debates that can bring political communities out of the current impasse. Third, any healing requires political leaders to have the decency to conduct a fair appraisal of claims and not to hide behind the law, since the legitimacy of the institutions in place is based on the rule of law and constitutionalism as key principles in their own right. Neither principle can take precedence over the other. Constitutionalist Francesco Palermo further fleshes out this point when he states, "Contemporary constitutionalism requires much more elaborate rules than in the past, as it has to ensure democratic, transparent, inclusive, and effective decision-making, taking into account different claims, different interests, and different legitimacies" (Palermo 2019). Fourth, the legitimacy that ought to reside behind political actions cannot be taken for granted. It has to be earned and deserved. In this sense, "the nation is a daily plebiscite."

Thinking Outside the Box

A key question about the situation in Spain is to ask ourselves if there is enough political will to transform the state of autonomies into an authentic federal state with an appropriate balance between shared rule and self-rule.

It has become clear over the last decade in connection with Spain that the state of autonomies, with its non-sharing of state sovereignty and its lack of flexibility, is no longer delivering on its promise of bringing together all Spanish citizens, nations, and nationalities.

Spain is paralyzed in its ability to change and evolve as the result of an excessive focus on the unity of the state. All potential reforms are appraised through this singular lens and, as a consequence, proposals that move away from the status quo are considered to be destabilizing for the state itself, when not simply depicted as being unpatriotic or, of late, as acts of sedition and even acts of rebellion.

Potential reforms have been described as direct and immediate challenges to the state's existence. Even the simple idea that an autonomous region can initiate and lead a potential constitutional reform is viewed with suspicion and denounced. With some hindsight, the Ibarretxe Plan, elaborated between 2001 and 2005 (as discussed in chapter 1), can be considered as an attempt to end the political impasse, since it advocated a form of sovereignty-association.

The question that arises is whether the situation can evolve to the point where political leaders are encouraged to invest time and energy into reshaping political institutions with a view to take deep diversity and diverse state traditions into account. I am thinking here especially of the Anglo-American, German, Swiss, and post-colonial traditions (Cardinal and Sonntag 2015, 4–5).

Three principles ought to be engaged to re-establish trust between the constituent power (the state central) and the constitutive components of the state (the autonomous communities, member states or provinces, depending on the context): autonomy, non-subordination of power, and co-decision/interdependence/co-sovereignty. I will come back to this below.

Political leaders in Spain might want to consider ways to implement federalism – coming together versus holding together, to use Alfred Stepan's terminology, and rather than being forced to stay together. The trends reveal different political heritages and different goals of state actors. The coming-together tradition is generally associated with America's territorial model, which insists on the overall objective of constituting a single sovereign people.

At one end of the spectrum are "relatively autonomous units that 'come-together' to pool their sovereignty while retaining their individual identities. The United States, Switzerland, and Australia are examples of such states. At the other end of the democratic continuum, we have India, Belgium, and Spain, as examples of 'holding together' federalism" (Stepan 1999, 23), which we consider to be a federalism that holds differentiated units together.

Since Alfred Stepan published his seminal article over twenty years ago, India, Belgium, and Spain have continued their internal transformation, with India and Spain using state power to contain their population to maintain the territorial integrity of the country. It can be said that, in Spain at least, the federal tradition has moved from a holding-together stance to a forcing-together mindset of the majority nation and its ancillary institutions, including the constitutional tribunal. The consequences of such a transformation are significant and have contributed to undermine the legitimacy of the Spanish state internally, in the eyes of the historic nations, and externally, in the eyes of the European Union and the international political community.

It is imperative to imagine political scenarios that do not simply mechanistically reproduce the status quo, since the current state of affairs imposes a straitjacket on the members of the minority nations. This comes with some uncertainty but, at the same time, the major political issues at stake cannot be resolved blindly through the use of coercive measures.

Something has to give. The central question for political leaders is what means are available to the protagonists in positions of authority, and what means ought to be institutionalized to create conditions conducive to democratic debates that can bring the political communities out of the current impasse.

I will try to identify the elements on which trust can be built or rebuilt.

Short of having political leaders able to mobilize the energy needed to revitalize trust relations among political leaders and state actors, a large part of the solution might reside within civil society itself. For some time, and with keen interest, I have been following the social movement under way in the Basque territory. The movement, "In our own hands/Gure Esku Dago," has produced encouraging results by asserting five things:

1 Changes ought to occur with peaceful means.
2 Political transition ought to be preceded by a vast societal introspection as well as an all-encompassing political mobilization that seeks to leave no one outside the political process.
3 Attaining consensus between political adversaries (nationalists, unionists, secessionists, etc.) is crucial before a major political move can be undertaken in order to avoid a divide-and-conquer strategy reminiscent of the British imperial tradition.
4 Acceptance that the state of autonomies is no longer in tune with political reality on the terrain in the Basque Country and, by extension, in Catalonia.
5 The four preceding elements help transform the Basque Country, and other national communities for that matter, into authentic political subjects that take the political community beyond its depiction, by the central state, as simply a singular culture or a sociological entity.

Initiatives such as "In Our Own Hands" invite political leaders to question the persistent Spanish doctrine that all rights stem from the Spanish constitution of 1978, in which historic rights are "consigned to an annex" (Keating 2018). However, these historic rights are not superfluous elements; they form the very foundation for the political compact that helped Spain put the authoritarian Franco period as a thing of the past.

The Supreme Court of Canada's decision in Reference re Secession of Quebec (1998) is particularly useful for us today, as it invites political actors and state managers to reappraise "constitutional democracy, not as a system that solves ... problems once and for all with some definitive ordering of its members, but as a complex set of practices in which the irreducible conflicts over the recognition of diversity and the requirements of unity are conciliated over time" (Tully 2000, 4). Unity and diversity are not opposing terms – they should be seen as compatible and even congruent. Indeed, they ought to be at the basis of any plural and decent society. "The opposite of unity is not diversity; it is disunity while the opposite of diversity is a single uniform homogeneity" (Gagnon and Burgess 2018b, xviii). In this connection, political philosopher James Tully judiciously identifies two contrasting paths that cohabit within constitutional democracies.

The first path is depicted as an "end-state" relation to democracy – "that is, a view of democracy as some definitive ordering of the members of a political association and of the relations among them ... [with the aim of] arriving at the 'just' ordering of the members and their relations once and for all" (Tully 2000, 4). This is often what the majority nation seeks to impose on the other members of an established political association. The situation prevailing in Catalonia under article 155 is a case of unusual intensity during which direct rule over Catalonia was imposed, suspending Catalonia's indirect political self-rule as a result.

The second path, and a promising response to the end-state relation to democracy, is the "activity-oriented" expression of democracy that, as its primary objective, pursues the goal of freedom. Under this second rendering, democracy is accomplished through "processes of discussion and change both in accordance with constitutional rules as well as over these rules" (Tully 2000, 4). In such a democratic endeavour, dissent and political resistance ought not to be considered as detrimental to the democratic expression but as a crucial and necessary component.[3]

This brings the right to decide to the forefront of the debate as a valid and legitimate concept. In my view, the right to decide is consistent with the goal of creating majority communities at various scales while pursuing the central objective of enlarging the democratic project. In other words, democracy is not limited to, for example, parliamentary institutions or the single will of a majority nation. In addition, the right to decide, as a mobilizing concept, covers a lot of ground as it encompasses both internal and external processes of self-determination. And for this reason it renders the concept much less effective than what some colleagues believe – I am thinking here, for example, of the body of work produced over the years by Jaume López (2011). The main shortcoming of the right to decide concept, and that ought to be identified as a significant flaw, is that it ends up reducing political claims founded on the principle of legitimacy to issues in the realm of legality that help buffer constitutional courts against potential criticisms or, to use the terminology of Torbisco Casals, to un-wisely support a form of politics founded on the "constitutional fetishism that dominates Spanish legal culture" (2017, 216).

I believe that we need to embrace the influential work of James Tully, who addresses the values that are supported and fed by the democratic project, and contrasts the logic driven by an end-state approach with the logic resting on the activity-oriented approach to democracy. These two distinct paths highlight particular features – political stability and political freedom – that cast light on the two sides of the same coin and allow us to insist on their capacity to manage conflicts jointly. These two processes do not evolve in silos; they need to be combined and reconciled. In my view, these two paths need one another to succeed. Either path taken alone does not possess the necessary qualities to take deeply divided polities out of their ongoing predicament. However, finding an adequate balance between these two paths appears to be the best option to select if political leaders and state managers are serious about finding a way out of a constitutional impasse.

James Tully (2000, 4–5) made another particularly insightful point when he stated that "a constitutional democracy will not be legitimate because it is completely just (which is never the case), but because it is free and 'flexible' – always open and responsive to dissent and amendment."

Ongoing debates in Spain, at least on Basque as well as Catalan po-litical claims, have tended to focus on an end-state view of democracy. Such a view is bound to make winners and losers. Such a position ap-pears not to be very conducive for the political stability of a political regime. I would even go so far as say that it can be detrimental to the maintenance of political trust between constitutional partners.

Rethinking Constitutional Arrangements

In any democratic political setting, political opposition and rival po-litical projects cannot be reduced to silence or eliminated. This is even more evident when a state is formed of several political communities – of several demoi – acting through democratic institutions. It is crucial that competing voices be heard and that debates take place to inform the public and put to the test the democratic qualities of a given society, even in situations during which such discussions may create political tensions. Such tensions are essential at different historical junctures in order to imagine ways to design a fairer partnership.

Arend Lijphart, to whom we owe the concept of consociational de-mocracy, reminds us that "although the replacement of segmental loyalties by common national allegiance appears to be a logical answer to the problems posed by a plural society, it is extremely dangerous to attempt it. Because of the tenacity of primordial loyalties, any effort to eradicate them not only is quite unlikely to succeed, especially in the short run, but may well be counterproductive and may stimulate segmental cohesion and intersegmental violence rather than national cohesion" (Lijphart 1977, 24). The work of Lijphart and, in his wake, Brendan O'Leary and John McGarry, have helped make the scientific community more aware of the urgency to pay attention (not only lip service) to the constitutional design of many segmented polities. Cases in point include South Tyrol, Flanders and Wallonia, Northern Ireland, and New Caledonia (Cetrà 2019; Mathieu 2020c; Lecours, Brassard-Dion, and Laforest 2021). They have in common that they have paid serious attention to the moral and political claims expressed by distinct national communities that came together to materialize and actualize historical arrangements (Tierney 2022).

The success experienced in these national contexts can be ascribed essentially to four reasons. First, a desire of political leaders to accommodate national communities rather than force their integration, at all costs, into a larger nation. Second, although this differs in quality from one region to the next, the possibility for member units of a given polity to have an authentic say in the making of public policies at the (supra) national level. Here, in descending order, Flanders, Wallonia, Northern Ireland, and New Caledonia have consistently seen their respective roles gain prominence in international forums. Third, in all cases, initiatives based on social harmony rather than coercive measures have led to a substantial increase of political trust among the constitutional partners. Fourth, and perhaps even more decisive, is the role played by the judiciary, which has to act as a fair arbiter and honest broker and be perceived as such by all. In the cases mentioned, the constitutional courts have been in a position to maintain and even consolidate their legitimate moral authority.

In the case of Canada, after intervening in what several authors consider to be a partial and inadvisable way during the repatriation of the Constitution in 1982 (Russell 1983; Rocher and Pelletier 2013), the Supreme Court was able to redeem itself when it ruled on the Reference re Secession of Quebec (1998). Jurist Robert Schertzer suggests that, since this recent constitutional event,

the [Supreme] Court's adopted role can be an integral part of a decision recognizing the legitimacy of multiple models and the federation as a process and outcome of negotiation ... paired with a role for the

Court as a broad facilitator of this negotiation, either explicitly or more indirectly....

It is in assuming this role that the Court ideally seeks to reinforce the legitimacy of the various parties' perspectives, to affirm the legitimacy of the political and institutional processes that allow negotiation and co-operation, and to induce the parties to use these processes.... Here, the ideal is to avoid imposing a particular party's perspective on another party, to reaffirm the legitimacy of the losing party's perspective, and to mitigate the loss for a party to the extent possible, while also seeking to emphasize that continued disagreement is reasonable and that the federal system can account for this situation as a flexible and dynamic association. (Schertzer 2016, 255)

I grant that this view might not portray exactly what the situation is in reality, since the Supreme Court was careful not to give free licence to any member state to act as it wished without paying attention to the presence and claims of other partners in the federation. Building on four principles – democracy, federalism, the rule of law and constitutionalism, and the protection of the rights of minorities – the Supreme Court made the point in paragraph 85 that "the Constitution is the expression of the sovereignty of the people of Canada. It lies within the power of the people of Canada, acting through their various governments duly elected and recognized under the Constitution to effect whatever constitutional arrangements are desired within the Canadian territory, including, should it be so desired, the secession of Quebec from Canada."

In contrast to the situation prevailing in Spain, it is possible for the government of Quebec or the people of Quebec to actively seek independence, but the conditions to be met remain hard to assemble. For example, two conditions are identified in paragraph 148: "a clear majority of Quebecers votes on a clear question in favour of secession." If these two conditions are met, then negotiation can be initiated. The Supreme Court specifies that the final decision resides not with voters but with the political actors themselves (Casanas Adam and Rocher 2014, 62). So, from this standpoint, there is no guarantee of success for Quebec in its capacity to achieve full self-determination as a political subject.[4] In addition, the four principles identified in the Supreme Court's reference with respect to Quebec secession constitute guarantees, but at the same time significant hurdles. In fact these principles can be viewed as representing powerful constitutional locks. In the end, though, the Supreme Court ruling was well received by the main parties to the constitutional conflict, thus helping attenuate ongoing political tensions.

Contestation and Resistance

Both Canada and Spain portray themselves as constitutional democracies, although their ways of accommodating national diversity appear to be at opposite ends of the constitutional spectrum. At one extreme is Canada, which, bluntly stated, appears to target "demos-enabling" (a politics of contentment) while, at the other extreme is Spain, whose strategy is more akin to "demos-constraining" (a politics of containment).

As I have highlighted in this book, the situation in Canada is not as open as some analysts have argued (including Pelletier 2006), but there is nonetheless much more room for manoeuvre than in Spain. This is largely because the exercise of sovereignty is not perceived in the same way among political actors, senior government officials, and magistrates.

Montesquieu was right to call for a separation of powers between the main holders of political authority: "So that power cannot be abused, it is necessary that, by the disposition of things, power stops power" (Ducharme 2010, 57). Much closer to us, the work of Jürgen Habermas is particularly relevant as he emphasizes the importance, for a political regime, of preserving its political legitimacy. According to Habermas (1991, 178), legitimacy corresponds to "a political order's worthiness to be recognized."

When people, minorities, or large segments of political communities no longer recognize the legitimacy of a given political regime to act on their behalf, political stability can be maintained only through coercive measures. From this point on, a regime can be maintained, but societal disintegration is clearly underway and the necessary cohesion for the state to succeed starts unravelling. Again, to quote Habermas (1991, 180), "Inasmuch as the state assumes the guarantee to prevent social disintegration by way of binding decisions, the exercise of state power is then measured against this; it must be recognized as legitimate if it is to last."

The legitimacy of a political regime must go beyond the existence and control of representative institutions, although the latter are essential to secure its political stability. But, on the basis of the principle of modern constitutionalism, certain conditions must be met. Pressing forward the work of Tully, I consider the following four conditions to be crucial in any sustainable relation between constitutional partners: historical continuity, political consent, hospitality, and reciprocity. I have discussed these four conditions at length in the first two books in the present triptych (Gagnon 2010, 2014).

Building on the work of philosophers such as Will Kymlicka, Philip Pettit, and Nancy Fraser, Neus Torbisco Casals considers a substantial deficit of legitimacy to be sufficient reason to consider the "exit option." She makes the point that "secession, even a unilateral one, should emerge as a legitimate action in a democratic context whenever the state insists on subjugating its national minorities, denying them equal recognition as collective subjects as well as the right to internal self-determination (including the attribution of the necessary powers to allow their cultural and linguistic development). Hence, the right to secession would work as a shield against the impulse of majorities to oppress minorities" (Torbisco Casals 2017, 221).

Drawing inspiration from the work of my colleagues in the Research Group on Plurinational Societies – in particular Eugénie Brouillet, Dimitrios Karmis, Guy Laforest, Geneviève Nootens, François Rocher, and James Tully – I have come to the conclusion that sovereignty must be seen as the expression of the political subjects that are called upon to evolve within democratically established territories. In short, what must be paramount is not so much the stability of political regimes as the development of democratic processes open to deliberation and respect for contrasting, even antagonistic, positions. As Nootens points out, "The idea that sovereignty (state or popular) is one and indivisible, that the state corresponds to a single and indivisible constituent power, and that people's ability to act is subordinated to the embodiment of autonomy of the political within the state, constitutes a hindrance to the democratization of relations between nations in multinational federations" (Nootens 2019, 139).

It is here, I believe, that the right to decide can achieve its full potential. If a political regime simply reproduces and even consolidates the preferences and political claims of the majority (nation), the democratic principle is not exercised in its full sense. Both federalism as a political contract and consociationalism as a political option offer some potent cues on how to, first, rally oppositional political forces around a series of common objectives and, second, negotiate a revamped constitutional order void as much as possible of a dominant mentality.[5]

Democratic federations and consociations provide pillars on which to build an all-encompassing society that is congruent with a plurality of cultures as well as a diversity of political and legal traditions. To be efficient and legitimate, a consociational democracy needs to uphold four principles: a grand coalition between political parties, segmental autonomy and federalism, proportionality, and a mutual veto (Lijphart 1977). In other words, majority rule is considered to be an unsatisfying way of governing.

We can return to the Canadian example at this point, since it casts some useful light. Even though there has been, over the years, major political tension between Quebec and Ottawa over constitutional arrangements, concrete efforts have been made to bring together two major traditions of federalism (territorial and multinational) as well as three legal traditions (common law, civil law, and more recently, Indigenous customary law). I believe that such an endeavour has helped extend legitimacy to political institutions.

For example, in paragraph 49 of Reference re Supreme Court Act (2014), the Supreme Court of Canada recognized the importance of appointing three of its nine judges from Quebec (see Taillon 2019, 168). As it states in its decision, "The purpose of s. 6 is to ensure not only civil law training and experience on the Court, but also to ensure that Quebec's distinct legal traditions and social values are represented on the Court, thereby enhancing the confidence of the people of Quebec in the Supreme Court as the final arbiter of their rights. Put differently, s. 6 protects both the *functioning* and the *legitimacy* of the Supreme Court as a general court of appeal for Canada."

The Canadian Supreme Court has taken upon itself to advance a constitutional philosophy that tends to favour federal practices, democratic values, constitutionalism, and the rule of law in addition to the protection of minority rights. Since the 1995 referendum in Quebec, this philosophy has helped ease political tensions and bring Quebecers and the Indigenous Peoples gradually back into the federal fold. It also suggests that the judiciary can offer a positive role model for the management of deep diversity (Schertzer 2016, 255).

Adhering to a Living Constitution

Constitutions exist to guide political actors as they manage societal diversity and elaborate schemes that will help establish the necessary conditions and instruments to protect minorities from potential abuses by the majority. To ignore the claims made by minority nations would be tantamount to saying that the institutions in place would inevitably take the side of the majority culture. Stated differently, if a constitution is too much out of step with the milieu it aims to manage, then it ceases to be a source of political legitimacy (Gagnon and Schwartz 2015, 252).

Gandhi once said, "A nation's greatness is measured by how it treats its weakest members." This idea has been reformulated in Canada in the context of Métis political claims and historical rights. Prime Minister Pierre Elliott Trudeau once stated in this respect, "Riel and his followers were protesting against the Government's indifference to their problems and its refusal to consult them on matters of their vital interest.... Questions of minority rights have deep roots in our history.... We must never forget that, in the long run, a democracy is judged by the way the majority treats the minority. Louis Riel's battle is not yet won" (quoted in Miller 1992, 189).

This is why I stated at the very beginning of this chapter that we need to think outside the box since, in many countries, there is no lever for action that is immediately available to reform state institutions. The case of Spain has made it clear that the executive is concerned about making decisions with political opponents for fear of alienating voters. At the same time, the Constitutional Court of Spain has been unable to demonstrate that it can act as an impartial arbiter to help resolve a constitutional impasse. Last, although the European Union could provide political leadership, the major state actors are afraid that their own minorities could follow the Catalan example and advance political projects that support pro-independence nationalist demands.

In sum, thinking outside the box would mean that:

- Democracy is not reducible to "majority rule." In the modern era, democracy means that minorities deserve protection and ought to get equal protection, equal opportunities, and equal conditions of existence to achieve fulfilment as full members of society;
- The First Peoples must be able to make their voices heard and have a real influence on the socio-political transformations underway at regional and national levels, as well as in international organizations and in other national contexts.
- Civil society has to be considered a legitimate actor in developing political consensus and imagining constitutional arrangements – and its leaders cannot be thrown in jail without the due process of a fair hearing.
- Political projects emanating from the autonomous communities ought to be welcomed rather than condemned. This should be evident in a "free and democratic society."
- The European Union ought to play a much more active role when national minorities and minority nations in one of its member states display distress in response to an unfair hearing or unfair treatment.

As a consequence, it is crucial to develop a meta-normative theory focusing on three aspects: federalism rather than unilateralism, constitutional pluralism rather than monism, and subsidiarity rather than centralization. In sum, only a shared vision of constitutional categories can pave the way for reconciliation of the parties and consolidation of the political system. Assuming these conditions are met, loyalty would become a natural path. Recasting the dominant centralist stand in favour of a vision founded on the principles of coordination, non-subordination, and consent appears to be the best political and societal investment a country could make in this new century. Such an endeavour would help appease political tensions as states, formed of distinctive demoi, give a fairer and more equal hearing to their constitutive parts. And, to conclude, it is important not to be content with an approach based solely on the "right to choose," since – in such a scenario – political communities are trapped in a legal straitjacket that limits their ability to act. In other words, I am of the view that it is crucial to assess conflicting claims on the basis of the notion of legitimacy rather than legality.

On Future Horizons

I may have completed this trilogy, but I am not planning to abandon the field of multinational federalism, where so much remains to be done. It is the area of research with the best resources for providing complex sovereign states with normative anchoring and effective approaches to meet the challenges of this new century.

Significant work by members of the Research Group on Plurinational Societies (whose members have been finalists four times for the Social Sciences and Humanities Council Insight Award) has shown that special attention needs to be paid to the federalism-secession dyad. This is a topic too rarely addressed by specialists of federalism. Yet secession is an issue that must be debated openly in order to define realistic, responsible scenarios that will allow the most fragile federations to find solutions that are both fair and democratic. Secession is a fundamental question that must be examined frankly and with open eyes.

My colleague Jorge Cagiao y Conde and I were given the opportunity to launch a publishing project to explore the interconnections between the notion of federalism and secessionist plans. This led to the publication of *Fédéralisme et sécession* with an English version, entitled *Federalism and Secession* (Cagiao y Conde and Gagnon 2019, 2021). The challenge was considerable: we had to review the work of several major contributors to theories of federalism who understood that the principle of sovereignty itself needs to be clarified if the societies that are present at the foundation of a federal pact are to continue their existence. This helps guarantee the political stability of political regimes through strong recognition policies.

In March 2018, the establishment of the new Centre d'analyse politique: constitution – fédéralisme (CAPCF) at the Université du Québec à Montréal, where I have the privilege of being the first director, opened five major lines of research: (1) cooperative federalism, asymmetry and solidarity; (2) energy and the environment; (3) fiscal federalism and decentralization; (4) Indigenous peoples, rights and social justice; and (5) political and constitutional history. Our first findings are encouraging and show promise for the years to come.

My colleague Arjun Tremblay and I hosted the CAPCF's inaugural conference and then published the initial findings (Gagnon and Tremblay 2020). The researchers brought together around this project explored three broad issues:

1 How do multinational democracies with deep diversity adopt (or transform) federal models that reflect, represent, and empower national differences?
2 How can we properly assess the quality of a multinational federation?
3 What can federal democracies do to recognize and accommodate national diversity and other forms of collective identity?

Each of these questions opens the way to various interpretations, depending on whether the focus is on Southeast Asia, South America, North America, Europe, or Africa.

The CAPCF, in association with the Canada Research Chair in Quebec and Canadian Studies, which I have held since 2003, also launched an international project with colleagues at Canterbury Christ Church University to delve deeper into the many forms federalism can take. Back in Québec, I had great pleasure in working with Félix Mathieu and Dave Guénette. Together we published a summary of fifty studies by experts on federalism from around the world (Mathieu, Guénette, and Gagnon 2020). This work will continue to inform our discussions in the years to come. On the initiative of Soeren Keil and Paul Anderson, English, Burmese, Catalan, and Spanish versions of many of these contributions have been or will soon be published.

Likewise, in connection with the research conducted at the CAPCF, I would like to thank Antoine Brousseau Desaulniers and Stéphane Savard, who published *La pensée fédéraliste contemporaine au Québec* (Brousseau Desaulniers and Savard 2020). It focused on constitutional history while exploring the tensions between sovereigntist approaches and federalism, which has been the principal point of friction between Québec and Canada since 1960. It is a multidisciplinary book that looks in particular at the roles of political players in – and contributions of intellectuals to – competing currents of federalism in Canada. Some twenty authors were brought together, and the result is a lucid work on the values and representations of political players trying to make their visions of society a reality.

I would also like to mention a new collaboration between the CAPCF and research centres across Canada. It involves a major survey to pinpoint and measure the expectations of political communities. It is led by the Environics Institute for Survey Research, in partnership with the CAPCF, the Canada West Foundation, the Institute for Research on Public Policy (IRPP), and the Brian Mulroney Institute of Government at St. Francis Xavier University. The survey primarily addresses three broad concerns: relations between Indigenous and non-Indigenous people, regional perspectives on the economy and climate change, and social programs, immigration, and cultural and national diversity. Each of those concerns will lead to the publication of a specialized study.

I would be remiss if I did not mention the research I am conducting with José Maria Sauca at Universidad Carlos III de Madrid. Since 2000, we have carried out a number of joint projects and we are now coordinating research on linguistic diversity as a priority concern for advanced democracies acting on different scales and with institutional architecture sheltering multiple demoi. Our work will complement the findings we published in *Negotiating Diversity: Identity, Pluralism and Democracy* (Gagnon and Sauca 2014), in which we focused on constitutional and legal pluralism, recognition policies, and democratic practices in federal contexts.

In coming years the CAPCF will increase collaboration with members of the International Association of Centers for Federal Studies. A summer seminar "Negotiating and Sharing Power(s): Autonomy, Recognition and Cooperation" was held in 2019. The next seminar is planned for spring 2023 to focus on issues raised by recognition and redistribution in fragmented societies, among other themes. This project owes a debt to close collaboration with our Canadian partners, first and foremost John McGarry at Queen's University, and our European partners, with the support of Joseph Marko and Francesco Palermo at the European Academy of Bolzano/Bozen in South Tyrol.

Each of these initiatives is testimony to the work that has been completed, but especially to the arduous task that researchers in federal studies are facing in coming years. It is with great enthusiasm, surrounded by graduate students and faculty colleagues at the Université du Québec à Montréal and beyond, that I am looking forward to the future.

Allow me to draw attention to the work done with my colleagues James Bickerton, Eugénie Brouillet, Guy Laforest, Johanne Poirier, and Brian Tanguay. It will continue to bear fruit, given the projects we are carrying out in federal and constitutional studies. In 2020, James Bickerton and I had the pleasure of publishing the seventh edition of *Canadian*

Politics – a book that has been standard fare in Canadian universities for over three decades. Similarly, Johanne Poirier and I published recent GRSP findings (Gagnon and Poirier 2020a; 2020b). Everything is now in place for Brian Tanguay and me to begin tidying up the fifth edition of *Canadian Parties (Still) in Transition*.

Lastly, my work will continue to question the way state sovereignty operates, with a view to document claims made by First Peoples intending to assume political authority over their own communities and territories. There is an urgent need to redress past injustices towards First Peoples by ending their historical exclusion from the political process. My work on multinational federalism is intended to establish decent and fair operative principles that can contribute to bring communities to care for each other. This will require much effort in reconceptualizing citizenship, democracy, and the meaning of territory and state authority. The work of John Borrows, Robert Hamilton, Joshua Nichols, and Kiera Ladner is particularly relevant, as they ask why Indigenous peoples should limit their constitutional demands to section 35 of the Canadian Charter of Rights and Freedoms. Like for Quebec, I would argue, First Peoples ought to inscribe their claims in the language of self-determination. This would contribute to building a new and necessary road away from colonialism and contribute to advance a constitutional path (1) that feeds a much deeper diversity and (2) that treats First Peoples as constituting a new majority in Canada rather than being considered one among many ethnic communities. The terms of the Canadian conversation ought to evolve in a significant way if claims made by First Peoples are to be taken seriously. Hamilton and Nichols illustrate the issue at stake particularly well: "The colonial pillar is thus employed to determine the legal dimension of the box of rights that section 35 'recognized and affirmed.' It functions to silently and completely strip away the political rights of Aboriginal peoples.... This unilateral diminishment of Indigenous peoples from self-governing nations to a racialized minority is entangled with the *thick* version of sovereignty that the [Supreme] Court attributes to the Crown.... It facilitates the perception of Indigenous peoples as holders of *rights* rather than *jurisdiction*" (Hamilton and Nichols 2021, 230).

I feel my work offers the necessary ingredients to engage in a conversation among researchers, policymakers, members of diverse nations, and citizens in general – potential partners who could draw on normative considerations to develop a literature that leads to a concrete emulation between multinational federalism and pre-colonial treaty federalism studies. Some authors, including Taiaiake Alfred and Jeff Corntassel (2005), might have be too quick to reject the potency of federalism as an instrument of unveiling and empowerment for partners in Canada's federal pact.

As I have illustrated throughout this book, the legitimacy clash cannot be more obvious than the one between Canada's constitutional order and claims made by First Peoples. Majority rule – though important – is insufficient to provide the state with a full legitimate authority to act on behalf of all constituent peoples (Tierney 2022). To the extent Canada intends to abandon its colonial features, it is crucial that Canada revisit its formal foundation by finding a much-needed equilibrium between the current constitutional order (legality) and peoples' most decent claims to the origins of the country (legitimacy).

The next step for authors concerned with political and moral issues that I have raised and discussed in this book ought to be an exploration into the exercise of sovereignty and democracy. While it might sound highly disputable for many, why should sovereignty in Canada rest exclusively with the Crown? I feel we ought to walk in the footsteps of scholars such as John Borrows, Kent McNeil, and James Tully who have opened new domains of enquiry and questioned the way state authority has been conceived and enforced by dominant groups and interests. Kent McNeil (2018) brilliantly questions what he terms the relativity of de jure sovereignty in Canada. This is a refreshing thought that can lead to a much more promising future for all partners in the Canadian federation. This calls for our immediate attention, as it requires much-needed and sophisticated studies from philosophers, political scientists, and legal experts. My hope is that many will be in a position to concentrate their efforts on this essential task so that Indigenous political organizations can evolve in a proper setting and work on an equal footing with trustworthy partners.

It looks as though there will be a lot of work ahead. Completing this trilogy is not so much a culmination as it is the opening of the door to many more projects, each more exciting and stimulating than the last.

Notes

Introduction

1 The book was first published in 2006 by the Catalan government's Institut d'Estudis as *Au-delà de la nation unificatrice : plaidoyer pour le fédéralisme multinational* (Gagnon 2006a). The same year, it won the Josep Maria Vilaseca i Marcet Award, named after the institute's first director.

2 The founding members of the team are Dominique Arel, Alain-G. Gagnon, Guy Laforest, James Tully, and François Rocher. Over the years, other researchers have joined the GRSP and, in several cases, have made it their primary scientific group. Political scientists, jurists, and philosophers including José Woehrling, Dimitrios Karmis, Geneviève Nootens, André Lecours, Pierre Noreau, Jocelyn Maclure, Eugénie Brouillet, Johanne Poirier, Geneviève Motard, Martin Papillon, Antoine Bilodeau, Dominique Leydet, and Luc Turgeon have been associated with the GRSP for projects and grant applications submitted to the Social Sciences and Humanities Research Council and to the Fonds québécois de recherche Culture et société (formerly the FCAR). It is also important to mention the contribution made by two outstanding research professionals to the day-to-day work of the GRSP: Stéphan Gervais from 1994 to 2003, when the team was hosted by McGill University, and Olivier De Champlain, who quickly took up the role after the group transferred to the Department of Political Science at Université du Québec à Montréal following the creation of the Canada Research Chair in Quebec and Canadian Studies in 2003.

3 Throughout this book I use the notions of multinational federalism and plurinational federalism interchangeably. A few authors distinguish between the two, such as Michael Keating. In Keating's view, "The plurinational state extends the concept of plurinationality, referring to the existence of multiple political communities rather than to a single, unitary *demos*" (Keating 2001b, 78), whereas the multinational state is "a complex

state in which several communities, defined by identity or interest, coexist" (64). This distinction is relevant at the taxonomic level but provides no extra value in this book since my analysis focuses on the demoi – the political subjects – rather than on the identities involved.

4 For a detailed analysis, see Guénette and Gagnon (2021, 147–74).

5 Seymour (2017) has continued Rawls's work by transposing the concepts he uses into a liberal theory of individual rights for the establishment of a liberal theory of collective rights.

6 Although they offer very different perspectives, Beauchemin (2002, 2011) and Létourneau (2000) support this statement.

1. Laying the Groundwork: Legality, Legitimacy, Fair Democracy

1 Twenty years after the publication of the *Reference* decision, Mathieu and Guénette (2019) edited a collective work as doctoral candidates associated with the Canada Research Chair in Quebec and Canadian Studies to measure how each of the four principles supporting the Canadian constitutional compact has infused and influenced political relationships in the country.

2 This perspective resembles the approach to constitutional interpretation known as "originalism," defended in the United States by conservative Republicans who want to interpret the constitution on the basis of the intent of the founding fathers in the eighteenth century. Behind this stance, of course, lie highly partisan interests.

3 Readers should consult Gagnon (2014, 59–62) for a longer discussion of this theme.

4 The trust/mistrust dynamic in the Belgian, British, Canadian, and Spanish contexts has been explored in detail by the members of the Research Group on Plurinational Societies, and I commend their sustained modelling efforts over the long term. See, in particular, Karmis and Rocher (2012, 2018).

5 I refer readers to Gagnon (2014), which forms the second part of this triptych.

6 More recent work in this area includes Burelle (2005, 2020) and Bastien (2013).

7 Citing paragraph 59 in the *Reference*, Nootens considers that the Supreme Court merely recognized Quebec as a cultural and linguistic minority. See "Démocratie et pouvoirs constituants dans les sociétés plurinationales" (Nootens 2019, 124).

8 More on this topic is found in Payero-López (2020, especially 74–6). On the basis of analysis by Pérez-Royo (2018), the author highlights the weak original legitimacy of the Spanish state. This was able to pass unnoticed

during the years of major social investment in education and health care, as the welfare state emerged and Spain joined the European Union in the post-Franco period.

9 I will come back to this in more detail in chapters 4 and 5.

10 See Mathieu (2020b), where he lists and analyses several contributions made by the members of the school.

11 Note that the concept of nation may be attached simultaneously to the political and cultural domains, as illustrated by Lecours and Nootens (2011, 3–18).

12 The Institute for Democracy and Electoral Assistance (2017) argues that the fragility of society comes from the lack of an inclusive governance.

13 Ryan (1976), quoted in Sanschagrin (2021). See also Loranger (1884).

14 See chapter 3.

15 Even Switzerland, known for its outstanding capacity to recognize the diversity of the cantons, cannot escape this trend. See, in this connection, Belser (2020).

16 The case of Germany is useful here because, although they can be classified under the territorial federalism label, the *Länder* have their own constitutions and can appeal to the Supreme Court to arbitrate disputes over powers.

17 Naturally there are counter-examples, including Czechoslovakia, the Soviet Union, and Yugoslavia, all federations where coercion was the rule.

18 See Taylor (1993).

19 For a discussion of the situation in multi-ethnic and multinational federal states that broke apart following decolonization in Africa and Asia in the late 1950s and early 1960s, or after the fall of the Berlin Wall in 1989 and a movement towards democracy (for example, the Soviet Union, Yugoslavia, Czechoslovakia), see also O'Leary (2001). He argues that the stability of a political regime in a context of national diversity is proportional to the existence of a Staatsvolk that guarantees the stability of the encompassing state. In O'Leary's words, "The theory that I wish to advance and explore is that *a stable democratic majoritarian federation, federal or multinational, must have a Staatsvolk, a national or ethnic people, who are demographically and electorally dominant* – though not necessarily an absolute majority of the population – and who will normally be the co-founders of the federation" (284–5).

2. Foundations of and Changes to the Federal Project in Canada

1 Some key studies in the field of political economy need to be mentioned here: Mackintosh (1964) and Easterbrook and Aitken (1956).

2 See Brown (1966) on this topic. Smiley (1975) also refers to the creation of the first national policy in 1879, when he explains Ottawa's strategy, which

involved creating new economic infrastructures to promote growth and ensure its political leadership. Canada was in the first stages of genuine economic nationalism.

3 The Act also gave effect to the Policy on Bilingualism in the civil service that Prime Minister Lester B. Pearson had tabled in the House of Commons in April 1966 (Gélinas 2019) to ensure that English-speakers and French-speakers had equal access to government services.

4 For two contrasting analyses of these language disputes, see Poirier (2016) and MacMillan (1998). It is interesting to note that while the Laurendeau-Dunton Commission was continuing its work, the government of Jean-Jacques Bertrand in Quebec set up its own Commission of Inquiry on the Position of the French Language and on Language Rights in Quebec (Gendron Commission 1972). Its findings eventually led the Quebec government to introduce an affirmed language policy that made French the main language in the educational, cultural, social, economic, and communications fields.

5 The only gap in the federal government's long-standing desire to take control in the language field resulted from the pressure exerted by the Quebec government to extend the application of Bill 101 to federally chartered businesses operating in Quebec. The central government always opposed this measure except, in the fall of 2020, when Prime Minister Justin Trudeau – surprising everybody – stated, "With regard to Bill 101, we recognize that, in order for Canada to be bilingual, Quebec must first and foremost be francophone. That is why we support Bill 101 in what it does for Quebec, and that is why it is important to manage official bilingualism across the country" (*House of Commons Debates* 2020, 2046).

6 More light is provided by the research I conducted with my colleague Raffaele Iacovino (Gagnon and Iacovino 2007) and the work of Rocher and Pelletier (2013).

7 Taken from Constitutional Committee of the Quebec Liberal Party (1980, 68), quoted in Pelletier (2008, 20).

8 Elmerich (2021) describes this period as "a long constitutional winter."

9 Translated under the title of *Contemporary Canadian Federalism: Foundations, Traditions, Institutions* (Gagnon 2009).

10 See Blache (1993), Sauvé (2008), and the analysis published following the work of the Séguin Commission on fiscal imbalance (Commission Séguin sur le déséquilibre fiscal 2001; Commission sur le déséquilibre fiscal [Séguin Commission] 2002).

11 Other jurists, such as Brouillet (2005), have noted the same phenomenon.

12 These research institutes include the Canada West Foundation and the Business Council on National Issues. For researchers in federal studies in Canada but outside Quebec, this position is increasingly taken as a given and no longer debated.

13 For a defence of the principle of provincial equality, see Morton (2005).
14 The Acadian nation in New Brunswick, under the leadership of Louis Robichaud, experienced a similar period of levelling up, although to a lesser degree, during the 1960s. See Belliveau and Boily (2005).
15 Stevenson (1977, 83–4) adds the cases of Alberta, Manitoba, and Nova Scotia to those of Quebec and New Brunswick.
16 For a more in-depth analysis, see Young, Faucher, and Blais (1984).
17 For a discussion of this period, see Clarkson and McCall (1990–4) and Clarkson (2002).
18 For the pre-1990 period, the most exhaustive research has been conducted by Tanguay (1990). For the post-1990 period, see Lévesque and Bourque (2013) and Rioux (2020).

3. Conceptual Advances in Multinationality and the Definition of Shared Sovereignty

1 See Pierré-Caps (1995) and Seymour (2002) for a clearer view of the relationship between "state" and "nation." For these authors, the idea of "multination" opens the way to new forms of political and constitutional arrangements that can provide inspiration to "manage" and mitigate inter-community conflicts.
2 Rousseau (1762) has some interesting thoughts to offer, in particular in connection with the social contract.
3 Lord Acton's goal was not so much to endorse democracy as to ensure the advent of a multinational empire in which the European nations could coexist peacefully. See Lang (2002).
4 The following studies appear to me to be particularly relevant: Tully (1995b), Alfred (1999, 2005), Sioui (1999), Cairns (2000), Borrows (2016), Rodon (2019), along with dissertations and theses: Ladner (2000), Motard (2013), Germain (2015), Hansen (2019), and Woons (2020).
5 Chevrier (2019) devoted a substantial book to a study of how the imperial culture was maintained in Canada. He states, "Canada provides a perfect illustration of the empire in action, as it claims to have achieved a synthesis of a postnational microcosm in which cultures, peoples and beliefs coexist harmoniously thanks to multicultural law and a special way of governing." The phrase is found on the back cover.
6 See Burelle (2005). There would be a federal union but, at least as it was imagined by George-Étienne Cartier, the federated communities would not be merged into a single entity (Laforest and Mathieu 2016, 125–30).
7 More detail is provided in the work I completed recently with my colleague and McGill University jurist Johanne Poirier on the first 150 years of the Canadian federation, as part of the work of the Research Group on

Plurinational Societies. The work led to a collective work published in English and French, respectively by McGill-Queen's University Press and Presses de l'Université Laval (Gagnon and Poirier 2020a, 2020b). Similarly, after the thirtieth anniversary of repatriation, Rocher and Pelletier (2013) reviewed the constitutional tensions it caused in Canada.

8 This section is largely based on Gagnon (2015a), in which I discussed the existence of a "Quebec school of federalism."

9 For an analysis of the experiences of various states, including Belgium, Canada, Ethiopia, India, Malaysia, Nigeria, Russia, and Switzerland, and the European Union, see Burgess and Pinder (2007), Burgess and Gagnon (2010a), Seymour and Gagnon (2012b), Gagnon and Burgess (2018b), and Mathieu, Guénette, and Gagnon (2020).

10 Another key contribution is Carbonneau (2019).

11 This book is the original version of *The Case for Multinational Federalism: Beyond the All-Encompassing Nation* (Gagnon 2010).

12 Louis Cornellier (2020) concluded his opinion piece on "theoretical federalism" as follows: "[Félix] Mathieu knows that his plan [for multinational federalism] is uncertain. One can at least hope that, despite Canada turning a deaf ear, federalists with some interest in Quebec will draw inspiration from it instead of taking cowardly pleasure in the crepuscular comfort of exile."

13 For an in-depth analysis of the contribution made by the members of this school, see Mathieu (2020b).

14 For a historical analysis of tensions between Indigenous nations and the Crown, see Culhane Speck (1998) and Miller (2009).

15 See, in particular, the work of jurist John Borrows.

16 It is possible to identify situations in which representatives of the First Peoples are finally forced to accept the government position. One example is the Apuiat wind energy project, supported by the Innu on Quebec's North Shore, at a standstill, for a long period, for lack of clear "political" willingness of the Quebec government. This kind of deadlock can only make the bond of trust between Indigenous communities and government authorities more fragile.

17 The Oka Crisis is especially revealing. For seventy-eight days, Mohawk demonstrators, who had erected barricades in opposition, among other things, to the planned expansion of a golf course and residential construction, called for the enlargement of the "protected territory" of Kanesatake.

18 Waskaganish is a symbolic location for closer relations between the Cree nation and the Quebec nation. Premier René Lévesque went there in 1977 to testify to his willingness to build a nation-to-nation connection.

19 The work of Salée (2003) or, more recently, Woons (2020) looks at ways to rethink the Indigenous/non-Indigenous relationship.

20 Nadasdy (2017) highlights the postulates on which the Indigenous concept of sovereignty is founded, which are often divorced from the markers the Indigenous peoples have given themselves to understand the conceptual universe in which they live. Other authors, including Alfred and Corntassel (2005), claim the concept of sovereignty should not be used in the relations that the Indigenous peoples maintain with the government authorities, since it plays into the colonizer's hands and confirms that the Indigenous peoples have been colonized (Flamand 2020). In a similarly critical spirit, David Strang (1996) points out that the concepts of state, nation, and sovereignty are often the weapons used by the colonial forces to dispossess the First Peoples.

21 Analysis has been conducted by jurists, philosophers, and political scientists such as Borrows (2016), Coyle (2019), Ladner (2019), Nichols (2018), Russell (2017), and Seymour (2017).

4. The Canadian Political Order and Constitutional Nationalism

1 This section was initially presented as a keynote address on 15 February 2020 in Grainau, at the annual convention of Canadian studies specialists in German-speaking countries. My special thanks go to Professor Christian Lammert at the John F. Kennedy Institute for North American Studies at the University of Berlin for his judicious comments on a previous version of this chapter, which is an updated version of the article published in the winter of 2021 in issue 71 of *Zeitschrift für Kanada-Studien* (Gagnon 2021b).

2 For an assessment of the contribution made by historians to Canadian nation-building, see Berger (1976).

3 Some Quebec historians have defended a similar position, including Bastien (2013) and Bédard (2014).

4 Careless (1969) offers a view that was well in advance of its time.

5 The initiative was funded by the wealthy Bronfman family. See "Heritage Minutes" (2018). In 1999, the series was renamed as *Historica Minutes* when the Bronfman Foundation set up the Historica Foundation. The Historica Foundation later merged with the Dominion Institute in 2009 to form the Historica-Dominion Institute.

6 In 2020, the two books were released in a fourth edition.

7 I have borrowed this concept from Ovidiu Cristian Ionita (2014), whose doctoral thesis directed by Samir Saul was defended at Université de Montréal.

8 The principle of federalism is the first of the four constitutional principles defined by the Supreme Court of Canada in Reference re Secession of Quebec (1998). The three others are the principles of democracy, constitutionalism, and the rule of law, as well as respect for minorities.

9 The Reference re Secession of Quebec (1998) has become something of a mandatory reference for all Western democracies.

10 Pettit (1997, chap. 3) is especially relevant here.

11 The *Act respecting the laicity of the State* (Bill 21) was passed on 15 June 2019 under a parliamentary guillotine. It prohibits the wearing of religious symbols by teachers and principals in public schools, and also by people in situations of authority (such as police officers, prison guards, lawyers, and judges). It includes a clause that contravenes both the *Canadian Charter of Rights and Freedoms* and Quebec's *Charter of Human Rights and Freedoms*. For an extremely critical analysis of the position taken by the Legault government, see Bouchard (2020).

12 This aspect of the question has also been noted by Karmis and O'Toole (2018, 105).

13 To provide more protection for human rights, Stacy supports relational sovereignty, which relies on a fairer sharing of authority between states and the international community.

14 For a more recent and enlightening contribution on this topic, see Levy et al. (2018).

15 Strangely, the throne speech that followed Justin Trudeau's taking of power in the fall of 2015 mentions that nation-to-nation relations with the First Peoples must be given priority. This is, at the very least, a paradoxical statement from a government that also believes that Canada has entered a new era with the emergence of a post-national political order. "We will keep our diverse communities strong and will renew Canada's nation-to-nation relationship with Indigenous peoples." See Trudeau (2015b).

5. Diversity in Advanced Liberal Democracies

1 This chapter constitutes a synthesis of many of the arguments I have previously presented on this topic. The first version was drafted as a keynote presentation at the Fifteenth Conference of the Israel Association for Canadian Studies, "Rethinking Diversity and Multiculturalism: Global and Local Challenges," Hebrew University, 23–6 May 2016. The chapter contains practically all of the text published in French in Mathieu and Guénette (2019).

2 It is worth returning to a key text that acknowledges the emergence of a multinational Canada: Cairns (1994, 26–9).

3 Garth Stevenson argues that there might be fewer differences than we think between the two models, as they seem to have produced similar results: "Many Canadians in Ontario and the western provinces wanted all minorities (including French Canadians) to be submerged in a melting pot that would be uniformly English-speaking and culturally homogeneous.

To a large extent, with the help of their provincial governments, the sup-porters of homogeneity achieved the kind of Canada they wanted, except in Quebec" (Stevenson 2014, 262).

4 It is important to note here that the Quebec government refused to take part in the process before the Supreme Court of Canada.

5 For development of this point, see Erk and Anderson (2009).

6 For two summaries of Hans Kelsen's philosophy in English and in French, see Baume (2012) and Cagiao y Conde (2011).

7 My thanks to David Sanschagrin for bringing to my attention this aspect that I had not noticed in the work of Kelsen.

8 In addition, since the late 1990s, support for multiculturalism among the Canadian population outside Quebec has been eclipsed by a discourse centred more on citizen participation. See Tremblay (2019, 1–14, 215–27).

9 For an analysis of all aspects of the Bouchard-Taylor report, see St-Louis (2018) and Lefebvre and St-Laurent (2018).

10 Taken from Diefenbaker Papers, MGOI/XII/F/408, Library and Archives Canada. Justin Trudeau (2015a) echoed this sentiment during a speech in London following his election.

11 For a development of this point, see Gagnon and Iacovino (2007, 3–19).

12 I will come back to this in more detail in chapter 7.

13 For an exhaustive account of distinct federal traditions in Quebec, refer to Gagnon (2009) and Brousseau Desaulniers and Savard (forthcoming).

14 I will limit myself to two major collections of essays on this theme: Bur-gess and Pinder (2007), especially the chapters by Ismail Bakar, Michael Burgess, Patrick Peeters, and Ronald Watts; and Seymour and Gagnon (2012b), especially the chapters by Rajeev Bhargava, Raffaele Iacovino and Jan Erk, and Philip Resnick.

15 Pettit (1997) is especially relevant to our analysis here: see chapter 3.

16 Tully (1995a) has accurately depicted a growing discomfort and a major federal deficit that affect first and foremost Quebec's political development.

17 I am indebted to Jack Minz and Richard Simeon for these two concepts; see Minz and Simeon (1982).

6. The International Context and the All-Important Question of Rights

1 This fourteen-point declaration was made even more important by the fact that the political actors of the time were attempting to define the essential principles for restoring peace between the nations on a sustainable basis at the end of the First World War.

2 In 1948, fifty-six countries were UN members. Forty-eight supported the declaration, while the USSR, Belarus, Poland, Czechoslovakia, Ukraine,

Yugoslavia, Honduras, South Africa, Saudi Arabia, and Yemen abstained. See Amnesty International France (n.d.).

3   For an analysis of the situation in South Tyrol, see Mathieu (2020c, chap. 5).

4   Territorial autonomy was first given to the Trentino-Alto Adige region, with its Italian-speaking majority, before being established at the local community level in 1972. See Mathieu (2020c) for a more detailed discussion.

5   For an analysis of the situation in Sudan, see Giraudeau (2012), who notes that North Sudan has a mixed population, thanks to the presence of a black Muslim community known as the *Fur*, giving the region its name of Darfur (63). We should add that the Somaliland region in Somalia, which declared independence in 2011, was unable to obtain any form of international recognition despite its democratic stability and relative peace compared to the encompassing state of Somalia (see Felter 2018).

6   For contrasting analyses of the right to self-determination, see Crawford (2001), Summers (2007), Courtois (2014), Levrat et al. (2017), and Cagiao y Conde and Gagnon (2019, 2021).

7   See the work of Valerie Bunce, including *Subversive Institutions* (Bunce 1999b), in which she relates the events leading to the disintegration of the Soviet Union and the role played by nationalism.

8   For the start of this far-reaching process of change, see Carrère-D'Encausse (1991), and Lévesque (1995).

9   The commission's objectives are set out on the UN's own website: "The United Nations Commission on Human Rights was established in 1946 to weave the international legal fabric that protects our fundamental rights and freedoms. Composed of 53 States members, its brief expanded over time to allow it to respond to the whole range of human rights problems and it set standards to govern the conduct of States. It also acted as a forum where countries large and small, non-governmental groups and human rights defenders from around the world voiced their concerns" (United Nations Human Rights Council 2020).

10   For example, in 2014 the Council of Europe introduced its Framework Convention for the Protection of National Minorities, which came into force in 1998 and is recognized by thirty-nine states.

11   The Venice Commission has published opinions and recommendations on referendum law, judicial independence, the rights of national minority members, the issues connected with secession, the relations established between federated entities, and international treaties, to give only a few examples. See St-Hilaire (2017) for a detailed analysis.

12 From 1995 to 2004, Eide chaired a new working group within the sub-commission with the goal of providing more protection for minorities in an increasingly tense international context (Pharo 2019).

13 There is a consensus on this point. See the analyses by Núñez (2001) and Fossas (2007) supporting this interpretation at a time when Catalonia and the Basque Country were seeking to update and give more force to their autonomy status at the cultural, linguistic, political, and even para-diplomatic levels on the basis of their territorial autonomy (Guibernau, 2003, 2004; Garcia Segura 2019, 53–62).

14 Some interesting comments are made by Kagan (2002), who points out that Americans believe that their power authorizes them to promote the principles underlying "liberal" civilization and, at the same time, the world order. This attitude appears to apply at the level of several sovereign states, as illustrated by the situation in Spain. The analysis by Buchanan (1991) of the right to secede still remains highly relevant.

15 However, Cetrà (2017) notes, "Devolution processes in the second half of the twentieth century have contributed to strengthening minority nations' languages, while the European trend towards minority protection is noteworthy in moving away from monolingual frames but less significant in its implications."

16 The inability of the political elites in Ottawa to endorse the cause of the First Peoples may explain, in part, why Canada has fallen behind as an intermediate political power on the international state and why it finds it difficult to obtain respect from other states in the concert of nations, as reflected in its renewed failure to obtain a seat on the UN Security Council in June 2020. Bill C-262, tabled by former New Democratic Party MP Roméo Saganash, died on the Order Paper in June 2019, after being blocked in the Senate. On 12 August 2020, with a general election a possibility in Canada following accusations of conflict of interest by member of the ruling Liberal Party, the minister of Indigenous services, Marc Miller, stated that the implementation of the UNDRIP remained an "absolute priority" for the government (Wright 2020).

17 It appears that Canada's member states are more proactive in the recognition of the rights of the First Peoples, based on several recent initiatives. For example, the government of British Columbia amended its environmental assessment legislation to take Indigenous requirements into account, referring directly to the United Nations Declaration on the Rights of Indigenous Peoples (UNDRIP). Ottawa appears more likely to follow this example (Hudson 2020).

18 It would be a good time for younger researchers to closely analyse the two groups of researchers to highlight points where they converge and diverge

and identify areas that should be explored to promote inter-community dialogue and a better understanding of others.

19 They include the Hawthorn-Tremblay survey of the contemporary Indians of Canada (1964–70), the Berger Mackenzie Valley pipeline inquiry (1974–7), the Erasmus-Dussault Royal Commission on Aboriginal Peoples (1991–6), the Truth and Reconciliation Commission of Canada on residential schools for Indigenous children (2008–15), the National Inquiry into Missing and Murdered Indigenous Women and Girls (2016–19), and the Public Inquiry Commission (Viens Commission) on relations between Indigenous Peoples and certain public services in Quebec: listening, reconciliation, and progress (2017–19).

20 See the documentary *Les vies d'Albert Camus* (Benamou 2020). The documentary returns to his call for a civilian truce made in Algers on 22 January 1956, in the presence of many Algerian and French representatives. See also Pierré-Caps (2014).

7. Multinational Federalism: Challenges, Shortcomings, and Promises

1 With special thanks to Dan Freeman-Maloy and Félix Mathieu, respectively a post-doctoral student and an associate researcher for the Canada Research Chair in Quebec and Canadian Studies (CREQC) at Université du Quebec à Montréal, for comments that were especially useful in preparing the preliminary version of this chapter.

2 This chapter is largely inspired by Gagnon (2021a).

3 Readers interested in cases beyond these regions should see Gagnon and Tremblay (2020) in which cases of Bosnia Herzegovina, Ethiopia, China, Hong Kong, and several others are examined, as well as Cetrà and Brown Swan (2020), in which, among various cases, India and the United Kingdom are studied.

4 For more on this subject, consult Karmis and Rocher (2018).

5 Tim Logan (2014, 12–13) makes the valid point that "many theories have been advanced about which of these most effectively explain secession.… Bunce … has theorized that in the former U.S.S.R., as international support for a minority and the power of local nationalists in relation to communists increase, the likelihood of minority leaders seeking significant changes in their autonomy also increases. But although international support was a crucial determinant, the initial leaders of the Gagauz and Transnistrian movements were not nationalists, but members of the Soviet-era nomenklatura. This casts doubt on Bunce's theory. Elite incentives, not local political competition, are the other significant variable. Taken together, international support and elite incentives explain the current situation in Moldova."

6 We owe this notion to Taylor (1991). He indicated that to be inclusive "Canada would have to allow for a second-level or 'deep' diversity, where a plurality of ways of belonging would also be acknowledged and accepted" (75–6).

7 A thin conception would pay attention to cultural differences among ethnic communities forming a country, whereas a thick conception would insist on the importance to provide specific political communities with the necessary tools to grow and fully emancipate themselves within a democratic multinational political setting.

8 For a study of recent developments with respect to tensions between Catalonia and Spain, see Gagnon and Sanjaume-Calvet (2017).

9 Among the powers exercised by the state of Jammu and Kashmir under Article 370, one notes the rights reserved to its residents to buy land and property in the region, hold government positions, and obtain welfare benefits.

Conclusion

1 The following sections summarize the findings and recommendations I have made at forums in Bosnia and Herzegovina (Mostar, Neum), Spain (Barcelona, Bilbao, Madrid, Valencia), Iraq (Koja), and Italy (Bolzano – Bozen), as well as at activities organized under the auspices of the United Nations in recent years.

2 "Es que el referendum legal y pactado, ni es legal ni es pactado. Es imposible. No es legal porque la Constitucion no lo permite, puesto que se modifica el sujeto de la soberania nacional. Y no es pactado porque ne se pacta nada, ya que la pregunta viene dada."

3 In Canada, this is what happened when Quebec contested Canadian institutions through the referendums of May 1980 and October 1995.

4 For an in-depth analysis of the accession to sovereignty process for Quebec, see Guénette and Gagnon (2021, 147–74).

5 This point was brought to my attention by jurist Dave Guénette.

References

Abu-Laban, Yasmeen. 1994. "The Politics of Race and Ethnicity: Multiculturalism as a Contested Arena." In *Canadian Politics*, edited by James P. Bickerton and Alain-G. Gagnon, 242–63. 2nd ed. Peterborough, ON: Broadview.

– 2020. "Diversity in Canada." In *Canadian Politics*, edited by James Bickerton and Alain-G. Gagnon, 349–71. 7th ed. Toronto: University of Toronto Press.

Abu-Laban, Yasmeen, and Christina Gabriel. 2002. *Immigration, Employment Equity, and Globalization*. Toronto: University of Toronto Press.

Abu-Laban, Yasmeen, and Daiva Stasiulis. 1992. "Ethnic Pluralism under Siege: Popular and Partisan Opposition to Multiculturalism." *Canadian Public Policy* 18, no. 4 (December): 365–86. http://doi.org/10.2307/3551654.

An Act for the Preservation and Enhancement of Multiculturalism in Canada, chap. 31, ratified 21 July 1988.

Acton, John Emerich. 1949. "Nationality." In *Essays on Freedom and Power*, edited by Gertrude Himmelfarb, 183–4. New York: Noonday.

Adeney, Katharine, and Harihar Bhattacharyya. 2018. "Current Challenges to Multinational Federalism in India." *Regional and Federal Studies* 28, no. 4 (August): 409–25. https://doi.org/10.1080/13597566.2018.1473855.

Akkerman, Tjitzke. 2016. *Radical Right-Wing Populist Parties in Western Europe*. London: Routledge.

Alfred, Taiaiake. 1999. *Peace, Power Righteousness: An Indigenous Manifesto*. Toronto: Oxford University Press.

– 2005. *Wagase*. Toronto: University of Toronto Press.

Alfred, Taiaiake, and Jeff Corntassel. 2005. "Being Indigenous: Resurgence against Contemporary Colonialism." *Government and Opposition* 40, no. 4 (Autumn): 597–614. https://doi.org/10.1111/j.1477-7053.2005.00166.x.

Amnesty International France. n.d. "Qu'est-ce que la Déclaration universelle des droits de l'homme (DUDH) ?" https://www.amnesty.fr/focus/declaration -universelle-des-droits-de-lhomme.

Anderson, Benedict. 1996. *L'imaginaire national : réflexions sur l'origine et l'essor du nationalisme*. Paris: Découverte.

Arendt, Hannah. 1958. *The Human Condition*. Chicago: University of Chicago Press.

Bacon, Alexandre. 2020. "Préface : Réflexions et perspectives historiques sur les participations autochtones aux processus politiques canadiens." In Guimont Marceau, Roy, and Salée 2020, ix–xxiii.

Baker, Johanne, ed. 2005. *Sovereignty Matters: Locations of Contestation and Possibility in Indigenous Struggles for Self-Determination*. Lincoln: University of Nebraska Press.

Bakvis, Herman, and Grace Skogstad, eds. 2002. *Canadian Federalism: Performance, Effectiveness and Legitimacy*. Toronto: Oxford University Press.

–, eds. 2020. *Canadian Federalism: Performance, Effectiveness and Legitimacy*. 4th ed. Toronto: University of Toronto Press.

Banting, Keith, and Richard Simeon, eds. 1983. *And No One Cheered: Federalism, Democracy and the Constitution Act*. Toronto: Methuen.

Barlow, Maude, and Bruce Campbell. 1991. *Take Back the Nation*. Toronto: Key Porter.

Barry, Brian. 2001. *Culture and Equality: An Egalitarian Critique of Multiculturalism*. Cambridge: Polity.

Bastien, Frédéric. 2013. *La Bataille de Londres : dessous, secrets et coulisses du rapatriement constitutionnel*. Montreal: Boréal.

Baume, Sandrine. 2012. *Hans Kelsen and the Case for Democracy*. Colchester, UK: European Consortium for Political Research Press.

Beauchemin, Jacques. 2002. *L'histoire en trop : la mauvaise conscience des souverainistes québécois*. Montreal: VLB éditeur.

– 2007. *La société des identités : éthique et politique dans le monde contemporain*. Outremont, QC: Athéna.

–, ed. 2011. *Mémoire et démocratie en Occident : concurrence des mémoires ou concurrence victimaire*. Collection Diversitas. Brussels: Peter Lang.

Beaud, Olivier. 1994. *La puissance de l'État*. Paris: Presses universitaires de France.

Bédard, Éric. 2014. "Défendre l'histoire « nationale »." *Bulletin d'histoire politique* 22, no. 3 (Spring–Summer): 158–64. https://doi.org/10.7202/1024153ar.

Béland, Daniel, and André Lecours. 2008. *Nationalism and Scoial Policy: The Politics of Territorial Solidarity*. Oxford: Oxford University Press.

– 2012. *Nationalisme et protection sociale*. Ottawa: Presses de l'Université d'Ottawa.

Belliveau, Joël, and Frédéric Boily. 2005. "Deux révolutions tranquilles ? Transformations politiques et sociales au Québec et au Nouveau-Brunswick (1960–1967)." *Recherches sociographiques* 56, no. 1 (January–April): 11–34. http://doi.org/10.7202/012088ar.

Belser, Eva-Maria. 2020. "Heading Together: Intergovernmental Relations and Horizontal Law-Making by Swiss Cantons." In Gagnon and Poirier 2020b, 251–90.

Benamou, Georges-Marc, dir. 2020. *Les vies d'Albert Camus.* YouTube video, 21 January, 1:38 :18. https://youtu.be/5CIBtVu17_U.

Benz, Arthur, and Jared Sonnicksen. 2017. "Patterns of Federal Democracy: Tensions, Friction, or Balance between Two Government Dimensions." *European Political Science Review* 9, no. 1 (February): 3–25. https://doi.org/10.1017/S1755773915000259.

Berger, Carl. 1976. *The Writing of Canadian History*. Toronto: University of Toronto Press.

Berlin, Isaiah. 2002. "Two Concepts of Liberty." In *Liberty: Incorporating "Four Essays on Liberty*, edited by Henry Hardy, 166–217. Oxford: Oxford University Press.

Bernier, Luc. 2013. "La Caisse de dépôt et placement du Québec: Straddling between Two Worlds." Working Papers, CIRIEC, July.

Bertrand, Jacques. 2012. "Autonomy and Nationalist Demands in Southeast Asia." In Gagnon and Keating 2012, 200–19.

Bickerton, James. 2019. "Rebalancing Federal Citizenship in Canada." 50 Shades of Federalism. http://50shadesoffederalism.com/case-studies/rebalancing-federal-citizenship-in-canada/.

Bickerton, James, and Alain-G. Gagnon. 2020. "Regions." In *Comparative Politics*, edited by Daniele Caramani, 267–80. 5th ed. Oxford: Oxford University Press.

Bickerton, James, Stephen Brooks, and Alain-G. Gagnon. 2006. "The Universal Liberalism of Pierre Trudeau." In *Freedom, Equality, Community: The Political Philosophy of Six Influential Canadians*, 119–46. Montreal and Kingston: McGill-Queen's University Press.

Bickerton, James, Alain-G. Gagnon, and Patrick Smith. 1999. *Ties That Bind: Parties and Voters in Canada*. Don Mills, ON: Oxford University Press.

Bieber, Florian. 2005. "Power-Sharing after Yugoslavia: Functionality and Dysfunctionality of Power-Sharing Institutions in Post-war Bosnia, Macedonia and Kosovo." In *From Power-Sharing to Democracy: Post-Conflict Institutions in Ethnically Divided Societies*, edited by Sid Noel, 85–103. Montreal and Kingston: McGill-Queen's University Press.

Bieber, Florian, and Roland Bieber. 2021. *Negotiating Unity and Diversity in the European Union*. Cham: Palgrave Macmillan.

Blache, Pierre. 1993. "Le pouvoir de dépenser au cœur de la crise constitutionnelle canadienne." *Revue générale de droit* 24, no. 1 (March): 29–64. https://doi.org/10.7202/1057015ar.

Bonenfant, Jean-Charles. 1963. "L'esprit de 1867." *Revue d'histoire de l'Amérique française* 17, no. 1 (June): 19–38. https://doi.org/10.7202/302251ar.

Borrows, John. 2015. "The Durability of Terra Nullius: Tsilhqot'in Nation v British Columbia." *University of British Columbia Law Review* 48, no. 3 (October): 701–42.

– 2016. *Freedom and Indigenous Constitutionalism*. Toronto: University of Toronto Press.

Bossacoma i Busquets, Pau. 2020. *Morality and Legality of Secession: A Theory of National Self-Determination*. London: Palgrave Macmillan.

Bouchard, Gérard. 2013. *Genèse des nations et cultures du Nouveau Monde*. Montreal: Boréal.

– 2019. *Les nations savent-elles encore rêver : les mythes nationaux à l'ère de la mondialisation*. Montreal: Boréal.

– 2020. "M. Legault et la nationalisation de la laïcité : la loi 21 a été adoptée aux dépens du droit, dans le mépris des tribunaux." *Le Devoir*, 18–19 January, B-9.

Bouchard, Gérard, and Charles Taylor. 2008. *Fonder l'avenir : le temps de la conciliation*. Report of the Commission de consultation sur les pratiques d'accommodement reliées aux différences culturelles, Quebec, Gouvernement du Québec.

Bradbury, Bettina, and Tamara Myers. 2006. *Negotiating Identities in Nineteenth- and Twentieth-Century Montreal*. Vancouver: University of British Columbia Press.

Brooks, Stephen, and Brian Tanguay. 1985. "Quebec's Caisse de dépôt et placement: Tool of Nationalism." *Canadian Public Administration* 28, no. 1 (March): 99–119. http://doi.org/10.1111/j.1754-7121.1985.tb00363.x.

Brouillet, Eugénie. 2005. *La négation de la nation : l'identité culturelle québécoise et le fédéralisme canadien*. Quebec: Septentrion.

Brouillet, Eugénie, and Louis-Philippe Lampron, eds. 2013. *La mobilisation du droit et la protection des collectivités minoritaires*. Quebec: Presses de l'Université du Québec.

Brouillet, Eugénie, Alain-G. Gagnon, and Guy Laforest. 2018. "Introduction: 1864, a Pivotal Year in the Advent of the Canadian Confederation." In *The Quebec Conference of 1864: Understanding the Emergence of the Canadian Federation*, 3–25. Montreal and Kingston: McGill-Queen's University Press.

Brousseau Desaulniers, Antoine, and Stéphane Savard, eds. 2020. *La pensée fédéraliste contemporaine au Québec*. Collection Politeia. Quebec: Presses de l'Université du Québec.

– Forthcoming. *Contemporary Federalist Thought in Quebec: Historical Perspectives*. Montreal and Kingston: McGill-Queen's University Press.

Brown, Craig. 1966. "The Nationalism of the National Policy." In *Nationalism in Canada*, edited by Peter Russell, 155–63. Toronto: McGraw-Hill Ryerson.

Brown Swan, Coree, and Daniel Cetrà. 2020. "Why Stay Together? State Nationalism and Justifications for State Unity in Spain and the UK?" In "State and Majority Nationalism in Plurinational States," special issue,

Nationalism and Ethnic Politics 26, no. 1 (January): 45–65. https://doi.org /10.1080/13537113.2020.1716443.

Brubaker, Rogers. 1992. *Citizenship and Nationhood in France and Germany.* Cambridge, MA: Harvard University Press.

– 2004. *Ethnicity without Groups.* Cambridge, MA: Harvard University Press.

– 2011. "Nationalizing States Revisited: Projects and Processes of Nationalization in Post-Soviet States." *Ethnic and Racial Studies* 34, no. 11 (November): 1785–1814. https://doi.org/10.1080/01419870.2011.579137.

Buchanan, Allen. 1991. *Secession: The Morality of Political Divorce from Fort Sumter to Lithunia and Quebec.* Boulder, CO: Westview.

Bumsted, John M. 1992a. *The Peoples of Canada: A Post-Confederation History.* Toronto: Oxford University Press.

– 1992b. *The Peoples of Canada: A Pre-Confederation History.* Toronto: Oxford University Press.

Bunce, Valerie 1999a. "Peaceful versus Violent State Dismemberment: A Comparison of the Soviet Union, Yugoslavia and Czechoslovakia." *Politics & Society* 27, no. 2 (June): 217–37. https://doi.org/10.1177 %2F0032329299027002003.

– 1999b. *Subversive Institutions: The Design and the Destruction of Socialism and the State.* Cambridge: Cambridge University Press.

– 2007. *Minority Politics in Ethnofederal States: Cooperation, Autonomy or Secession?* Ithaca, NY: Mario Einaudi Center for International Studies.

Bunce, Valerie, Stephen Watts, Philip G. Roeder, and Donald Rothchild. 2005. "Managing Diversity and Sustaining Democracy: Ethnofederal versus Unitary States in Postcommunist World." In *Sustainable Peace: Power and Democracy after Civil Wars*, edited by Philip G. Roeder and Donald Rothchild, 133–58. Ithaca, NY: Cornell University Press.

Burelle, André. 2005. *Pierre Elliott Trudeau : l'intellectuel et le politique.* Montreal: Fides.

– 2020. "Le pressant besoin d'une pensée fédéraliste prospective au Québec et dans le ROC." In Brousseau Desaulniers and Savard 2020, 519–30.

Burg, Steven L., and Lachen T. Chernyha. 2013. "Asymmetric Devolution and Ethnoregionalism in Spain." *Nationalism and Ethnic Politics* 19, no. 3 (July): 255–86. https://doi.org/10.1080/13537113.2013.818351.

Burgess, Michael. 2012. *In Search of the Federal Spirit: New Comparative Empirical and Theoretical Perspectives.* Oxford: Oxford University Press.

– 2015a. "Conclusion: Understanding Federalism and Federation. My Magnificient Obsession." In *Understanding Federalism and Federation*, edited by Alain-G. Gagnon, Soeren Keil, and Sean Mueller, 265–87. Farnham, UK: Ashgate.

– 2015b. "Divided We Stand: Autonomy or Secession in Federation?" In *States Falling Apart? Secessionist and Autonomy Movements in Europe*, edited by Eva

Maria Belser, Alexander Fang-Bär, Nina Massüger, and Rekha Oleschak Pillai, 15–35. Bern: Stämpfli Verlag.

Burgess, Michael, and Alain-G. Gagnon, eds. 1993. *Comparative Federalism and Federation: Competing Traditions and Future Directions*. London and Toronto: Harvester and Wheatsheaf and University of Toronto Press.

–, eds. 2010a. *Federal Democracies*. London: Routledge.

– 2010b. "Introduction: Federalism and Democracy." In Burgess and Gagnon 2012a, 1–25.

Burgess, Michael, and John Pinder. 2007. *Multinational Federations*: London: Routledge.

Cagiao y Conde, Jorge. 2011. "Démocratie et théorie du droit fédératif chez Proudhon et Kelsen." In *Proudhon : droit ou morale?*, edited by Anne-Sophie Chambost, 84–115. Paris: Société P.-J. Proudhon.

– 2012. "Autorité et conflit d'autorités en droit fédératif." *L'Europe en formation : revue d'études sur la construction européenne et le fédéralisme* 1, no. 363: 121–42. https://doi.org/10.3917/eufor.363.0121.

– 2014. "Introduction." In Cagiao y Conde and Gomez Muller 2014, 293–300.

– 2015. "Pour une approche sociologique du fédéralisme." *Revue d'études proudhoniennes* 1:114–29.

Cagiao y Conde, Jorge, and Alain-G. Gagnon, eds. 2019. *Fédéralisme et sécession*. Collection Diversitas. Brussels: Peter Lang.

– 2021. *Federalism and Secession*. Brussels: Peter Lang.

Cagiao y Conde, Jorge, and Alfredo Gomez Muller, eds. 2014. *Le multiculturalisme et la reconfiguration de l'unité et de la diversité dans les démocraties contemporaines*. Collection Diversitas. Brussels: Peter Lang.

Cairns, Alan, C. 1994. "The Charlottetown Accord: Multinational Canada v. Federalism." In *Constitutional Predicament: Canada after the Referendum of 1992*, edited by Curtis Cook, 25–62. Montreal and Kingston: McGill-Queen's University Press.

– 2000. *Citizens Plus: Aboriginal Peoples and the Canadian State*. Vancouver: University of British Columbia Press.

Calame, Pierre. 2003. "De la légalité à la légitimité de la gouvernance : définition de cinq principes de base pour un enjeu essentiel." Paris: Institut de recherche et débat sur la Gouvernance. http://www.institut-gouvernance .org/fr/analyse/fiche-analyse-24.html.

Calame, Pierre, in collaboration with Jean Freys and Valery Garandreau. 2002. *La démocratie en miettes : pour une révolution de la gouvernance*. Paris: Descartes.

Caminal, Miquel i Badia. 2002. *El Federalismo pluralista: Del federalismo nacional al federalismo plurinacional*. Barcelona: Paidos.

Canada Health Act. 1985. RSC, c. C-6, ss 7–12, https://laws-lois.justice.gc.ca /eng/acts/c-6/page-1.html.

Canadian Multiculturalism Act. 1985. RSC, c 24 (4th Supp.). https://laws-lois. justice.gc.ca/eng/acts/c-18.7/page-1.html.

Canovan, Margaret. 1998. "Crusaders, Sceptics and the Nation." *Journal of Political Ideologies* 3, no. 3 (October): 237–53. https://doi.org/10.1080 /13569319808420779.

Carbonneau, Jean Rémi. 2019. "Traditions étatiques et légitimation des langues minoritaires dans les systèmes fédéraux : les trajectoires divergentes de la Lusace et des Pays catalans." PhD diss., Université du Québec à Montréal.

Cardinal, Linda, and Claude Couture. 1998. "L'immigration et le multiculturalisme au Canada." In *Les politiques publiques canadiennes*, edited by Manon Tremblay, 239–62. Quebec: Presses de l'Université Laval.

Cardinal, Linda, and Selma K. Sonntag, eds. 2015. *State Traditions and Language Rights*. Montreal and Kingston: McGill-Queen's University Press.

Careless, J.M.S. 1969. "Limited Identities in Canada." *Canadian Historical Review* 50, no. 1 (March): 1–10. https://doi.org/10.3138/CHR-050-01-01.

Carrère-D'Encausse, Hélène. 1991. *La gloire des nations ou la fin de l'Empire soviétique*. Paris: Fayard.

Casanas Adam, Elisenda, and François Rocher. 2014. "(Mis)recognition in Catalunya and Quebec: The Politics of Containment." In *Constitutionalism and the Politics of Accommodation in Multinational Democracies*, edited by Jaime Lluch, 46–69. New York: Palgrave Macmillan.

Cassese, Antonio. 1995. *Self-Determination of Peoples: A Legal Reappraisal*. Cambridge: Cambridge University Press.

Cetrà, Daniel. 2017. "Linguistic Diversity in Plurinational States." 50 Shades of Federalism. http://50shadesoffederalism.com/policies/linguistic -diversity-plurinational-states/.

– 2019. *Nationalism, Liberalism and Language in Catalonia and Flanders*. Basingstoke, UK: Palgrave Macmillan.

Cetrà, Daniel, and Coree Brown Swan. 2020. "State and Majority Nationalism in Plurinational States: Responding to Challenges from Below." In "State and Majority Nationalism in Plurinational States," special issue, *Nationalism and Ethnic Politics* 26, no. 1 (January): 1–7. https://doi.org/10.1080/13537113 .2020.1716435.

Chevrier, Marc. 2019. *L'empire en marche : des peuples sans qualités, de Vienne à Ottawa*. Quebec: Presses de l'Université Laval.

Chouinard, Stéphanie. 2020. "L'étude des petites nations par la lunette juridique : un exercice périlleux." In Laniel and Thériault 2020, 163–77.

Clarkson, Stephen. 2002. *Canada's Secret Constitution: NAFTA, WTO and the End of Sovereignty*. Ottawa: Canadian Centre for Policy Alternatives.

Clarkson, Stephen, and Christina McCall. 1990–4. *Trudeau and Our Times*, 2 vols. Toronto: McClelland & Stewart.

Coakley, John. 2011. "National Majorities in New States: Managing the Challenge of Diversity." In Gagnon, Lecours, and Nootens 2011, 101–24.

Cohen, Mitchell. 1995. "Rooted Cosmopolitanism." In *Toward a Global Civil Society*, edited by Michael Walzer, 223–33. Oxford: Berghahn Books.

Commission Séguin sur le déséquilibre fiscal. 2001. *Le pouvoir fédéral de dépenser*. Quebec: Quebec Government.

Commission sur le déséquilibre fiscal (Séguin Commission). 2002. *Pour un nouveau partage des moyens financiers au Canada*. Québec: Gouvernement du Québec.

Constitutional Committee of the Quebec Liberal Party. 1980. *A New Canadian Federation*. Montreal: Quebec Liberal Party.

Coquery-Vidrovitch, Catherine. 2016. *Petite histoire de l'Afrique : l'Afrique au sud du Sahara, de la préhistoire à nos jours*. Paris: Découverte.

Cornellier, Louis. 2008. "Le fédéralisme utopique d'Alain-G. Gagnon." *Le Devoir*, 27 September. https://www.ledevoir.com/opinion/chroniques /207727/le-federalisme-utopique-d-alain-g-gagnon.

– 2019. "L'autre fédéralisme." *Le Devoir*, 14 September. https://www.ledevoir .com/opinion/chroniques/562531/essai-l-autre-federalisme.

– 2020. "Fédéralisme théorique." *Le Devoir*, 14 March. https://www.ledevoir .com/opinion/chroniques/574835/federalisme-theorique.

Cornstassel, Jeff. 2012. "Re-envisioning Resurgence: Indigenous Pathways to Decolonization and Sustainable Self-Determination." *Decolonization: Indigeneity, Education & Society* 1 (1): 86–101.

Coulthard, Glen Sean. 2007. "Subjects of Empire: Indigenous Peoples and the 'Politics of Recognition' in Canada." *Contemporary Political Theory* 6, no. 4 (November): 437–60. https://doi.org/10.1057/palgrave.cpt.9300307.

– 2014. *Red Skin, White Masks: Rejecting the Colonial Politics of Recognition*. Minneapolis: University of Minnesota Press.

– 2018. *Peau rouge, masques blancs : contre la politique coloniale de la reconnaissance*. Montreal: Lux.

Council of Europe. 2008. *Living Together as Equals in Dignity*. https://search. coe.int/cm/Pages/result_details.aspx?ObjectID=09000016805d37c2.

Courchene, Thomas. 2018. *Indigenous Nationals, Canadian Citizens: From First Contact to Canada 150 and Beyond*. Montreal and Kingston: McGill-Queen's University Press.

Courtois, Stéphane. 2014. *Repenser l'avenir du Québec : vers une sécession tranquille?* Montreal: Liber.

Coyle, Michael. 2019. "Balancing Sovereignties through Treaty Federalism." Paper presented at the International Conference on Sovereignties and Autochtonous Self-Determination: tiayoriho'ten, Wendake, QC, 24–5 October.

Crawford, James. 2001. "The Right of Self-Determination in International Law: Its Developments and Future." In *Peoples' Rights*, edited by Philip Alston, 7–68. Oxford: Oxford University Press.

– 2006. *The Creation of States in International Law*. Oxford: Clarendon.

CRÉ Saguenay–Lac-Saint-Jean/Conseil des Montagnais du Lac-Saint-Jean. 2008. *Avis régional concerté entre la Conférence des élus du Saguenay-Lac-Saint-Jean et la Première nation des Pekuakamiulnuatsh sur le livre vert La forêt, pour construire le Québec de demain*, 10 April.

Crocker, Chester A., Fen Osler Hampson, and Pamela Aall. 2004. *Taming Intractable Conflicts: Mediation in the Hardest Cases*. Washington, DC: US Institute of Peace.

Culhane Speck, Dara. 1998. *The Pleasure of the Crown: Anthropology, Law, and First Nations*. Vancouver: Talonbooks.

Curko, Hrvoje. 2016. "Can Institutions of Autonomy Become Potentially 'Subversive Institutions'?" *Croatian International Relations Review* 22, no. 76 (October): 52–84. https://doi.org/10.1515/cirr-2016-0006.

Dabin, Simon. 2020. "Le fédéralisme par traités et les peuples autochtones au Canada : une voie vers la réconciliation ou une utopie philosophique ?" In Mathieu, Guénette, and Gagnon 2020, 295–310.

Day, Shane. 2018. "How Unity and Diversity Affect Political Asymmetries of Indigenous Groups in Federations: Heterogenous Institutional Practices in Australia, Canada, and the United States." In Gagnon and Burgess 2018b, 326–61. Boston and Leiden: Brill and Nijhoff.

Delâge, Denys, and Jean-Philippe Warren. 2017. *Le piège de la liberté : les peuples autochtones dans l'engrenage des régimes coloniaux*. Montreal: Boréal.

Dieckhoff, Alain. 2004a. "Introduction : Nouvelles perspectives sur le nationalisme." In Dieckhoff 2004b, 11–31.

– 2004b. *La constellation des appartenances*. Paris: Presses de Sciences Po.

Ducharme, Michel. 2010. *Le concept de liberté au Canada à l'époque des révolutions atlantiques, 1776–1838*. Montreal and Kingston: McGill-Queen's University Press.

Dumont, Micheline. 2001. *Découvrir la mémoire des femmes*. Montreal: Remue-Ménage.

Easterbrook, W.T., and Hugh C.J. Aitken. 1956. *Canadian Economic History*. Toronto: Macmillan.

Eide, Asbjorn. 1993. *Possible Ways and Means of Facilitating Peaceful and Constructive Solution of Problems Involving Minorities*. Commission of Human Rights, Sub-Commission of Discrimination and Protection of Minorities, 45th session, 19 July. https://digitallibrary.un.org/record/170889?ln=en.

– 2014. "United Nations Standard-Setting Regarding Rights of Minorities and Indigenous Peoples." *Europa Ethnica* 71 (3–4): 51–61. https://doi.org/10.24989/0014-2492-2014-34-51.

Elazar, Daniel, ed. 1979a. *Federalism and Political Integration*. Ramat Gan, IL: Turtledove Publishing.

– 1979b. *Self-Rule/Shared Rule*. Ramat Gan, IL: Turtledove Publishing.

– 1991. *Exploring Federalism*. Tuscaloosa: University of Alabama Press.

Elmerich, Jeremy. 2021. "Constitutional Memories in Canada: Devising the Revision in the Peril of Disunion." In *Canadian Political, Social and Historical (Re)visions in the 20th and 21st Century*, edited by Marcin Gabrys, Magdalena Marczuk-Karbownik, and Magdalena Paluszkiewicz-Misiaczek, 145–72. Berlin: Peter Lang.

Erk, Jan, and Lawrence Anderson. 2009. "The Paradox of Federalism: Does Self-Rule Accommodate or Exacerbate Ethnic Divisions?" *Regional and Federal Studies* 19, no. 2 (May): 191–202. https://doi.org/10.1080/13597560902753388.

Evans, Peter B., Dietrich Rueschemeyer, and Theda Skocpol, eds. 1985. *Bringing the State Back In*. Cambridge: Cambridge University Press.

Fazi, André. 2020. "La résistance de l'État unitaire, ou un nouveau défi pour le nationalisme corse." In *L'Union européenne et les nationalismes régionaux*, edited by Nicolas Levrat, Dusan Sidjanski, and François Saint-Ouen, 107–26. Geneva: Centre de compétences Dusan Sidjanski en études européennes.

Felter, Claire. 2018. "Somaliland: The Horn of Africa's Breakaway State." Council on Foreign Relations, 1 February. https://www.cfr.org/backgrounder/somaliland-horn-africas-breakaway-state.

Fessha, Yonatan. 2016. *Ethnic Diversity and Federalism: Constitution Making in South Africa and Ethiopia*. London: Routledge.

FitzGibbon, John. 2014. "Euroscepticism and the 2014 European Parliamentary Elections." *L'Europe en formation : revue d'études sur la construction européenne et le fédéralisme* 3 (373): 29–44. https://doi.org/10.3917/eufor.373.0029.

Flamand, Sipi. 2020. "La nouvelle gouvernance autochtone." In Marceau Guimont, Roy, and Salée 2020, 49–56.

Fleras, Augie. 2009. *The Politics of Multiculturalism: Multicultural Governance in Comparative Perspective*. New York: Palgrave.

Forsyth, Murray. 1994. "Towards the Reconciliation of Nationalism and Liberalism." In *Integration and Fragmentation: The Paradox of the Late 20th Century*, edited by Guy Laforest and Douglas Brown, 7–23. Kingston, ON: Institute of Intergovernmental Relations.

Fossas, Enric. 2007. "Autonomie et plurinationalité en Espagne : vingt-cinq ans d'expérience constitutionnelle." In Gagnon, Lecours, and Nootens 2007, 291–306.

Friedrich, Carl. 1968. *Trends of Federalism in Theory and Practice*. New York: Praeger.

Gagnon, Alain-G. 1991a. "Égalité ou indépendance : un tournant dans la pensée constitutionnelle au Québec." In *Daniel Johnson : rêve d'égalité et projet d'indépendance*, edited by Robert Comeau, Michel Lévesque, and Yves Bélanger, 173–81. Sillery: Presses de l'Université du Québec.

– 1991b. "Other Federal and Nonfederal Countries: Lessons for Canada." In Watts and Brown 1991, 207–34.

– 2000. "Canada: Unity and Diversity." *Parliamentary Affairs: A Journal of Comparative Politics* 53, no. 1 (January): 12–26. http://doi.org/10.1093/pa/53.1.12.

– 2002. "La condition canadienne et les montées du nationalisme et du régionalisme." In *Le débat qui n'a pas eu lieu : la commission Pepin-Robarts, quelque vingt ans plus tard,* edited by Jean-Pierre Wallot, 105–21. Ottawa: Presses de l'Université d'Ottawa.

– 2006a. *Au-delà de la nation unificatrice : plaidoyer pour le fédéralisme multinational.* Barcelona: Institut d'Estudis Autonomics.

–, ed. 2006b. *Le fédéralisme canadien contemporain : fondements, traditions, institutions.* Montreal: Presses de l'Université de Montréal.

–, ed. 2009. *Contemporary Canadian Federalism: Foundations, Traditions, Institutions.* Toronto: University of Toronto Press.

– 2010. *The Case for Multinational Federalism: Beyond the All-Encompassing Nation.* London: Routledge.

– 2011. *L'âge des incertitudes : essais sur le fédéralisme et la diversité nationale.* Quebec: Presses de l'Université Laval.

– 2014. *Minority Nations in the Age of Uncertainty: New Paths to National Emancipation and Empowerment.* Toronto: University of Toronto Press.

– 2015a. "L'École québécoise du fédéralisme." *Le Devoir,* 25 September. https://www.ledevoir.com/opinion/idees/450932/une-ecole-quebecoise-du-federalisme.

– 2015b. "Multilevel Governance and the Reconfiguration of Political Space: Theoretical Considerations from a Multinational Perspective." In *Federalism as Decision-Making: Changes in Structures, Procedures and Policies,* edited by Francesco Palermo and Elisabeth Alber, 5–19. Boston and Leiden: Brill and Nijhoff.

– 2020a. "Majority, State Nationalism, and New Research Pathways." In "State and Majority Nationalism in Plurinational States," special issue, *Nationalism and Ethnic Politics* 26, no. 1 (January): 85–93. https://doi.org/10.1080/13537113.2020.1716445.

– 2020b. "Pandémie, fédéralisme et concertation." *La Presse+,* 28 April. https://plus.lapresse.ca/screens/66aa4987-d346-4dbd-afb2-43283567af7a__7C__0.html.

– 2021a. "Multinational Federalism: Challenges, Shortcomings and Promises." *Regional and Federal Studies* 30, no. 1 (January): 1–16. https://doi.org/10.1080/13597566.2020.1781097.

2021b. "Surmonter le nationalisme patriotique au Canada." *Zeitschrift für Kanada-Studien* 41 (71): 10–27.

Gagnon, Alain-G., and Michael Burgess. 2018a. "Introduction: Revisiting Unity and Diversity in Federal Countries." In Gagnon and Burgess 2018b, xviii–xx.

–, eds. 2018b. *Revisiting Unity and Diversity in Federal Countries: Changing Concepts, Reform Proposals and New Institutional Realities.* Boston and Leiden: Brill and Nijhoff.

Gagnon Alain-G., and Raffaele Iacovino. 2007. *Federalism, Citizenship, and Quebec: Debating Multinationalism*. Toronto: University of Toronto Press.

Gagnon Alain-G., and Michael Keating, eds. 2012. *Political Autonomy and Divided Societies: Imagining Democratic Alternatives in Complex Settings*. Basingstoke, UK: Palgrave Macmillan.

Gagnon, Alain-G., and Guy Lachapelle. 1996. "Québec Confronts Canada: Two Competing Societal Projects Searching for Legitimacy." *Publius: The Journal of Federalism* 26, no. 3 (Summer): 177–91. https://doi.org/10.1093/oxfordjournals.pubjof.a029862.

Gagnon, Alain-G., and Guy Laforest. 1993. "The Future of Federalism: Lessons from Canada and Quebec." In "Ethnic Tension & Nationalism," special issue, *International Journal* 48, no. 3 (Summer): 470–91. https://doi.org/10.1177/002070209304800304.

Gagnon, Alain-G., André Lecours, and Geneviève Nootens, eds. 2007. *Les nationalismes majoritaires contemporains : identité, mémoire, pouvoir*. Collection Débats. Montreal: Québec Amérique.

–, eds. 2011. *Contemporary Majority Nationalism*. Montreal and Kingston: McGill-Queen's University Press.

Gagnon, Alain-G., and Félix Mathieu. 2020. "La richesse des (petites) nations et l'agir hospitalier." In Laniel and Thériault 2020, 261–80.

Gagnon, Alain-G., and Mary Beth Montcalm. 1990. *Quebec: Beyond the Quiet Revolution*. Scarborough, ON: Nelson Canada.

Gagnon, Alain-G., and Johanne Poirier, eds. 2020a. *L'avenir du fédéralisme canadien : acteurs et institutions*. Quebec: Presses de l'Université Laval.

–, eds. 2020b. *Canadian Federalism and Its Future: Actors and Institutions*. Montreal and Kingston: McGill-Queen's University Press.

Gagnon, Alain-G., and Ferran Requejo, eds. 2010. *Nations en quête de reconnaissance : regards croisés Québec-Catalogne*. Collection Diversitas. Brussels: Peter Lang.

Gagnon, Alain-G., and Guy Rocher, eds. 2002. *Reflections on the James Bay and Northern Quebec Agreement*. Montreal: Québec Amérique.

Gagnon Alain-G., and José Maria Sauca, eds. 2014. *Negotiating Diversity: Identity, Pluralism and Democracy*. Brussels: Peter Lang.

Gagnon, Alain-G., and Marc Sanjaume-Calvet. 2016. "Trois scénarios pour la Catalogne au xxie siècle : autonomie, fédéralisme et sécession." In Seymour 2016, 135–74.

– 2017. "Clash of Legitimacies in Catalonia and Spain: The Imperial Logic of Modern Constitutionalism versus Multinational Federalism." In Kraus and Vergès Gifra 2017, 275–302.

Gagnon, Alain-G., and Alex Schwartz. 2015. "Canadian Federalism since Patriation: Advancing a Federalism of Empowerment." In *Patriation and*

Its Consequences: Constitution-Making in Canada, edited by Lois Harder and Steve Patten, 244–66. Vancouver: University of British Columbia Press.

Gagnon, Alain-G., and Richard Simeon. 2010. "Canada." In *Diversity and Unity in Federal Countries: A Global Dialogue on Federalism,* edited by Luis Moreno and César Colino, 7:110–38. Montreal and Kingston: McGill-Queen's University Press.

Gagnon, Alain-G., and A. Brian Tanguay, eds. 1992. *La juste démocratie : mélanges en l'honneur de Khayyam Zev Paltiel.* Montreal and Kingston: McGill-Queen's University Press.

Gagnon, Alain-G., and Arjun Tremblay, eds. 2020. *Federalism and National Diversity in the 21st Century.* Basingstoke, UK: Palgrave Macmillan.

Gagnon, Alain-G., and James Tully, eds. 2001. *Multinational Democracies.* Cambridge: Cambridge University Press.

Gagnon, Bernard, ed. 2010. *La diversité québécoise en débat : Bouchard, Taylor et les autres.* Collection Débats. Montreal: Québec Amérique.

Garcia Segura, Caterina. 2019. "Catalogne en quête d'indépendance : l'outil de la diplomatie publique." In Massie and Lamontagne 2019, 51–75.

Gatti, Luigi. 2017. "Idéologie et déconstruction de l'État: la Yougoslavie communiste, 1941–1991." PhD diss., Institut de recherche Montesquieu.

Gélinas, Xavier. 2019. *La loi sur les langues officielles : une naissance mouvementée (1962–1969).* Gatineau, QC: Canadian Museum of History.

Gendron Commission. 1972. *Rapport de la commission d'enquête sur la situation de la langue française et sur les droits linguistiques au Québec.* Vol. 1. Québec: Gouvernement du Québec.

Germain, Alexandre. 2015. "La question territoriale et le fédéralisme multinational : Uashat mak Mani-Utenam et la planification territoriale autochtone au Canada." PhD diss., Université du Québec à Montréal.

Giraudeau, Géraldine. 2012. "La naissance du Soudan du Sud : la paix impossible?" *Annuaire français de droit international,* no. 58, 61–82. https://doi.org/10.3406/afdi.2012.4671.

Gourdeau, Éric. 1993. "Québec and the Aboriginal Question." In Quebec: State and Society, edited by Alain-G. Gagnon, 349–71. 2nd ed. Scarborough. ON: Nelson Canada.

Graefe, Peter. 2014. "L'État canadien." In *La politique québécoise et canadienne : une approche pluraliste,* edited by Alain-G. Gagnon, 37–65. Collection Politeia. Quebec: Presses de l'Université du Québec.

Grafstein, Robert. 1981. "The Failure of Weber's Conception of Legitimacy: Its Causes and Implications." *Journal of Politics* 43, no. 2 (May): 456–72. https://doi.org/10.2307/2130377.

Granatstein, Jack. 1998. *Who Killed Canadian History?* Toronto: HarperCollins.

Groupe de réflexion sur les institutions et la citoyenneté (GRIC). 1994. "D'égal à égal : nous devons refaire notre réflexion sur la nature des relations à établir avec les peuples autochtones." *Le Devoir*, 28 March, A7.

Guénette, Dave, and Alain-G. Gagnon. 2021. "From Referendum to Secession: Québec's Self-Determination Process and Its Lessons." In Cagiao y Conde and Gagnon 2021, 147–74.

Guibernau, Montserrat. 2003. "Between Autonony and Secession: The Accommodation of Minority Nationalism in Catalonia." In *The Conditions of Diversity in Multinational Democracies*, edited by Alain-G. Gagnon, Montserrat Guibernau, and François Rocher, 115–33. Montreal: Institute for Research on Public Policy.

– 2004. "Catalanism: A Non-Secessionist Nationalism." In *The Fate of the Nation-State*, edited by Michel Seymour, 234–47. Montreal and Kingston: McGill-Queen's University Press.

Habermas, Jürgen. 1991. *Communication and the Evolution of Society*. Cambridge: Polity.

– 1998. *L'intégration européenne*. Paris: Fayard.

Hamilton, Robert, and Joshua Nichols. 2021. "Reconciliation and the Straitjacket: A Comparative Analysis of the *Secession Reference* and *R v Sparrow*." *Ottawa Law Review* 52 (2): 403–53.

Hansen, Paul. 2019. "Conceptions of Sovereignty." MA thesis, University of Western Ontario.

Hatzfeld, Hélène. 2013. "Légitimité." In *Dictionnaire critique et interdisciplinaire de la participation*, edited by Ilaria Casillo, Jean-Michel Fourniau, Catherine Neveu, Rémi Lefebvre, Loïc Blondiaux, Denis Salles, Francis Chanteauraynaud, and Rémi Barbier, 1–13. Paris: GIS Démocratie et participation.

Henders, Susan J. 2010. *Territoriality, Asymmetry, and Autonomy: Catalonia, Corsica, Hong Kong, and Tibet*. New York: Palgrave Macmillan.

"Heritage Minutes." 2018. *The Canadian Encyclopedia*. Historica Canada. Article published 25 October. https://www.thecanadianencyclopedia.ca/en /article/heritage-minutes-editorial.

Hoehn, Felix. 2012. *Reconciling Sovereignties: Aboriginal Nations and Canada*. Saskatoon: Native Law Center, University of Saskatchewan.

Hombrado, Angustias. 2011. "Learning to Catch the Wave? Regional Demands for Constitutional Change in Contexts of Asymmetrical Arrangements." *Regional and Federal Studies* 21, no. 4–5 (December): 479–501. https://doi.org /10.1080/13597566.2011.578943.

House of Commons Debates, 43-2, No 031 (18 November 2020) at 2046 (Hon Justin Trudeau).

Hudson, Michael. 2020. "New Tools for Reconciliation: Legislation to Implement the UN Declaration on the Rights of Indigenous Peoples." *Institute for Research on Public Policy Insights* 32, 16 June. https://centre.irpp.org/research-studies/new-tools-for-reconciliation-legislation-to-implement-the-un-declaration-on-the-rights-of-indigenous-peoples/.

Iacovino, Raffaele, and Jan Erk. 2012. "The Constitutional Foundations of Multination Federalism: Canada and Belgium." In Seymour and Gagnon 2012b, 205–30.

Institute for Democracy and Electoral Assistance (IDEA). 2017. *Overview: The Global State of Democracy. Exploring Democracy's Resilience.* Stockholm: IDEA International

Ionita, Ovidiu Cristian. 2014. "Nationalisme, construction nationale et « action extérieure » : les entités nationales non souveraines espagnoles et l'Union européenne (1992–2008)." PhD diss., Université de Montréal.

Jenson, Jane. 1995. "Mapping, Naming, and Remembering: Globalization at the End of the Twentieth Century." *Review of International Political Economy* 2, no. 1 (Winter): 91–116. https://doi.org/10.1080/09692299508434311.

Johnson, Daniel. 1965. *Égalité ou indépendance.* Montreal: Éditions Renaissance.

Joppke, Christian. 2012. *The Role of the State in Cultural Integration: Trends, Challenges, and Ways Ahead.* Washington, DC: Migration Policy Institute.

Kagan, Robert. 2002. "Power and Weakness." *Policy Review*, no. 113 (June–July): 3–28. https://www.hoover.org/research/power-and-weakness.

Kallen, Evelyn. 1982. "Multiculturalism: Ideology, Policy and Reality." *Journal of Canadian Studies* 17, no. 1 (Spring): 51–63. https://doi.org/10.3138/jcs.17.1.51.

Karmis, Dimitrios. 2004. "Pluralism and National Identity(ies) in Contemporary Québec." In *Quebec: State and Society*, edited by Alain-G. Gagnon, 69–96. 3rd ed. Toronto: University of Toronto Press.

– 2009. "Multiples Voices of the Federal Tradition and the Turmoil of Canadian Federalism." In Gagnon 2009, 53–79.

Karmis, Dimitrios, and Alain-G. Gagnon. 2001. "Federalism. Federation and Collective Identities in Canada and Belgium: Different Routes, Similar Fragmentation." In Gagnon and Tully 2001, 137–75.

Karmis, Dimitrios, and Darren O'Toole. 2018. "Vigilance, Trust and 'Fine Risks' in the Minefield of Multinational Democracies." In Karmis and Rocher 2018, 86–110.

Karmis, Dimitrios, and François Rocher, eds. 2012. *La dynamique confiance/méfiance dans les démocraties : le Canada sous l'angle comparatif.* Quebec: Presses de l'Université Laval.

–, eds. 2018. *Trust, Distrust, and Mistrust in Multinational Democracies: Comparative Perspectives.* Montreal and Kingston: McGill-Queen's University Press.

Katzenstein, Peter J. 1985. *Small States in World Markets: Industrial Policy in Europe.* Ithaca, NY: Cornell University Press.

Keating, Michael. 2001a. *Nations against the State: The New Politics of Nationalism in Quebec, Catalonia and Scotland.* 2nd ed. London: Palgrave Macmillan.

– 2001b. "Par-delà la souveraineté : La démocratie plurinationale dans un monde post-souverain." In *Repères en mutation : identité et citoyenneté dans le Québec contemporain*, edited by Jocelyn Maclure and Alain-G. Gagnon, 58–86. Collection Débats. Montreal: Québec Amérique.

– 2001c. *Plurinational Democracy: Stateless Nations in a Post-Sovereignty Era*. Oxford: Oxford University Press.

– 2004. "European Integration and the Nationalities Question." *Politics & Society* 3, no. 1 (September): 367–88. https://doi.org/10.1177 %2F0032329204267295.

– 2018. "The Basque Statute of Autonomy." Centre for Constitutional Change. Researching the Issues. Informing the Debate, 22 October.

Keating, Michael, and Alain-G. Gagnon. 2012. "Introduction." In Gagnon and Keating 2012, 1–10.

Kraus, Peter. 2008. *A Union of Diversity: Language, Identity and Polity-Building in Europe*. Cambridge: Cambridge University Press.

Kraus, Peter A., and Joan Vergès Gifra, eds. 2017. *The Catalan Process: Sovereignty, Self-Determination and Democracy in the 21st Century*. Barcelona: Institut d'Estudis de l'Autogovern.

Kymlicka, Will. 1996. *Multicultural Citizenship: A Liberal Theory of Minority Rights*. Oxford: Oxford University Press.

– 1998. *Finding Our Way: Rethinking Ethnocultural Relations in Canada*. Toronto: Oxford University Press.

– 2004a. "Justice and Security in the Accommodation of Minority Nationalism." In *Ethnicity, Nationalism and Minority Rights*, edited by Stephen May, Tarid Modood, and Judith Squires, 144–75. Cambridge: Cambridge University Press.

– 2004b. "La justice et la sécurité dans la prise en compte du nationalisme minoritaire." In Dieckhoff 2004b, 181–223.

– 2008. "The Internationalization of Minority Rights." In *Constitutional Design for Divided Societies*, edited by Sujit Choudhry, 114–26. Oxford: Oxford University Press.

Labelle, Micheline, and François Rocher. 2008. "Pluralisme national et souveraineté du Canada : luttes symboliques autour des identités collectives." In *Diversité et identités au Québec et dans les régions d'Europe*, edited by Jacques Palard, Alain-G. Gagnon, and Bernard Gagnon, 145–68. Brussels: Peter Lang.

Labelle, Micheline, and Daniel Salée. 1999. "La citoyenneté en question : l'État canadien face à l'immigration et à la diversité nationale et culturelle." *Sociologie et sociétés* 31, no. 2 (Fall): 125–44. https://doi.org/10.7202/001395ar.

Ladner, Kiera. 2017. "Taking the Field: 50 Years of Indigenous Politics in the *CJPS*." *Canadian Journal of Political Science* 50, no. 1 (March): 163–79. https://doi.org/10.1017/S0008423917000257.

– 2019. "Indigenous Constitutional Resurgence: Under the Cloak of Possum & Buffalo Robes, or: Ruminations and Machinations on Self-Determination, Sovereignty and Territoriality." Paper presented at the International Conference on Sovereignties and Autochtonous Self-Determination: tiayoriho'ten, Wendake, QC, 24–5 October.

– 2000. "When Buffalo Speaks: Creating an Alternative Understanding of Traditional Blackfoot Governance." PhD diss., Carleton University.

Laforest, Guy. 1990. "La Révolution glorieuse, John Locke et l'impasse constitutionnelle au Canada." *Les Cahiers de droit* 31 (2): 621–40. https://doi.org/10.7202/043027ar.

– 1995. *De l'urgence*. Montreal: Boréal.

Laforest, Guy, Eugénie Brouillet, Alain-G. Gagnon, and Yves Tanguay, eds. 2015. *The Constitutions That Shaped Us: A Historical Anthology of the Pre-1867 Canadian Constitutions*. Montreal and Kingston: McGill-Queen's University Press.

Laforest, Guy, and Alain-G. Gagnon. 2017. "Comprendre la vie politique au Québec et au Canada." In *La politique québécoise et canadienne : acteurs, institutions, sociétés*, edited by Alain-G. Gagnon and David Sanschagrin, 9–31. 2nd ed. Collection Politeia. Quebec: Presses de l'Université du Québec.

– 2020. "The Canadian Political Regimes from a Quebec Perspective." In *Canadian Politics*, edited by James Bickerton and Alain-G. Gagnon, 21–44. 7th ed. Toronto: University of Toronto Press.

Laforest, Guy, and Félix Mathieu. 2016. "Le fiduciaire, le financier et le poète : Cartier, Galt et D'Arcy McGee." In *La conférence de Québec de 1864, 150 ans plus tard : comprendre l'émergence de la fédération canadienne*, edited by Eugénie Brouillet, Alain-G. Gagnon, and Guy Laforest, 123–48. Quebec: Presses de l'Université Laval.

Laforest, Guy, in collaboration with Oscar Mejia Mesa. 2014. *Interpreting Quebec's Exile within the Federation: Selected Political Essays*. Collection Diversitas. Brussels: Peter Lang.

Lajoie, Andrée. 2005. "Le fédéralisme canadien : science politique fiction pour l'Europe." *Lex Electronica* 10, no. 1 (Winter): 3. https://www.lex-electronica.org/s/955.

– 2006. "Le fédéralisme au Canada : Provinces et minorités, même combat." In Gagnon 2006b, 183–209.

Lang, Timothy. 2002. "Lord Acton and the 'Insanity of Nationality.'" *Journal of the History of Ideas* 63, no. 1 (January): 129–49. http://doi.org/10.1353/jhi.2002.0005.

Langlois, Simon. 2018. *Refondations nationales au Canada et au Québec*. Quebec: Septentrion.

Laniel, Jean-François. 2020. "Remarques sur le « nouveau nationalisme » des petites nations en contexte de mondialisation néolibérale." In Laniel and Thériault 2020, 235–58.

Laniel, Jean-François, and Joseph Yvon Thériault. 2020. *Les petites nations : culture, politique et universalité*. Paris: Classiques Garnier.

Lapointe-Gagnon, Valérie. 2018. *Panser le Canada : une histoire intellectuelle de la commission Laurendeau-Dunton*. Montreal: Boréal.

LaSelva, Samuel, V. 2018. *Canada and the Ethics of Constitutionalism: Identity, Destiny, and Constitutional Faith*. Montreal and Kingston: McGill-Queen's University Press.

Lawson, Tim. 2015. "Trudeau's Canada, Again." *New York Times*, 8 December. https://www.nytimes.com/2015/12/13/magazine/trudeaus-canada-again.html.

Lazaro, Julio, M. 2008. "El Constitucional liquida la consulta soberanista de Ibarretxe." *El Pais*, 11 September. https://elpais.com/diario/2008/09/12/espana/1221170407_850215.html.

Lecours, André. 2012. "Sub-State Nationalism in the Western World: Explaining Continued Appeal." *Ethnopolitics* 11, no. 3 (September) 268–86. https://doi.org/10.1080/17449057.2010.507114.

– 2021. *Nationalism, Secessionism, and Autonomy*. Oxford: Oxford University Press.

Lecours, André, Nikola Brassard-Dion, and Guy Laforest, eds. 2021. *Constitutional Politics in Multinational Democracies*. Collection Diversity, Democracy, and Citizen Engagement. Montreal and Kingston: McGill-Queen's University Press.

Lecours, André, and Geneviève Nootens. 2011. "Understanding Majority Nationalism." In Gagnon, Lecours, and Nootens 2011, 3–18.

Lefebvre, Solange, and Guillaume St-Laurent, eds. 2018. *Dix ans plus tard : la commission Bouchard-Taylor, succès ou échec ?* Collection Débats. Montreal: Québec Amérique.

Legaré, Anne. 2020. "Société et nation : Du culturel au politique." In Laniel and Thériault 2020, 137–66.

Létourneau, Jocelyn. 2000. *Passer à l'avenir : histoire, mémoire, identité dans le Québec d'aujourd'hui*. Montreal: Boréal.

Lévesque, Benoît, and Gilles L. Bourque. 2013. "Repenser le modèle québécois." In *L'innovation sociale : les marches d'une construction théorique et pratique*, edited by Benoît Lévesque, Jean-Marc Fontan, and Juan-Luis Klein, 317–32. Quebec: Presses de l'Université du Québec.

Lévesque, Carole. 2015a. "Peuples autochtones : la réconciliation passe d'abord par la reconnaissance." In *L'État du Québec, 2016*, edited by Annick Poitras, 233–9. Montreal: Del Busso.

– 2015b. "Promouvoir la sécurisation culturelle pour améliorer la qualité de vie et les conditions de santé de la population autochtone." In "Décolonisation et droits des peuples autochtones," special issue, *Ligue des droits et libertés* 24, no. 2 (Autumn): 16–19.

Lévesque, Jacques. 1995. *1989, la fin d'un empire : l'URSS et la libération de l'Europe de l'Est*. Paris: Presses de Sciences Po.

Levrat, Nicolas. 2017. "La complexe mise en œuvre du droit à l'autodétermination" (Opinion). *Le Temps* (Geneva), 28 September. https://www.letemps.ch/opinions/complexe-mise-oeuvre-droit-lautodetermination.

Levrat, Nicolas, Sandrina Antunes, Guillaume Tusseau, and Paul Williams. 2017. *Catalonia's Legitimate Right to Decide: Paths to Self-Determination*. https://www.unige.ch/gsi/files/9315/0461/7440/CATALONIAS _LEGITIMATE_RIGHT_DECIDE.pdf.

Levy, Ron, Hoi Kong, Graeme Orr, and Jeff King, eds. 2018. *The Cambridge Handbook of Deliberative Constitutionalism*. Cambridge: Cambridge University Press.

Lijphart, Arend. 1977. *Democracy in Plural Societies: A Comparative Exploration*. New Haven, CT: Yale University Press.

– 1999. *Patterns of Democracy: Government Forms and Performance in Thirty-Six Countries*. New Haven, CT: Yale University Press.

– 2008. *Thinking about Democracy: Power Sharing and Majority Rule in Theory and Practice*. New York: Routledge

Ljubljana Guidelines on Integration of Diverse Societies & Explanatory Notes. 2012. Organization for Security and Co-operation in Europe, High Commissioner on National Minorities.

Logan, Tim. 2014. "Moldova: Autonomy and Conflict." *McGill International Review*, April, 10–14.

López, Jaume. 2011. "From the Right to Self-Determination to the Right to Decide / Del dret a l'autodeterminacio al dret a decidir." *Quaderns de Recerca*, no. 4 (November): 1–37.

Loranger, T.J.-J. 1884. *Lettres sur l'interprétation de la constitution fédérale*. Montreal: A. Périard.

Macdonald Commission. 1985. *Report of the Royal Commission on the Economic Union and Development Prospects for Canada*. 3 vols. Ottawa: Supply and Services Canada.

Mackintosh, W.A. 1964. *The Economic Background of Dominion-Provincial Relations*. Carleton Library Series. Montreal: McClelland & Stewart.

MacMillan, C. Michael. 1998. *The Practice of Language Rights in Canada*. Toronto: University of Toronto Press.

Mallory, James. 1954. *Social Credit and the Federal Power in Canada*. Toronto: University of Toronto Press.

Marceau Guimont, Stéphane, Jean-Olivier Roy, and Daniel Salée, eds. 2020. *Peuples autochtones et politique au Québec et au Canada : identités, citoyennetés et autodétermination*. Collection Politeia. Quebec: Presses de l'Université du Québec.

Marko, Joseph, ed. 2019a. *Human and Minority Rights Protection by Multiple Diversity Governance: History, Law, Ideology and Politics in European Perspective*. Abingdon, UK: Routledge.

– 2019b. "Introduction." In Marko 2019a, 1–11.

– 2019c. "Law and Ideology: The Ideological Conundrums of the Liberal-Democratic State." In Marko 2019a, 96–137.

Marko, Joseph, Edith Marko-Stöckl, Benedikt Harzl, and Hedwig Unger. 2019. "The Historical-Sociological Foundations: State Formation and Nation Building in Europe and the Construction of the Identitarian Nation-Cum-State Paradigm." In Marko 2019a, 33–95.

Massie, Justin, and Marjolaine Lamontagne, eds. 2019. *Paradiplomatie identitaire : nations minoritaires et politique extérieure*. Collection Politeia. Quebec: Presses de l'Université du Québec.

Mathieu, Félix. 2017. *Les défis du pluralisme à l'ère des sociétés complexes*. Collection Politeia. Quebec: Presses de l'Université du Québec.

– 2020a. "L'agir fédéral multinational : vers l'enthousiasme de Bono ?" In *La Confédération et la dualité canadienne*, edited by Valérie Lapointe-Gagnon, Rémi Léger, Serge Dupuis, and Alex Tremblay Lamarche, 333–51. Quebec: Presses de l'Université Laval.

– 2020b. "L'école québécoise de la diversité : émergence, déploiement et renouvellement d'une pensée fédéraliste authentique." In Brousseau Desaulniers and Savard 2020, 377–404.

– 2020c. "Les nations fragile : trajectoires sociopolitiques comparées." Thèse de doctorat, Université du Québec à Montréal.

Mathieu, Félix, and Alain-G. Gagnon. 2021. "(Still) in Search of the Federal Spirit: Autonomy and Self-Determination in Multinational Federations." In *Beyond Autonomy? Federalism and Democracy in the 21st Century*, edited by Tracy Fenwick and Andrew C. Banfield, 69–87. Boston and Leiden: Brill and Nijhoff.

Mathieu, Félix, and Dave Guénette, eds. 2019. *Ré-imaginer le Canada : vers un Canada multinational ?* Collection Diversité et démocratie. Quebec: Presses de l'Université Laval.

Mathieu, Félix, Dave Guénette, and Alain-G. Gagnon, eds. 2020. *Cinquante déclinaisons de fédéralisme : théorie, enjeux et études de cas*. Collection Politeia. Quebec: Presses de l'Université du Québec.

May, Paul. 2016. *Philosophies du multiculturalisme*. Paris: Presses de Sciences Po.

McCall, Christina, Frank Cunningham, Abraham Rotstein, Stephen Clarkson, Pat Armstrong, Roberto Perin, Kenneth McRoberts, Leo Panitch, Daniel Drache, and Reg Whitaker. 1992. "Three Nations." *Canadian Forum*, March, 4–6.

McCrone, David. 1998. *The Sociology of Nationalism: Tomorrow's Ancestors*. London: Routledge.

McGarry, John. 2005. "Asymmetrical Arrangements and the Plurinational State." Position paper for the Third International Conference on Federalism, Forum of Federations, Brussels, 3–5 March.

McGarry, John, and Brendan O'Leary. 2004. *The Northern Ireland Conflict: Consociational Engagements*. Oxford: Oxford University Press.

McKillop, A.B. 1999. "Who Killed Canadian History? A View From the Trenches." *Canadian Historical Review* 80, no. 2 (June): 269–300. https://doi.org/10.3138/CHR.80.2.269.

McNeil, Kent. 2018. "Indigenous and Crown Sovereignty in Canada." In *Resurgence and Reconciliation: Indigenous-Settler Relations and Earth Teachings*, edited by Michael Ash, John Borrows, and James Tully, 293–314. Toronto: University of Toronto Press.

McRae, Kenneth. 1998. *Conflict and Compromise in Multilingual Societies: Switzerland*. Waterloo, ON: Wilfrid Laurier University Press.

– 2000. *Conflict and Compromise in Multilingual Societies: Finland*. Waterloo, ON: Wilfrid Laurier University Press.

– 2006. *Conflict and Compromise in Multilingual Societies: Belgium*. Waterloo, ON: Wilfrid Laurier University Press.

McRoberts, Kenneth. 2017. "Undermining Catalonia's Referendum Is a Threat to Democracy." *Globe and Mail*, 2 October. https://www.theglobeandmail.com/opinion/undermining-catalonias-referendum-is-a-threat-to-democracy/article36457810/.

Medda-Windischer, Roberta, and Patricia Popelier, eds. 2016. *Pro-Independence Movements and Immigration: Discourse, Policy and Practice*. Boston and Leiden: Brill and Nijhoff.

Meier, Olivier. 2019. "Max Weber et la légitimité du pouvoir." RSE – Magazine Gouvernance, éthique et développement, 17 September. https://www.rse-magazine.com/Max-Weber-et-la-legitimite-du-pouvoir_a3424.html.

Mejia Mesa, Oscar. 2020. "Le livre blanc et l'autodétermination des peuples autochtones au Canada." In Guimont Marceau, Roy, and Salée 2020, 113–35.

Mendez, Lucia. 2018. "Nicolas Sartorius: 'El Derecho a Decidir es Reaccionario." *El Mundo*, 12 November. https://www.elmundo.es/espana/2018/11/12/5be8780346163fc74c8b45a1.html.

Miller, J.R. 1992. "From Riel to the Métis." In *The Prairie West: Historical Readings*, edited by R. Douglas Francis and Howard Palmer, 185–203. Edmonton: University of Alberta Press.

– 2009. *Compact, Contract, Covenant: Aboriginal Treaty-Making in Canada*. Toronto: University of Toronto Press.

Minz, Jack, and Richard Simeon. 1982. "Conflict of Taste & Conflict of Claim in Federal Countries." Discussion Paper no. 13, Kingston, Institute of Intergovernmental Relations.

Morton, F.L. 2005. "Equality or Asymmetry? Alberta at the Crossroads." Asymmetry Series 2005. Kingston: Institute of Intergovernmental Relations.

Motard, Geneviève. 2013. "Le principe de personnalité des lois comme voie d'émancipation des peuples autochtones : analyse critique des ententes d'autonomie gouvernementale du Canada." PhD diss., Université Laval.

Muro, Diego, and Eckart Woertz, eds. 2018. *Secession and Counter-Secession: An International Relations Perspective*. Barcelona: Centre for International Affairs (CIDOB).

Nadasdy, Paul. 2017. *Sovereignty's Entailments: First Nation State Formation in the Yukon*. Toronto: University of Toronto Press.

Napoleon, Val. 2009. "Living Together: Gitksan Legal Reasoning as a Foundation for Consent." In *Challenges of Consent: Consent as the Foundation of Political Community in Indigenous/Non-Indigenous Contexts*, edited by Jeremy Webber and Colin McLeod, 45–76. Vancouver: University of British Columbia Press.

Neumann, Franz L. 1955. "Federalism and Freedom: A Critique." In *Federalism: Mature and Emergent*, edited by Arthur W. Macmahon, 44–57. New York: Doubleday.

Nichols, Joshua. 2018. "Sui Generis Sovereignties: The Relationship between Treaty Interpretation and Canadian Sovereignty." Centre for International Governance Innovation, no. 1, January.

Nimni, Ephraim, ed. 2005. *National Cultural Autonomy and Its Contemporary Critics*. London: Routledge.

Nincic, Miroslav. 1999. "The National Interest and Its Interpretation." *Review of Politics* 61, no. 1 (Winter): 29–55. https://doi.org/10.1017/S0034670500028126.

Noël, Alain. 2013. "Ideology, Identity, Majoritarianism: On the Politics of Federalism." In *The Global Promise of Federalism*, edited by Grace Skogstad, David Cameron, Martin Papillon, and Keith Banting, 166–87. Toronto: University of Toronto Press.

Noël, Alain, and Gagnon, Alain-G. 1995. "Le Québec et le nouvel ordre mondial." In *L'Espace québécois*, edited by Alain-G. Gagnon and Alain Noël, 13–29. Montreal: Québec Amérique.

Nootens, Geneviève. 2002. "État et nation : fin d'un isomorphisme ?" *Politique et Sociétés* 21 (1): 25–41. https://doi.org/10.7202/040299ar.

– 2019. "Démocratie et pouvoirs constituants dans les sociétés plurinationales : quelques problèmes de théorie politique." In Mathieu and Guénette 2019, 119–40.

Núñez, Xosé-Manoel. 2001. "What Is Spanish Nationalism Today? From Legitimacy Crisis to Unfulfilled Renovation (1975–2000)." *Ethnic and Racial Studies* 24, no. 5 (January): 719–52. https://doi.org/10.1080/01419870120063954.

O'Leary, Brendan. 2001. "An Iron Law of Nationalism and Federation? A (Neo-Diceyan) Theory of the Necessity of a Federal Staatsvolk, and of Consociational Rescue." *Nations and Nationalism* 7, no. 3 (July): 273–96. http://doi.org/10.1111/1469-8219.00017.

Orban, Edmond. 1984a. *La dynamique de la centralisation dans l'État fédéral : un parcours irréversible ?* Montreal: Québec Amérique.

– 1984b. "Quebec Alienation and the Trend toward Centralization." In *Quebec: State and Society*, edited by Alain-G. Gagnon, 31–44. Scarborough, ON: Methuen.

Pal, Leslie. 1993. *Interests of State: The Politics of Language, Multiculturalism, and Feminism in Canada*. Montreal and Kingston: McGill-Queen's University Press.

Palermo, Francesco. 2009. "When the Lund Recommendations Are Ignored: Effective Participation of National Minorities through Territorial Autonomy." *International Journal on Minority and Group Rights* 16, no. 4 (December): 653–63. https://doi.org/10.1163/15718115_016_04-12.

– 2019. "What Does the EU Tell Us about Federalism?" 50 Shades of Federalism. http://50shadesoffederalism.com/theory/what-does-the-eu-tell-us-about-federalism/.

Papillon, Martin. 2019. "Les traités avec les peuples autochtones : un 5ᵉ pilier de l'ordre constitutionnel canadien ?" In Mathieu and Guénette 2019, 395–417.

Paquin, Stéphane. 1999. *L'invention d'un mythe : le pacte entre deux peuples fondateurs*. Montreal: VLB éditeur.

– 2005. *Économie politique internationale*. Paris: Montchrestien.

Paquin, Stéphane, Louise Beaudoin, Robert Comeau, and Guy Lachapelle, eds. 2006. *Les relations internationales du Québec depuis la doctrine Gérin-Lajoie (1965–2005)*. Quebec: Presses de l'Université du Québec.

Parent, Christophe. 2011. *Le concept d'État fédéral multinational : essai sur l'union des peuples*. Collection Diversitas. Brussels: Peter Lang.

Payero-López, Lucia. 2020. "Assessing the Spanish State's Response to Catalan Independence: The Application of Federal Coercion." In Gagnon and Tremblay 2020, 73–103.

Peleg, Ilan. 2007. *Democratizing the Hegemonic State: Political Transformation in the Age of Identity*. Cambridge: Cambridge University Press.

Pelletier, Alexandre. 2019. "Majority Nationalisms and the Accommodation of Ethnic Minority in Myanmar." Paper presented at the Center for Constitutional Change, University of Edinburgh, Edinburgh, 25 February.

Pelletier, Benoît. 2006. "L'avenir du Québec au sein de la fédération canadienne." In Gagnon 2006b, 535–48.

Pelletier, Réjean. 2008. *Le Québec et le fédéralisme canadien : un regard critique*. Quebec: Presses de l'Université Laval.

Pérez-Royo, Javier. 2018. "Anexo : Reforma constitucional o period constituyente ?" In *Constitucion: la reforma invisible. Monarquia, plurinacionalidad y otras batallas*, edited by Anton Losada and Javier Pérez-Royo, 211–86. Barcelona: Roca Editorial de Libros.

Pettit, Philip. 1997. *Republicanism: A Theory of Freedom and Government*. New York: Oxford University Press.

Pharo, Helge Øystein. 2019. "Peace with a Human Rights Perspective: Asbjørn Eide Interviewed by Helge Øystein Pharo." *PRIO Blogs*, 5 November. https://blogs.prio.org/2019/11/peace-with-a-human-rights-perspective -asbjorn-eide-interviewed-by-helge-oystein-pharo/.

Picard, Ariane. 2020. "À la croisée des chemins : crise autochtone et fédéralisme exécutif au Canada."Centre d'analyse politique: constitution et fédéralisme, 20 May. https://capcf.uqam.ca/publication/a-la-croisee-des -chemins-crise-autochtone-et-federalisme-executif-au-canada/.

Pierré-Caps, Stéphane. 1995. *La multination : l'avenir des minorités en Europe centrale et orientale*. Paris: Éditions Odile Jacob.

– 2014. "Albert Camus, le fédéralisme et l'Algérie." *Civitas Europa* 1, no. 32 (June): 197–212. https://doi.org/10.3917/civit.032.0197.

Pirro, Andres. 2015. *The Populist Radical Right in Central and Eastern Europe: Ideas, Impact and Electoral Performance*. London: Routledge.

Poirier, Éric. 2016. *La Charte de la langue française : ce qu'il reste de la loi 101 quarante ans après son adoption*. Quebec: Septentrion.

Popelier, Patricia, and Maja Sahadžić, eds. 2019. *Constitutional Asymmetry in Multinational Federalism: Managing Multinationalism in Multi-Tiered Systems*. Cham: Palgrave Macmillan.

Public Inquiry Commission on Relations between Indigenous Peoples and Certain Public Services in Quebec (Viens Commission). Quebec: Government of Quebec.

Québec. 2017. *Secrétariat aux affaires intergouvernementales canadiennes*. Quebec: Direction des communications, ministère du Conseil exécutif.

Reference re Secession of Quebec. 1998. CanLII 793 (SCC), [1998] 2 SCR 217.

Reference re Supreme Court Act. 2014. ss 5 and 6, 2014 SCC 21, [2014] 1 SCR 433.

Requejo, Ferran. 2005. *Multinational Federalism and Value Pluralism: The Spanish Case*. London: Routledge.

Requejo, Ferran, and Klaus-Jürgen Nagel, eds. 2011. *Federalism beyond Federations: Asymmetry and Processes of Resymmetrisation in Europe*. Farnham, UK: Ashgate.

Resnick, Philip. 1994. "Toward a Multinational Federalism: Asymmetrical and Confederal Alternatives." In *À la recherche d'un nouveau contrat politique : options asymétriques et options confédérales*, edited by Leslie Seidle, 71–90. Montreal: Institut de recherche en politique publique.

– 2012. "What Theorists of Nationalism Have to Learn from Multinational States." In Seymour and Gagnon 2012b, 69–80.

Richez, Emmanuelle, and Tejas Pandya. 2020. "Ensuring a Future for Indigenous Languages in Canada: Can 'Consequentialist' Multinational Federalism Provide an Answer?" In Gagnon and Tremblay 2020, 289–313.

Riker, William. 1964. *Federalism: Origin, Operation, Significance*. Boston: Little Brown.

Rioux, Hubert. 2020. *Small Nations, High Ambitions: Economic Nationalism and Venture Capital in Quebec and Scotland*. Toronto: University of Toronto Press.

Rioux, Marcel. 1969. *La question du Québec*. Paris: Seghers.

Rivard, Étienne. 2013. "L'approche commune ou l'irrésistible élan vers une définition interethnique de la planification." *Recherches amérindiennes du Québec* 43 (1): 25–38. http://doi.org/10.7202/1024470ar.

Rocher, François, and Benoît Pelletier, eds. 2013. *Le nouvel ordre constitutionnel canadien : du rapatriement de 1982 à nos jours*. Collection Politeia. Quebec: Presses de l'Université du Québec.

Rodon, Thierry. 2019. *Les apories des politiques autochtones au Canada*. Collection Politeia. Quebec: Presses de l'Université du Québec.

Roeder, Philip, G. 2009. "Ethnofederalism and the Mismanagement of Conflicting Nationalisms." *Regional and Federal Studies* 19, no. 2 (May): 203–19. https://doi.org/10.1080/13597560902753420.

Rousseau, Jean-Jacques. 1762. *Du contrat social ou Principes du droit politique*. Paris: Union générale d'éditions.

Roy, Arundhati. 2020. "Modi's Brutal Treatment of Kashmir Exposes His Tactics – and Their Flaws." *Guardian*, 5 August. https://www.theguardian.com/commentisfree/2020/aug/05/modi-brutal-treatment-of-kashmir-exposes-his-tactics-and-their-flaws.

Roy, Jean-Olivier. 2020. "Autonomie individuelle et collective chez les Autochtones : l'action politique créatrice d'espaces de liberté démocratique." In Guimont Marceau, Roy, and Salée 2020, 215–38.

Royal Commission on Aboriginal Peoples. 1993. *Partners in Confederation: Aboriginal Peoples, Self-Government and the Constitution (Erasmus-Dussault Commission)*. Ottawa: Minister of Supply and Services Canada.

Rupnik, Jacques, ed. 1995. *Le déchirement des nations*. Paris: Seuil.

Russell, Peter. 1983. "Bold Statecraft, Questionable Jurisprudence." In Banting and Simeon 1983, 210–38.

– 2017. *Canada's Odyssey: A Country Based on Incomplete Conquests*. Toronto: University of Toronto Press.

Ryan, Claude. 1976. "Le rapatriement de la Constitution : le rêve vain de M. Trudeau." *Le Devoir*, 8 March.

– 2000. "The Agreement on the Canadian Social Union as Seen by a Quebec Federalist." In *The Canadian Social Union without Quebec: 8 Critical Analyses*, edited by Alain-G. Gagnon and Hugh Segal, 209–25. Montreal: Institute for Research on Public Policy.

Salée, Daniel. 2003. "L'État québécois et la question autochtone." In *Québec : État et société*, edited by Alain-G. Gagnon, 2:117–47. Collection Débats. Montreal: Québec Amérique.

Sanjaume-Calvet, Marc. 2018. "Secession and Federalism: A Chiaroscuro." Fifty Shades of Federalism. http://50shadesoffederalism.com/diversity-management/secession-federalism-chiaroscuro/.

Sanschagrin, David. 2019. "Le Renvoi de 1998 et la gouvernance judiciaire : légitimer la domination." In Mathieu and Guénette 2019, 199–260.

– 2021. "L'avènement du nationalisme constitutionnel au Canada : une analyse socio-historique des champs juridique et étatique." PhD diss., Université du Québec à Montréal.

Santafé, Gustavo Gabriel, and Félix Mathieu. 2019. "Les récits du fédéralisme au Parti libéral du Québec." In Mathieu and Guénette 2019, 65–89.

Sauca, José Maria. 2010. Identidad y Derecho: Nuevas Perspectivas para Vieyos Debates. Valencia, Spain: Tirant lo Blanch.

Sauvé, Marc. 2008. "Le pouvoir fédéral de dépenser et la nature centralisatrice de la Constitution canadienne de 1867." MA thesis, Université du Québec à Montréal.

Savard, Rémi. 1985. La voix des autres. Collection Positions anthropologiques. Montreal: L'Hexagone.

– 1996. L'Algonquin Tessouat et la fondation de Montréal : Diplomatie franco-indienne en Nouvelle-France. Montreal: L'Hexagone.

Savard, Stéphane. Forthcoming. "The Search for a Third Option in a Time of Crisis: Constitutional Positions of Federalist Pressure Groups, 1977–1981." In Brousseau Desaulniers and Savard, forthcoming.

Schertzer, Robert. 2016. The Judiciary Role in a Diverse Federation: Lessons from the Supreme Court of Canada. Toronto: University of Toronto Press.

Schmitt, Étienne. 2016. "Rendre une voix aux nations aphones : un modèle de coopération plurinationale." PhD diss., Université du Québec à Montréal.

Schmitter, Philippe. 1974. "Still the Century of Corporatism." Review of Politics 36, no. 1 (January): 85–131. https://doi.org/10.1017/S0034670500022178.

Schwartz, Alex. 2011. "Patriotism or Integrity? Constitutional Community in Divided Societies." Oxford Journal of Legal Studies 31, no. 3 (September): 503–26. https://doi.org/10.1093/ojls/gqr010.

Secrétariat aux affaires intergouvernementales canadiennes. 2017. Quebecers, Our Way of Being Canadian: Policy on Québec Affirmation and Canadian Relations. Quebec: Bibliothèque et Archives nationales. https://www.sqrc.gouv.qc.ca/documents/relations-canadiennes/politique-affirmation-en.pdf.

Seymour, Michel, ed. 2002. États-nations, multinations et organisations supranationales. Montreal: Liber.

–, ed. 2016. Repenser l'autodétermination interne. Montreal: Thémis.

– 2017. A Liberal Theory of Collective Rights. Collection Democracy, Diversity, and Citizen Engagement. Montreal and Kingston: McGill-Queen's University Press.

Seymour, Michel, and Alain-G. Gagnon. 2012a. "Introduction: Multinational Federalism: Questions and Queries." In Seymour and Gagnon 2012b, 1–19.

–, eds. 2012b. *Multinational Federalism: Problems and Prospects*. London: Palgrave Macmillan.

Sichra, Inge. 2014. "Estado plurinacional – sociedad plurilingüe? solamente una ecuacion simbolica?" In Cagiao y Conde and Gomez-Muller 2014, 245–78.

Simeon, Richard. 2002. "Federalism and Decentralization in Canada." Paper presented at the Second International Conference on Decentralisation, Forum of Federations, Manila, 25–7 July.

Simeon, Richard, and Jack Minz. 1982. *Conflict of Taste and Conflict of Claim in Federal Countries*. Kingston, ON: Institute of Intergovernmental Relations.

Simon, René. 1980. "Minutes of the Proceedings: Special Joint Committee of the Senate and the House of Commons, 17 December.

Simpson, Betasamosake Leanne. 2011. *Dancing on Our Turtle's Back: Stories of Nishnaabeg Re-Creation, Resurgence, and a New Emergence*. Winnipeg: Arbeiter Ring Publishing.

Sioui, Georges. 1999. *Pour une histoire amérindienne de l'Amérique*. Quebec: Presses de l'Université Laval.

– 1995. *For an Amerindian Autohistory: An Essay on the Foundations of a Social Ethic*. Montreal and Kingston: McGill-Queen's University Press.

Smiley, Donald V. 1975. "Canada and the Quest for a National Policy." *Canadian Journal of Political Science* 8, no. 1 (March): 40–62. https://doi.org /10.1017/S0008423900045224.

Snyder, Jack. 2000. *From Voting to Violence: Democratization and Nationalist Conflict*. New York: Norton.

Soloch, Krzystof. 2009. "Les pays d'Europe centrale entre solidarité européenne et préférence atlantique." *Politique étrangère* 3 (Fall): 541–51. https://doi.org/10.3917/pe.093.0541.

Stacy, Helen. 2005. "Relational Sovereignty." In *Proceedings of the Annual Meetings (American Society of International Law)*. 99:396–400. Cambridge: Cambridge University Press. https://doi.org/10.1017/S0272503700072001.

Stepan, Alfred. 1999. "Federalism and Democracy: Beyond the U.S. Model." *Journal of Democracy* 10, no. 4 (October): 19–34. http://doi.org/10.1353/jod .1999.0072.

Stevenson, Garth. 1977. "Federalism and the Political Economy of the Canadian State." In *The Canadian* State, edited by Leo Panitch, 71–100. Toronto: University of Toronto Press.

– 2014. *Building Nations from Diversity: Canadian and American Experience Compared*. Montreal and Kingston: McGill-Queen's University Press.

St-Hilaire, Maxime. 2017. "Standards constitutionnels mondiaux : épistémologie et méthodologie." In *Les standards constitutionnels mondiaux,* edited by Mathieu Disant, Gregory Lewkowicz, and Pauline Türk, 11–75. Brussels: Bruylant.

St-Louis, Jean-Charles. 2018. "Parler de la « diversité » au Québec : une étude généalogique des discussions récentes sur le pluralisme et la citoyenneté." PhD diss., Université du Québec à Montréal.

Strang, David. 1996. "Contested Sovereignty: The Social Constructions of Colonial Imperialism." In *State Sovereignty as Social Construct*, edited by Thomas J. Biersteker and Cynthia Weber, 22–49. Cambridge: Cambridge University Press.

Strong-Boag, Veronica. 2019. *The Last Suffragist Standing: The Life and Time of Laura Marshall Jamieson*. Vancouver: University of British Columbia Press.

Summers, James. 2007. *Peoples and International Law: How Nationalism and Self-Determination Shape a Contemporary Law of Nations*. Leiden: Nijhoff.

Taillon, Patrick. 2019. "Une démocratie sans peuple, sans majorité et sans histoire : De la démocratie par le peuple à la démocratie par la Constitution." In Mathieu and Guénette 2019, 141–72.

Tamir, Yael. 1993. *Liberal Nationalism*. Princeton, NJ: Princeton University Press.

– 2019. *Why Nationalism?* Princeton, NJ: Princeton University Press.

Tanguay, Brian. 1990. "Rediscovering Politics: Organized Labour, Business, and the Provincial State in Quebec, 1960–1985." PhD diss., Carleton University.

Taylor, Charles. 1991. "Shared and Divergent Values." In Watts and Brown 1991, 53–76.

– 1992. *Reconciling the Solitudes: Essays on Canadian Federalism and Nationalism*. Edited by Guy Laforest. Montreal and Kingston: McGill-Queen's University Press.

– 1993. "The Deep Challenge of Dualism." In *Quebec: State and Society*, edited by Alain-G. Gagnon, 82–95. 2nd ed. Scarborough, ON: Nelson Canada.

Thériault, Joseph Yvon. 2007. *Faire société : société civile et espaces francophones*. Sudbury, ON: Prise de parole.

– 2019. *Sept leçons sur le cosmopolitisme : agir politique et imaginaire démocratique*. Collection Débats. Montreal: Québec Amérique.

Tierney, Stephen. 2004. *Constitutional Law and National Pluralism*. Oxford: Oxford University Press.

– 2019. "Courts in Federal Systems: Consolidating or Subverting the Federal Idea." Paper presented at the International Conference: Defensive Federalism: How Self-Government Can Be Protected from "the Tyranny of the Majority"?, Institut d'Estudis de l'Autogovern, Barcelona, 28–9 November.

– 2022. *The Federal Contract: A Constitutional Theory of Federalism*. Oxford: Oxford University Press.

Tilly, Charles. 2005. *Trust and Rule*. Cambridge: Cambridge University Press.

Todorov, Tzvetan. 2008. *Le siècle des Lumières*. Paris: Gallimard.

Tolstov, Sergii. 2019. "Сепаратизм і сецесіонізм: Концептуальні особливості в умовах Європейського інтеграційного проекту" [Separatism and Secessionism: Conceptual Features in the Context of European Integration Project]. *Ideology and Politics Journal* 1 (12): 73–98.

Torbisco Casals, Neus. 2017. "National Minorities, Self-Determination and Human Rights: A Critique of the Dominant Paradigms in the Catalan Case." In Kraus and Gifra 2017, 195–225.

Tremblay, Arjun. 2019. *Diversity in Decline? The Rise of the Political Right and the Fate of Multiculturalism*. Basingstoke, UK: Palgrave Macmillan.

Tremblay, Jean-François. 2000. "L'autonomie gouvernementale autochtone, le droit et le politique, ou la difficulté d'établir des normes en la matière." *Politique et sociétés* 19 (2–3): 133–51. https://doi.org/10.7202/040228ar.

Trudeau, Justin. 2015a. "Diversity is Canada's Strength," 26 November. https://pm.gc.ca/en/news/speeches/2015/11/26/diversity-canadas-strength.

– 2015b. "Statement by the Prime Minister of Canada on the Speech from the Throne," 4 December. https://pm.gc.ca/en/news/statements/2015/12/04/statement-prime-minister-canada-speech-throne.

– 2016. "Statement by the Prime Minister of Canada on Vimy Ridge Day," 9 April. https://www.newswire.ca/news-releases/statement-by-the-prime-minister-of-canada-on-vimy-ridge-day-575126481.html.

Trudeau, Pierre Elliott. 1968. *Federalism and the French Canadians*. Toronto: Macmillan of Canada.

Trudel, Pierre. 2009. *Ghislain Picard : entretiens*. Collection Trajectoires. Montreal: Boréal.

Truth and Reconciliation Commission of Canada. 2015. *Honouring the Truth, Reconciling for the Future*. Ottawa: Queen's Printer.

Tully, James. 1995a. "Let's Talk: The Quebec Referendum and the Future of Canada." Austin and Hempel Lectures, Dalhousie University and University of Prince Edward Island.

– 1995b. *Strange Multiplicity: Constitutionalism in an Age of Diversity*. Cambridge: Cambridge University Press.

– 1999. "Liberté et dévoilement dans les sociétés multinationales." *Globe : revue internationale d'études québécoises* 2 (2): 13–36. https://doi.org/10.7202/1000467ar.

– 2000. "The Unattained Yet Attainable Democracy: Canada and Quebec Face the New Century." Paper presented at Les Grandes Conférences Desjardins, McGill University, 23 March.

Tupper, Allan. 1983. *Bill S-31 and the Federalism of State Capitalism*. Discussion Paper 19. Kingston, ON: Institute of Intergovernmental Relations, Queen's University.

Turgeon, Luc. 2004. "Interpreting Québec's Historical Trajectories: Between La Société Globale and the Regional Space." In *Quebec: State and Society*, edited by Alain-G. Gagnon, 51–67. 3rd ed. Toronto: University of Toronto Press.

Turgeon, Luc, and Alain-G. Gagnon. 2013. "The Politics of Representative Bureaucracy in Multilingual States: A Comparison of Belgium, Canada and Switzerland." *Regional and Federal Studies* 23, no. 4 (December): 407–23. https://doi.org/10.1080/13597566.2013.765866.

UNESCO. 2001. "Universal Declaration on Cultural Diversity." https://adsdatabase.ohchr.org/IssueLibrary/UNESCO%20Universal%20Declaration%20on%20Cultural%20Diversity.pdf.

United Nations. 1966. "International Covenant on Civil and Political Rights." General Assembly resolution 2200A (XXI). https://www.ohchr.org/en/instruments-mechanisms/instruments/international-covenant-civil-and-political-rights.

– 2007. "United Nations Declaration on the Rights of Indigenous Peoples." https://www.un.org/development/desa/indigenouspeoples/wp-content/uploads/sites/19/2018/11/UNDRIP_E_web.pdf.

United Nations Human Rights Council. 2020. "Overview and Function." *Legal 60*, 25 September. https://legal60.com/united-nations-human-rights-council-overview-and-function/.

Van den Wijngaert, Mark. 2011. "D'une Belgique unitaire à une Belgique fédérale." In *D'une Belgique unitaire à une Belgique fédérale : 40 ans d'évolution politique des communautés et des régions (1971–2011)*, edited by Mark Van den Wijngaert, 19–38. Brussels: Vlaams Parlement/Academic and Scientific Publishers.

Vézina, Valérie. 2018. *Une île, une nation ? Le nationalisme insulaire à la lumière des cas de Terre-Neuve et Puerto Rico*. Quebec: Presses de l'Université du Québec.

Watts, Ronald L., and Douglas M. Brown, eds. 1991. *Options for a New Canada*. Toronto: University of Toronto Press.

Webber, Jeremy, and Colin M. Macleod, eds. 2011. *Between Consenting Peoples: Political Community and the Meaning of Consent*. Vancouver: University of British Columbia Press.

Weinstock, Daniel. 2004. "L'éducation à la citoyenneté dans les sociétés multiculturelles." In Dieckhoff 2004b, 153–77.

Wheare, Kenneth C. 1962. "Federalism and the Making of Nations." In *Federalism: Mature and Emergent*, edited by Arthur W. McMahon, 28–43. New York: Russell & Russell.

Whitaker, Reg. 1991. *A Sovereign Idea: Essays on Canada as a Democratic Community*. Montreal and Kingston: McGill-Queen's University Press.

Wiener, Antje. 2007. "Contested Meanings of Norms: A Research Framework." *Comparative European Politics* 5, no. 1 (April): 1–17. http://doi.org/10.1057/palgrave.cep.6110107.

– 2014. *A Theory of Contestation*. Heidelberg: Springer.

Woons, Marc. 2020. "Normativity, Power & Peripheral Nations." PhD diss., University of Leuven.

Wright, Teresa. 2020. "Droit des peuples autochtones : la Déclaration des Nations unies, une priorité du ministre Miller." *La Presse*, 12 August. https://www.lapresse.ca/actualites/national/2020-08-12/droits-des -peuples-autochtones-la-declaration-des-nations-unies-une-priorite-du -ministre-miller.php.

Xanthaki, Alexandra. 2014. "Indigenous Rights at the United Nations: Their Impact on International Human Rights Standards." *Europa Ethnica* 71 (3–4): 69–77. https://doi.org/10.24989/0014-2492-2014-34-69.

Young, Iris Marion. 1990. *Justice and the Politics of Difference*. Princeton, NJ: Princeton University Press.

Young, Robert, Philippe Faucher, and André Blais. 1984. "The Concept of Province-Building: A Critique." *Canadian Journal of Political Science* 17, no. 4 (December): 783–818. https://doi.org/10.1017/S0008423900052586.

Index

Note: Page numbers in italics indicate a figure.

Contributions by the Same Author

A Selection of Titles Associated with the Overall Subject

Bickerton, James, Stephen Brooks, and Alain-G. Gagnon. 2006. *Freedom, Equality, Community: The Political Philosophy of Six Influential Canadians*. Montreal and Kingston: McGill-Queen's University Press.

Bickerton, James, and Alain-G. Gagnon, eds. 2020. *Canadian Politics*. 7th ed. Toronto: University of Toronto Press.

Brouillet, Eugénie, Alain-G. Gagnon, and Guy Laforest, eds. 2018. *The Quebec Conference of 1864: Understanding Emergence of the Canadian Federation*. Quebec: Presses de l'Université Laval.

Burgess, Michael, and Alain-G. Gagnon, eds. 1993. *Comparative Federalism and Federation: Competing Traditions and Future Directions*. London and Toronto: Harvester and Wheatsheaf/University of Toronto Press.

Burgess, Michael, and Alain-G. Gagnon, eds. 2010. *Federal Democracies*. London: Routledge.

Cagiao y Conde, Jorge, and Alain-G. Gagnon, eds. 2021. *Federalism and Secession*. Brussels: Peter Lang.

Gagnon, Alain-G., ed. 2009. *Contemporary Canadian Federalism: Foundations, Traditions, Institutions*. Toronto: University of Toronto Press.

Gagnon, Alain-G. 2010. *The Case for Multinational Federalism: Beyond the All-Encompassing Nation*. London: Routledge.

Gagnon, Alain-G. 2014. *Minority Nations in the Age of Uncertainty: New Paths to National Emancipation and Empowerment*. Toronto: University of Toronto Press.

Gagnon, Alain-G., and Michael Burgess, eds. 2018. *Revisiting Unity and Diversity in Federal Countries: Changing Concepts, Reform Proposals and New Institutional Realities*. Boston and Leiden: Brill and Nijhoff, 2018.

Gagnon, Alain-G., Montserrat Guibernau, and François Rocher, eds. 2003. *The Conditions of Diversity in Multinational Democracies.* Montreal and Kingston: McGill-Queen's University Press.

Gagnon, Alain-G., and Raffaele Iacovino. 2007. *Federalism, Citizenship, and Quebec: Debating Multinationalism.* Toronto: University of Toronto Press.

Gagnon, Alain-G., and Michael Keating, eds. 2012. *Political Autonomy and Divided Societies: Imagining Democratic Alternatives in Complex Settings.* Basingstoke, UK: Palgrave Macmillan.

Gagnon, Alain-G., Soeren Keil, and Sean Mueller, eds. 2015. *Understanding Federalism and Federation: Essays in Honour of Michael Burgess.* London: Routledge.

Gagnon, Alain-G., André Lecours, and Geneviève Nootens, eds. 2011. *Contemporary Majority Nationalism.* Montreal and Kingston: McGill-Queen's University Press.

Gagnon, Alain-G., and Pierre Noreau, eds. 2017. *Constitutionnalisme, droits et diversité : mélanges en l'honneur de José Woehrling.* Montreal: Thémis.

Gagnon, Alain-G., and Johanne Poirier, eds. 2020. *Canadian Federalism and Its Future: Actors and Institutions.* Montreal and Kingston: McGill-Queen's University Press.

Gagnon, Alain-G., and Ferran Requejo, eds. 2011. *Nations en quête de reconnaissance : regards croisés Québec-Catalogne* Brussels: Peter Lang.

Gagnon, Alain-G., and David Sanschagrin, eds. 2017. *La politique québécoise et canadienne : acteurs, institutions, sociétés.* Quebec: Presses de l'Université du Québec.

Gagnon Alain-G., and José Maria Sauca, eds. 2014. *Negotiating Diversity: Identity, Pluralism and Democracy.* Brussels: Peter Lang.

Gagnon, Alain-G., and Arjun Tremblay, eds. 2020. *Federalism and National Diversity in the 21st Century.* Cham: Palgrave Macmillan.

Gagnon, Alain-G., and James Tully, eds. 2001. *Multinational Democracies.* Cambridge: Cambridge University Press.

Laforest, Guy, Eugénie Brouillet, Alain-G. Gagnon and Yves Tanguay, eds. 2014. *The Constitutions That Shaped Us: A Historical Anthology of Pre-1867 Canadian Constitutions.* Montreal and Kingston: McGill-Queen's University Press.

Mathieu, Félix, Dave Guénette, and Alain-G. Gagnon, eds. 2020. *Cinquante déclinaisons de fédéralisme : théorie, enjeux et études de cas.* Quebec: Presses de l'Université du Québec.

Seymour, Michel, and Alain-G. Gagnon, ed. 2012. *Multinational Federalism: Problems and Prospects.* Basingstoke, UK: Palgrave Macmillan.

Lightning Source UK Ltd.
Milton Keynes UK
UKHW041515291222
414576UK00005B/28